PARTIAL JUSTICE

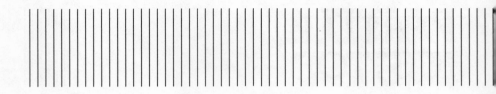

PARTIAL JUSTICE

Women in State Prisons
1800–1935

Nicole Hahn Rafter

Northeastern University Press
Boston

Designer: Catherine Dorin

Northeastern University Press

Copyright © 1985 Nicole Hahn Rafter

Library of Congress Cataloging in Publication Data

Rafter, Nicole Hahn, 1939–
    Partial justice, etc
    Bibliography: p.
    1. Women prisoners—United States—History. 2. Reformatories for women—United States—History. 3. Prisons—United States—History. I. Title
HV9466.R34 1985   365'.43'0973   84–7990

ISBN 0–930350–63–4

Composed in Bembo by Eastern Typesetting Co., South Windsor, Connecticut. Printed and bound by The Maple Press, York, Pennsylvania. The paper is Warren's #66 Antique, an acid-free sheet.

Manufactured in the United States of America

89 88 87 86 85   5 4 3 2 1

To Eleanor H. Little

Contents

Tables and Figures

Acknowledgments

So many colleagues, friends, and staff members in libraries and departments of correction throughout the country contributed to this project that I have sometimes felt more like a coordinator than an author.

Elizabeth Ann Mills and Elena Natalizia did much of the research for the national survey, and Nicolette Parisi handled all the computer work. My venerable friend Eleanor H. Little of Guilford, Connecticut, helped me understand the viewpoint of those who founded and operated women's reformatories. On numerous occasions, she shared with me her memories of her work in the early twentieth century at New Jersey's Clinton Farms, an institution first headed by Miss Little's lifelong companion, May Caughey. Miss Little also read and corrected parts of the manuscript, enlightening me in ways that published documents could not. She does not agree with all my points of view, but nevertheless she has graciously consented to my desire to recognize her many years of work on behalf of women in prison by dedicating this book to her.

I am grateful to Ronald A. Farrell of the Department of Sociology, State University of New York at Albany, for finding two students, Peggy Hobcroft and Roberta Tarkan, to help with data collection from prisoner records held by the New York State Archives. In Ohio, Brenda Chaney and Cindy Kohles helped code from prisoner registries. Deborah Veits and Phyllis Jo Baunach of the National Institute of Justice provided support and guidance at various points in the project. I was also much aided by colleagues at Northeastern University: Deans Norman Rosenblatt and Robert D. Croatti of the College of Criminal Justice, who found many ways to make my work easier; Laurie Mulcahy, who helped with the tedious task of compiling the code book; Gerald R. Murphy of the Office of Sponsored Programs; students in my courses on women and crime, who challenged my ideas and offered fresh ones; and above all, John H. Laub, whose seemingly endless capacity for sound criticism and supportive friendship I exploited mercilessly.

Others who contributed include Penny Bernhardt; John Berecochea; Charmarie Blaisdell; Lucy Freibert; Mary Ann Hawkes; Esther Heffernan; Vanessa Householder; Ronald Gold; Joan McDermott; Sheldon L. Messinger; John W. Mills; Janice E. Ryan, RSM; Julie Schlack; and Joseph A. Zillo. Archivists and other librarians in New York, Ohio, and Tennessee provided technical assistance and often friendship during my research trips. Moreover, I could not have completed this project without the aid of correspondents in a number of states who answered queries, often with copies of reports and searches for information.

Perhaps the greatest resource of any writer is colleagues willing to comment on drafts of a work while it is in progress. Those who read parts of the manuscript include Christopher R. Adamson, Mary Bularzik, John A. Conley, Laura Frader, Roger Gottlieb, Robert S. Hahn, Dorie Klein, Diane K. Lewis, Lucien X. Lombardo, Gary Marx, Lynn T. Sanford, Steven Spitzer, and Alexandra Todd. I was also fortunate to have three fine editors, Robilee Smith, Deborah Kops, and Ann Twombly.

The research was supported by Grant Number 79–NI–AX–0039 from the National Institute of Justice, U.S. Department of Justice. Points of view and opinions are my own and do not necessarily represent the official position or policies of the U.S. Department of Justice. Released time for writing and funds for secretarial assistance were provided by a grant from Northeastern University's Research and Scholarship Development Fund, whose support I also gratefully acknowledge. Any errors, of course, are solely my responsibility.

Earlier versions of parts of this work appeared as "Female State Prisoners in Tennessee: 1831–1979," *Tennessee Historical Quarterly* 39, 4 (Winter 1980): 485–97; "Prisons for Women, 1790–1980," in Michael Tonry and Norval Morris, eds., *Crime and Justice: An Annual Review of Research,* Vol. 5 (Chicago: University of Chicago Press, 1983); and "Chastizing the Unchaste: Social Control Functions of the Women's Reformatory System," in Andrew Scull and Stanley Cohen, eds., *Social Control and the State: Comparative and Historical Essays* (Oxford: Martin Robertson and Company, 1983).

It would have been impossible to complete—or even contemplate—this project without the patience, good humor, and support of my children, Charles and Sarah Hahn. And for his help with this, as with so many other undertakings, I owe my greatest debt to Robert S. Hahn.

Preface

In recent years historical research on crime and social control has grown rapidly and become an important field of inquiry in both the United States and Western Europe. Yet most of the new work ignores female criminals. As a result, even though studies have corrected some of "the misconceptions about crime that have been entrenched in our consciousness for many decades," their correction is only partial.[1] The focus on male subjects is characteristic of historical investigations of crime and social control in general and of histories of prisons in particular. By paying little attention to institutions for women and girls, even recent prison histories present a skewed picture of the evolution and nature of incarceration. In addition, they limit our access to a significant chapter in the history of women.

Partial Justice attempts to overcome some of these deficiencies by providing a history of the incarceration of women in the continental United States from the founding of the first state prisons in the late eighteenth century. It covers all types of state-supported penal institutions that held women—mixed-sex and all-female penitentiaries as well as the more open reformatories that have, until now, formed the subject of the scant historical literature that does exist on women's prisons. The few previous studies mainly focused on the Northeast and Midwest, regions where women's prisons of the reformatory type were concentrated; this work covers, also, institutions in the South and West. It concludes at 1935, a point when the women's prison system completed important ideological and structural changes.

The idea for this book germinated as I was doing research on a branch of the men's prison system. Reading through nineteenth- and early-twentieth-century documents on high security institutions for men, I occasionally ran across a section titled "Matron's Report" or a list of deceased inmates that included female names. It seemed that prisons such as Sing Sing and Pennsylvania's venerable Eastern Penitentiary held women as well as the men who, according to some accounts, were their sole occupants. I wondered how female prisoners had experienced confinement in these mainly-male institutions, what administrative problems they had posed for officials, and in what ways awareness of their presence might alter our understanding of the development of the prison system. Eventually I formulated the main goal of this study: to establish the basic contours of the history of incarceration of women in the United States, a foundation upon which theory and more detailed studies of individual prisons might be built. My secondary goal was to discover sources of some of the problems that afflict women's prisons today. I was familiar with these problems from my reading and visits to women's prisons. In particular, I wanted to uncover the origins of the well-documented failure of women's prisons to provide care as adequate as that available to men.[2] Third, I aimed at being sensitive to variations in the nature of imprisonment by region, race, and period. I had few indications of what I might find, but I felt sure that, just as "the" men's prison system is not a monolith, so too would women's prisons turn out to differ considerably among themselves in those three aspects.

Part I deals with the evolution of women's prisons, tracing the emergence of two major types: *custodial institutions,* which closely resembled penitentiaries for men, and *reformatory institutions,* predicated on the notion that women need special care. These developments naturally raise a number of important socio-historical questions, more than could be fully answered given the broad geographical and chronological spans of the study. The developments are tied, however, to broader penological trends and changing attitudes toward female criminals. Part II deals with the prisoners themselves, discussing demographic characteristics, offense and sentencing patterns, and issues of race, gender, and social class. Throughout, I try to discern ways in which women's experiences of imprisonment differed from those of men.

THE STUDY'S DESIGN AND SOURCES

Methodologically, I developed a two-pronged approach. The first consisted of a national survey, in the course of which I identified every semi-autonomous or entirely independent penal institution for women established in the United States between 1800 and 1935. For each institution, I investigated where female state prisoners had been held previously; what pressures had led to its founding; and the nature of its administration, program, and population during the first ten years of operation. The survey method foreclosed the possibility of following each institution through the entire course of its existence, but it offered the advantage of providing an overview of the development of the women's prison system as a whole. For the national survey I relied on legislation, documents of prison investigatory commissions, whatever firsthand accounts and secondary sources were available, and—above all—reports issued annually or biennially by the prisons themselves. All records pertaining to prisons have to be approached with mistrust. Reports by institutions to their legislatures often glossed over internal turmoil, for example, and the descriptions of purpose and administrative structure that appear in laws establishing new prisons seldom coincided with later realities. But I found that by studying each institution through records that flowed from a variety of sources, I was able to piece together a picture of its origins and early development. By keeping alert to discrepancies among the sources, moreover, I grew able to detect problems that the prisons themselves were reluctant to mention.

The second angle of approach, detailed studies of the ways in which three states handled female prisoners across time, was designed to compensate for the necessary cursoriness of my examination of individual institutions in the national survey. This aspect of the study utilized prisoner registries as well as the sources mentioned above. In the registries, clerks recorded information on each incoming prisoner. These data present difficulties of their own, but they are more reliable than the summary descriptions of inmates that can be found in published institutional reports. They are more "raw" than any other data available on entire prison populations; and the margin for error was small as clerks were recording brute facts such as sex, race, age, conviction offense, and sentence. For this study, the registry data were coded, computerized, and used in conjunction with full-scale histories of prisons in the selected states.

The states—New York, Ohio, and Tennessee—were chosen in part for their geographical diversity: I hoped that by studying prisoners of different areas of the country, I might discover regional differences in type of inmate and treatment. My selection of these states was also influenced by the knowledge that their archives held nearly complete series of prisoner registries dating back into the nineteenth century. Tennessee did not establish an entirely separate prison for women until the 1960s; thus it offered an opportunity to investigate how women incarcerated in a predominantly male institution were handled over an extensive period of time. Ohio and New York held female state prisoners in both custodial and reformatory institutions; thus they presented opportunities for comparing the treatment of women in different types of prisons within a single state. These were my selection rationales at the time the study began. Working by and large in the dark, I could not have predicted how fortunate the selections would turn out to be: they yielded richly diverse samples as well as instructive parallels.

Like others who have attempted to study prisoners of the past, I was constantly frustrated by lack of information on individual inmates. The registries give evocative but merely skeletal profiles. For instance, in the case of Estelle J., convicted in New York in 1931 of robbery, first degree, the registry reports only that she was a twenty-six-year-old black woman from South Carolina who had previously worked as a maid; that she was married but separated from her husband; and that she received a sentence of fifteen to sixteen years. The next two cases were nearly identical—same offense, dates of conviction and admission to prison, sentence, race, and almost the same ages—so in Estelle J.'s case I was able to flesh out the registry record with the assumption that she had acted in concert with two female crime partners. For some Tennessee cases I was able to match registry records with court documents that gave specific offense details; and on women imprisoned at New York's reformatory at Albion, I found case files that included (among many other types of documents) intercepted letters written by and to prisoners. But even for Albion's inmates, every morsel of information raised new questions; I was never able to satisfy my desire for fuller biographies of prisoners.

Readers will probably share my frustration with several other gaps in this study. I had hoped to be able to gather information on the places of birth of inmates and of their parents in order to determine if the prisons held disproportionate numbers of immigrants and first generation Americans. This proved impossible because the registries lacked the data. Then too, I would have liked to collect registry information on male prisoners in order to compare their demographic characteristics, offenses, and sentences with those of women, but constraints of time and funds ruled out this possibility. Had I included males, I would have had to reduce drastically my total of about 4,600 female cases; since men's prisons and their inmates have already received some attention, it seemed best to concentrate on women. I did, however, make an exception to my females-only rule when I dealt with race. Because the proportions of blacks appeared to be much greater in women's than in men's prisons, for the chapter on race I turned to census data that enabled me to confirm my suspicion and develop some explanations for the difference.

Several secondary sources provided support and direction as I worked on this project. One was Estelle B. Freedman's *Their Sisters' Keepers: Women's Prison Reform in America, 1830–1930* (1981), the only recent history of women's prisons. Freedman's sensitive analysis of the background of women who led the reformatory movement was of particular help as I formulated my ideas about the role of class conflict in the evolution of the women's prison system. I relied as well on Eugenia C. Lekkerkerker's *Reformatories for Women in the United States* (1931), the only other book-length account of the development of women's prisons. Despite its uncritical approach and exclusive focus on prisons of the reformatory type, Lekkerkerker's work includes a wealth of important detail, much of it collected from firsthand observation. I also turned frequently to recent studies of institutions for juveniles, particularly Steven L. Schlossman's *Love and the American Delinquent* and Barbara Brenzel's articles on the Lancaster, Massachusetts, training school for girls.* Because their administrators conceived of their inmates as developmentally akin to wayward children, women's reformatories had more in common with juvenile institutions than with prisons for adult males. Finally, I was much aided by two recent social histories of prostitution, Mark T. Connelly's *The Response to Prostitution in the Progressive Era* and Ruth Rosen's *The Lost Sisterhood*.[3]

As some of these examples suggest, the literature on prison history is starting to diversify. Freedman, Schlossman, Brenzel, and others have laid new groundwork for studies of prisons for women and children. By investigating regional and racial differences in crime and punishment, writers such as Christopher R. Adamson, John A. Conley, and Michael S. Hindus are shifting the focus away from the predominantly white prisoner populations of the Northeast and Midwest. Patricia O'Brien's recent study of French prisons in the nineteenth century provides a model for taking sex and age into account, and it gives us an example with which to compare American developments. Such signs of diversification in the study of prison history indicate that, in the years ahead, we will have much more opportunity for comparative work. Efforts to discriminate more finely among types of institutions and prisoner groups will help us shake off stereotypes of "the prison" and "prisoners." These efforts will increase accuracy and improve our ability to formulate and test theories about the origins and maturation of prisons. And they will make us more sensitive to ways in which place and period, age, race, and ethnicity, as well as the crucial factors of sex and gender, affect the nature and experience of incarceration.[4]

---

*Since this was written, Brenzel has published a book on the subject: *Daughters of the State: A Social Portrait of the First Reform School for Girls in North America, 1856–1905* (Cambridge, Mass.: The MIT Press, 1983). Her study indicates many correspondences between the movements to establish reformatories for girls and adult women.

Introduction

Histories of prisons frequently begin with architecture, for incarcerative concepts of punishment express themselves through institutional design; and design affects treatment, though often in ways not anticipated by those who drew the blueprints. Historical differences between the incarceration of women and men extended well beyond institutional structures, but they can be grasped most rapidly through a comparison of the architectural types of prisons in which the sexes were held. This comparison necessarily starts with prisons that mainly held men because for many decades they were the only type of state prison. They formed the trunk from which women's prisons eventually branched, some repeating the masculine model, others diverging from it.

Most states established a central prison for felons soon after joining the Union. The earliest of these institutions, founded shortly after the Revolutionary War, resembled large houses. Several stories high, they were divided by central corridors off which opened rooms where a number of prisoners resided together. Early in the nineteenth century, prison reformers became dissatisfied with this type of arrangement, for it encouraged communication among prisoners and thwarted discipline. Dissatisfaction led to design of an entirely different type of penal institution, the penitentiary, with massive walls and wings of individual cells. After 1820, when states constructed new prisons, they usually built penitentiaries. But in the late nineteenth century, disillusionment set in again: penologists grew critical not of the penitentiary's configuration but of its inability to reform convicts, many of whom seemed to leave the gate better schooled in crime than when they entered. Late nineteenth-century reformers developed a new plan for rehabilitating offenders, one based on education, vocational training, and a system of rewarding inmates for good behavior; and they set about founding "reformatory" prisons in which to implement it. But men's reformatories, like prisons built subsequently in the twentieth century, basically followed the penitentiary layout, consisting of high walls that enclosed cellblocks, workshops, and exercise yards.[1]

DEVELOPMENT OF THE WOMEN'S PRISON SYSTEM: AN OVERVIEW

The women's prison system evolved at a different pace and, unlike the men's system, it came to include two distinct types of state prison: custodial institutions that repeated the penitentiary plan, and unwalled reformatories comprising a number of small residential buildings scattered over large tracts of rural acreage. For many years after states began constructing prisons, females convicted of serious crimes served their sentences beside men at the central prisons. While prisons of the house design still prevailed, women were held together in one or more rooms of their own, and their care was similar to that received by men in adjoining rooms. When the penitentiaries came into vogue, women, too, were sent to these institutions, but the level of their care dropped below that accorded to men. There were few female convicts. Sometimes there were but one or two, and in any case they were vastly outnumbered by men. To administrators, women were a great nuisance. They had to be isolated to prevent sexual mischief, but there were too few women to fill a wing of cells. Therefore officials locked them in large rooms above the guardhouse or messhall. To these officials, it seemed extravagant to hire a matron to supervise a small number of women. These prisoners were thus often left entirely on their own, vulnerable to attacks by one another and male guards. Secluded from the main population, women had less access than men to the physician and chaplain. Unlike men, they were not marched to workshops, messhalls, or exercise yards. Food and needlework were brought to their quarters, where the women remained, day in and day out, for the years of their sentences.

In populous states, by the mid-nineteenth century the number of female prisoners had increased to the point that it became necessary to provide them with regular quarters of their own. These were often small buildings erected in a corner of the prison yard. Eventually matrons were hired to supervise the women, and sewing machines or laundry tubs were provided for their employment. When the female population again outgrew the capacity of its quarters, states constructed yet another female department, this time perhaps across the street from the penitentiary or a mile or two away on prison property. Through this mitotic process, semi-autonomous custodial prisons for women came into being.

As they separated from men's prisons, custodial units for women developed their characteristic tradition of inmate neglect. In them prisoners received care inferior to that given their male counterparts. The further they were removed, the more were women cut off from personnel, who left the main prison to visit the female department only in emergencies. Because officials economized in constructing buildings for females, women usually had no yard for exercise. In time, their small prisons became overcrowded, often appallingly so, but these yardless, self-contained structures could not easily be enlarged. Many were allowed to fall into sorry states of disrepair. Rain seeped in through cracked roofs while heating and plumbing systems decayed. Part of the problem lay with female departments' lack of administrative independence. The head matron received her orders and supplies from the warden of the neighboring prison for men. But the larger male populations consumed the attention and funds of wardens, who therefore tended to ignore their female prisoners.

By the late nineteenth century, nearly every state operated a custodial unit for women. In states with few female convicts, the women's quarters remained within the walls of the central prisons. Elsewhere the female department stood outside the walls, and a few had achieved a measure of autonomy through legislation establishing them as separate prisons. The thrust of change was toward making female departments independent. Though many began as offshoots of men's institutions, today most custodial prisons for women have as much administrative autonomy as prisons for men. But today, as in the past, women held in custodial institutions receive less adequate care than male state prisoners.

While its custodial branch was maturing, the women's prison system began to develop a second arm consisting of reformatories. In the late 1860s middle-class women who had been abolitionists and health-care workers during the Civil War turned their attention to new forms of social meliorism, joining campaigns against sexual immorality and delinquency, and crusades for suffrage and temperance. Some became interested in improving conditions of incarcerated women. They soon decided that traditional prison architecture was unsuitable for the care and treatment of women, whose milder, more passive nature required a gentler environment. Through a series of institutional experiments, these reformers arrived at what they considered the ideal design. Women's reformatories should be located in rural areas that would shield inmates from the corrupting influence of the city and provide ample opportunity for restorative exercise in fresh air. And they should resemble men's prisons as little as possible. Unwalled institutions, women's reformatories architecturally expressed their founders' belief that women, because more tractable, required fewer constraints than men. Rejecting large congregate buildings, women's reformatories came to adopt the "cottage" plan, holding groups of twenty or so inmates in small buildings where they could live with a motherly matron in a familial setting.

The women who campaigned for reformatories held strong convictions about inherent differences between the sexes. Starting from the premise that females needed greater protection, they desired to rescue as well as reform, to save as well as correct. In particular, they hoped to redeem women who had not sunk into the pit of confirmed criminality but as yet teetered on its brink. Thus those who lobbied for women's reformatories concerned themselves not with the female felons held in custodial prisons but with a group not yet subject to state punishment—vagrants, unwed mothers, prostitutes, and other "fallen" women who seemed more promising material for their attempts to uplift and retrain. Reformatories for men, which grew out of the same penology of rehabilitation, concentrated their efforts on young felons—offenders not yet hardened beyond the possibility of improvement, but nonetheless convicted of serious crimes. Women's reformatories, on the other hand, came to incarcerate misdemeanants—offenders who, in the relative mildness of their crimes, had no counterparts in state prisons for men. Both men's and women's reformatories were state prisons that could hold inmates for periods of years, but they held different kinds of offenders. And in the case of women's reformatories, these were mainly lawbreakers who, before the institutions were established, were liable to only brief terms in local jails. In the course of saving fallen women, then, the founders of women's reformatories institutionalized a double standard, one that made it possible to incarcerate women for minor offenses for which men were not subject to lengthy punishment by the state.[2]

In addition, women's reformatories initiated a convention of differential care based on gender. Reformatory designers adopted the late nineteenth-century penology of rehabilitation, but they tailored it to fit what they understood to be woman's special nature. To instill vocational skills, they used not prison industries but domestic training. Inmates were taught to cook, clean, and wait on table; at parole, they were sent to middle-class homes to work as servants. Whereas men's reformatories sought to inculcate "manliness,"[3] women's reformatories encouraged femininity—sexual restraint, genteel demeanor, and domesticity. When women were disciplined, they might be scolded and sent, like children, to their "rooms." Indeed, the entire regimen was designed to induce a childlike submissiveness. The staff of such institutions consisted solely of women, on the theory that only those of the same sex could respond effectively to the needs of female offenders. Officials were selected with an eye to both their administrative abilities and their power to provide examples of "true womanhood," models whom inmates might emulate. Through such measures, reformatories feminized prison treatment, establishing their own tradition of differential care.

The women's reformatory movement gathered momentum slowly. From its inception about 1870 to the century's close, it produced only four institutions. But this was a period of germination during which reformers experimented, venturing ever further from traditional concepts of the prison as they evolved their own model. By the turn of the century, they had fully articulated the design of the ideal reformatory, a plan that thereafter met with great success. Between 1900 and 1935, seventeen states opened women's reformatories.[4] Women who spearheaded the reformatory campaign had learned by 1900 how to organize legislative lobbies and gain leverage within prison supervisory boards. Then too, with four successful institutions behind them, they had proved to the public that women could indeed manage prisons. Because their ideology meshed well with other facets of Progressive reform, they were able in the early twentieth century to attract widespread support. The period's preoccupation with the "social evil" of prostitution also contributed to the prosperity of the reformatory plan, which offered a means of getting loose women off the streets and into institutions where they might be reclaimed.

By 1935, the women's reformatory movement had exhausted itself. It had achieved its goal in those states of the Northeast and Midwest most receptive to Progressive reforms in general, and it had produced a few reformatories in the South and West as well. Prostitution was no longer a national issue. Management of reformatories, moreover, had passed to a second or third generation of administrators who lacked the founders' zeal. And because of the Great Depression, states were no longer willing to maintain expensive institutions for the rehabilitation of petty offenders. With the demise of the reformatory movement came the end of the reformatory itself as a special type of penal institution. The physical plants remained, but their original population of misdemeanants was gradually replaced by felons. States that had been operating two penal units for women, one custodial and the other reformatory, decided to close the former, transferring its inmates to reformatory grounds. Misdemeanants were squeezed out, and former reformatories came to resemble men's prisons by restricting their populations to serious offenders.[5]

PARTIAL JUSTICE

Despite their heterogeneity, prisons that held women shared a common characteristic: in them, women usually received treatment different from that given men. Whether this was *unjust* treatment is a complicated issue. "Justice" has a variety of meanings. One of them—justice in the sense of deserved punishment—is not at issue here; we will not attempt to decide whether incarcerated women and men of the past merited their conditions of confinement. But we are concerned with "justice" in the sense of "fairness"—with whether the punishment of incarceration affected women and men equally—and we will find repeated instances in which women experienced unequal justice.

This justice was *partial,* in two ways. First, prison administrators often reacted with greater leniency toward women, excusing them from rules to which men were subjected in custodial institutions, providing female-specific care in reformatories. This partiality, however, did not produce better treatment. Women held in custodial prisons encountered conditions that were as unpleasant as those of men, though in different ways: they were assigned to less physically arduous labor but had fewer opportunities for exercise, fresh air, and changes of environment; they encountered lower levels of surveillance than men but also had less protection and less access to staff. Women held in reformatories, too, experienced conditions that were simultaneously milder and harsher than those of men in state prisons.

The other sense in which justice for women was partial is also paradoxical: even when, in custodial prisons, women and men were handled with seeming impartiality, women suffered more because these prisons were designed for men and held men in far greater numbers. The earliest penitentiaries housed both women and men, but in them women were sometimes entirely alone. Even when several women were held together, they doubtless felt lonelier and more stigmatized than men. They were more likely to be humiliated by lack of privacy from the opposite sex. Before matrons were hired, both sexes were supervised by men—another instance in which similar treatment actually meant greater vulnerability for women, in this case to forced prostitution and rape. Both male and female prisoners were cut off from their families, but women's greater responsibility for childcare created a major difference between the sexes in the subjective experience of incarceration. Child-related problems were particularly acute for women who were pregnant at the time of incarceration or who became pregnant within the walls. They might be locked in cells identical to those of men, but they had to deliver their infants and try to keep them alive. Thus even apparently evenhanded treatment worked to create different and less desirable circumstances for women than for men incarcerated in custodial prisons.

Today, as in the past, women in prison continue to experience partial justice, in both senses—treatment apparently less harsh than that of many male prisoners (though this "leniency" carries its own price tag) and care that is much less adequate than that available to men. A recent *New York Times* article declared, "The criminal justice system discriminates in two ways against women—for them and against them. And it is that double-edged treatment . . . that makes the experience of imprisonment worse for women than for men." Current studies of women's prisons have unanimously concluded that these institutions fall far short of men's in their standards of care. According to a report by the U.S. comptroller general, "Women in correctional institutions are not provided comparable services, educational programs, or facilities. . . ." They have fewer opportunities for job training and work-release; they have less access to social services, visitors, and lawyers; they are more likely to be treated as children. Such problems—and the list is a long one—are rooted in the past, in traditions engendered by the custodial and reformatory branches of the women's prison system.[6] States that never established a reformatory fell into the habit of neglecting female convicts held in custodial prisons. Those that established reformatories legitimated provision of specialized but restrictive programs. In the latter states, about 1935 the reformatory and custodial traditions fused, combining their drawbacks. As former reformatories filled with felons, they absorbed the custodial tendency to slight this population.

Relatively small numbers and gender: these were the sources of the problems that afflicted female prisoners in the past and continue to impose special burdens on them today. Women in nineteenth-century custodial units were neglected partly because their small numbers made it easy to brush them aside as insignificant. Today, few states confine enough female prisoners to warrant more than one institution for this population. Thus it is more difficult to place women than men near their families and social service agencies appropriate to their needs. Thus, too, women sometimes lack the possibility of placement in a medium or minimum security prison, for an institution that holds all types of offenders requires considerable security. "A woman qualified for a minimum security risk classification may be confined under maximum security control," reports the comptroller general's study, adding that unlike men, women nearing the ends of their sentences "have few opportunities to transfer to less secure environments offering outside activities and the opportunity to reestablish family and community ties." Finally, officials balk at the expense of providing the full range of programs available to men to a relatively small number of women.[7] balk at the expense of providing the full range of programs available to men to a relatively small number of women.[7]

But a group's status, in prison or out, is not merely a function of its size. Gender-stereotyping, too, has affected the handling of women at all stages of prison development. In the nineteenth century, women were commonly regarded as more moral than men; as a corollary, criminal females were considered more depraved than males and hence less deserving. Preconceptions about gender roles influenced job assignments. In nineteenth-century custodial prisons, women were often required to manufacture and wash uniforms for male convicts. Their work produced less income than the industrial labor of men, leading to a vicious cycle of inferior treatment:

women were assigned to unprofitable labor, and officials then used un-
profitability as justification for not providing matrons and other services.
Stereotyping took on a different cast in reformatories. Reformatory advocates retooled the image of the female offender from that of a morally
depraved monster to that of an errant child. This new image supported a
program of training in domesticity and sexual self-restraint that narrowed
job possibilities after release and required women to conform to a stricter
morality than that required of men. The reformatory program, as we shall
see, reflected a much broader struggle over the very definition of gender.
The middle-class women who formulated and implemented this program
were reacting to the move of working-class women into the industrial labor
force and away from traditional standards for female sexual propriety. Reformatories incarcerated working-class women for minor sexual misbehaviors and tried, often successfully, to instill middle-class values. Through
the reformatory movement, the criminal justice system became a mechanism for punishing women who did not conform to bourgeois definitions
of femininity.

In the words of one survey, "Correctional programs for the female
offender are still heavily steeped in the myths of appropriate female behavior
and traditional sex roles." Another recent survey reports that "Adequate,
specific funding for female offender programing is lacking. . . . [A]ll too
frequently, programs established to serve men and women are male oriented
and male dominated." Because "many officials" in the predominantly male
prison bureaucracy "feel that women do not need the same type of training
and vocational skills as men," men's institutions take precedence when funds
are allocated.[8] The tendency to fund women's prisons last is not just a
function of their smaller populations. It is also a result of devaluation by
sex. Partial justice remains the rule, today as in the first penitentiaries.

PART I

Development of the Women's Prison System

CHAPTER 1 ||||||||||||||||||||||||||||||

"Much and Unfortunately Neglected": Women in Early and Mid-Nineteenth-Century Prisons

The early nineteenth century witnessed the emergence of one of the most dramatic innovations in the history of punishment: the penitentiary, a fortress-like institution designed to subject prisoners to total control. Although historians argue about why the penitentiary came into existence at that time, most agree about the nature of convict life within such prisons. According to the usual picture, penitentiaries were designed to isolate inmates from the moral contamination of other felons; unlike the very first state prisons, in which several inmates were held together in one room, penitentiaries separated convicts into individual cells. Some held prisoners in perpetual solitary confinement, while others herded them together during the day for labor. But in both "separate" and congregate penitentiaries, speech and even eye contact were forbidden. In congregate institutions especially, strict routines governed every activity. Convicts with shaven heads and identical striped uniforms rose with the morning bell, marched in lockstep to their meals and workshops, and returned in the evening to their cells. Officials scorned idleness as corrupting; they scheduled every moment of their charges' lives, mainly for the labor that, in congregate penitentiaries, was expected to be financially profitable to the institution as well as morally profitable to the prisoners. "The doctrines of separation, obedience, and labor," writes David Rothman in a typical description, "became the trinity around which officials organized the penitentiary."[1]

Few historians of the penitentiary have noted that women as well as men inhabited these gloomy institutions. Had they investigated the treat-

3

ment of incarcerated women, they would have found that in nearly every respect, it contradicted the usual picture of penitentiary discipline. Women were punished in nineteenth-century prisons, but few officials tried to transform them into obedient citizens through seclusion and rigorous routines.[2]

Even after states replaced their original prisons with penitentiaries, many continued to hold a number of women en masse in old-fashioned large cells, inside penitentiary walls but away from the men's cellblocks. Women did not receive the supposed benefits of unbroken silence and individual isolation. Exempted from the most extreme forms of regimentation, they encountered other sorts of deprivation. Descriptions of women's conditions in Jacksonian prisons emphasize the intolerable noise and congestion of their quarters. Whereas male prisoners were closely supervised, women seldom had a matron. Often idleness rather than hard labor was their curse. As time went on and women were transferred from large rooms to individual cells, their treatment became more like that of men. But in general, female convicts in nineteenth-century prisons experienced lower levels of surveillance, discipline, and care than their male counterparts. Describing the situation of women in his institution as "inhuman—barbarous—unworthy of the age," one penitentiary chaplain concluded that "To be a *male* convict in this prison, would be quite tolerable; but to be a *female* convict for any protracted term, would be worse than death."[3]

To illustrate these differences between the sexes, we will look in some detail at the conditions of women incarcerated from the late eighteenth through the mid-nineteenth centuries in the prisons of New York, Ohio, and Tennessee—the three states that this study will use throughout to exemplify penal practices in the Northeast, Midwest, and South. (Because the southern prison system developed more slowly than that of the Northeast and Midwest, several late nineteenth-century changes are used to illustrate southern practices; because the prison system of the West developed later still, no western representative is included here.) These examples indicate diversity in regional styles of incarceration, but they also show that women imprisoned in the various regions had much in common. Their conditions of confinement, while outwardly resembling those of men held in the same institutions, were often inferior.

DIFFERENTIAL PUNISHMENT: WOMEN IN THE PRISONS OF NEW YORK, OHIO, AND TENNESSEE

New York's Newgate prison, opened in 1797 in the Greenwich Village section of New York City, was the first state institution established to hold felons only. In it, as in other prisons of the pre-penitentiary era, there were no marked differences in the handling of the sexes. Evenhandedness was not to remain the rule for long, but in Newgate and other original state prisons, officials had little alternative. Like Newgate's male convicts, women

were lodged in chambers "sufficient for the accommodation of eight persons." Their quarters were separated, for women resided in a north wing
with "a courtyard entirely distinct from that of the men"; yet the institution's small size did not permit women to be isolated from the mainstream
of prison life, as they were later isolated in penitentiaries. The women had
no matron, but as several lived together in each room, they could protect
one another from lascivious turnkeys. Thus they were less exposed to sexual
attack than women later held in individual penitentiary cells. Newgate's
women were required to wash and sew, while the males were assigned to
shoemaking and other manufactures. However, because profit making had
not assumed the importance that it later did in penitentiary management,
the women's apparently lower productivity did not yet furnish an excuse
for inequitable care.[4]

Treatment of both male and female felons changed radically when,
about 1820, the penitentiary system was inaugurated at New York's new
Auburn State Prison. Auburn's disciplinary methods—the individual cell,
lockstep, prohibition on prisoner communication, harsh punishments for
rule infractions, hard labor—captured the imagination of penologists
throughout the western world and soon became staples in penal regimens.
With the advent of penitentiary discipline, New York closed the outmoded
Newgate, transferring that prison's male inmates to Auburn. But women
did not receive the benefits thought to accrue to penitentiary discipline for
another decade. Instead they became pawns in a heated dispute between
Auburn and another New York state penitentiary that opened somewhat
later at Sing Sing. Neither wanted the women, who were shunned as a
particularly difficult type of prisoner; each made strenuous efforts to ensure
that females would be sent to the other location. While the men's prisons
engaged in this squabble, women formerly incarcerated at Newgate, along
with others subsequently committed from the New York City area, were
held at the city's Bellevue Penitentiary.

At Bellevue, standards sank far below those established at the state
penitentiaries, for aside from semiannual visits by the inspectors of Sing
Sing (who technically had custody of these women), the female prisoners
almost wholly lacked supervision. No matron was hired to attend to their
needs and maintain order. Visiting state officials lamented the wretchedness
of conditions at Bellevue: the impossibility of separating old from young,
and hardened criminals from novices; the women's "constant and unrestrained intercourse" (a fault of special seriousness at a time when most
penologists endorsed the silent system); the poor quality and quantity of
the food; the lack of a matron; and the absence of proper sanitary and
security precautions (during a cholera epidemic, eight women died and
eleven escaped). But these complaints had little effect on Bellevue's officials,
who also actively sought to avoid responsibility for the state's female
convicts.[5]

While these conditions prevailed for New York City-area women, courts in the western part of the state began, in 1825, to commit females to Auburn. There, however, they were housed not in cellblocks but in a third-floor attic above the penitentiary's kitchen. Like their Bellevue counterparts, they suffered extreme neglect. Until a matron was hired in 1832, women at Auburn had no supervision. Once a day a steward delivered food and removed the waste, but otherwise prisoners were left to their own devices. Their lack of protection from one another, and the psychological strain of being forced to share an overcrowded, unventilated space, sharply distinguished their care from that of men in the nearby cellblocks. Visiting in the early 1830s, Harriet Martineau reported a scene of almost complete chaos:

> The arrangements for the women were extremely bad. . . . The women were all in one large room, sewing. The attempt to enforce silence was soon given up as hopeless; and the gabble of tongues among the few who were there was enough to paralyze any matron. . . . There was an engine in sight which made me doubt the evidence of my own eyes; stocks of a terrible construction; a chair, with a fastening for the head and for all the limbs. Any lunatic asylum ought to be ashamed of such an instrument. The governor [warden] liked it no better than we; but he pleaded that it was his only means of keeping his refractory female prisoners quiet while he was allowed only one room to put them all into.[6]

Reports such as Martineau's—together with the scandal that ensued when one Auburn inmate became pregnant, was flogged while five months into her pregnancy, and later died—finally forced New York to construct regular quarters for its female felons. This was the Mount Pleasant Female Prison, to which Auburn and Bellevue inmates were transferred in 1839. Nearly two decades had passed since New York had indicated, at Auburn and Sing Sing, that individual cells, close supervision, and reformational discipline were desirable for prisoners.[7]

———————

The development of Ohio's prison system paralleled that of New York. Like Newgate, Ohio's first prisons resembled large houses; they were relatively small buildings, and their cells opened off central corridors. In 1834, Ohio abandoned this nonsecure type of structure, substituting a penitentiary patterned after Auburn. Like Auburn and Bellevue, the Ohio penitentiary segregated female prisoners into separate quarters. But in two respects, the penal practices of Ohio diverged from those of New York. First, Ohio had much lower standards for handling prisoners of both sexes: throughout the nineteenth century, observers ranked the Ohio penitentiary as one of the worst prisons in the country. Diseases ravaged the population, administrative corruption flourished, and, as Dorothea Dix put it in an indictment scathing even for her, the institution was "so totally deficient of the means of moral and mental culture . . . that little remains to be said, after stating the fact." Second, Ohio's prisoner population was smaller than New York's, reflecting its smaller general population. Whereas New York's relatively large number of female convicts pushed the state into creating a separate women's prison at mid-century, Ohio was able to wait until the early twentieth century to do so.[8]

The Ohio penitentiary developed a novel method of sequestering females, that of building a Women's Annex adjacent to the institution but outside its front wall. Constructed in 1837, the annex was one of the earliest extramural structures in the country designed specifically for female state prisoners. Originally the annex consisted of eleven two-person rooms and a yard. Crowding later necessitated construction of additional cells, but because the annex had been jammed between the perimeter wall and the street, it could not be expanded, and the women's quarters became increasingly cramped. Like the men's section, the annex sometimes fell into such disrepair that it was impossible to keep out the elements. The wings of the men's prison, "which have leaked for years," were recovered in 1850 with cement. "The female prison has been served in the same way," according to the annual report, but "Much more needs to be done by way of improvements." Similar observations about the miserable state of the annex were made for the next sixty years.[9]

As in New York, segregation of women led to their neglect. The men's section was patrolled by guards, but until 1846, the annex had no matron. Thereafter, owing to underfunding and political turmoil in the central administration, supervision remained sporadic and inadequate at best. As a result, discipline was often more lax for female than male prisoners. Lack of discipline was accompanied by absence of other forms of attention and control. Unguarded, the women were vulnerable to unwelcome sexual advances by male officials. Pandemonium sometimes prevailed. Gerrish Barrett, a representative of the Boston Prison Discipline Society who visited the Ohio penitentiary in the mid-1840s, reported that although there were only nine women, they gave more trouble than the five hundred male convicts. "The women fight, scratch, pull hair, curse, swear and yell, and to bring them to order a keeper has frequently to go among them with a horsewhip." That there was some accuracy in Barrett's description is indicated by Dorothea Dix's independent observation of about the same period: "There was no matron in the woman's wing at the time I was there, . . . and they were not slow to exercise their good and evil gifts on each other." Later in the century, former prisoner Sarah Victor wrote, "[T]he knives had all been taken from the female department, to prevent some refractory prisoners from cutting each other, which they had done, in a terrible manner, at times. . . ."[10]

Even at the Ohio penitentiary, strict rules were sometimes imposed on women. Sarah Victor reported that in the early 1870s the "discipline of the prison was very strict . . . , the prisoners not being allowed to speak to each other. . . ." And on occasion, women were punished severely. Victor describes one women beaten so terribly "that she was black-and-blue all over her body." She herself, when she arrived at the penitentiary about 1870, was kept in solitary confinement for five months. In 1880, a new matron alluded with awe to a brutal penalty used by her predecessor; she hoped never to resort to it herself. This was probably the "humming-bird," a form of punishment that forced the naked offender to sit, blind-folded, in a tub of water while steam pipes were made to shriek and electric current was applied to the body.[11]

At times, then, women in the annex did taste the bitterness of peni-tentiary discipline. At others, they were practically free of control. But because leniency often went hand in hand with anarchy, it was not neces-sarily preferable to the austerities of a solitary cell and close surveillance.

Tennessee's first prison, opened in Nashville in 1831, also adopted the Auburn system of convict discipline: inmates were brought together during the day for silent labor (for the women, mainly sewing), and at night they were locked in individual cells. For its first ten or fifteen years of operation, the Tennessee State Penitentiary was a relatively progressive institution. More than Ohio's prison, it attempted to approximate New York's stan-dards of care. By 1845, however, decline had set in. Concern with maxi-mizing profits from prison labor, combined with increasing preoccupation with the issue of slavery, corroded the quality of convict care. Tennessee started exhibiting the indifference to prisoner health and safety that came to characterize penal treatment throughout the South. On the eve of the Civil War the institution lacked an adequate water supply, and the warden was forced to inquire of the legislature, "What shall be done with the excrement arising in the prison in the future? You are aware it has been deposited on a vacant lot adjoining the prison property for the last fifteen years." The Civil War destroyed any possibility that Tennessee might have returned to northern standards. As in other Southern states, the conflict severely damaged the prison system, and prisoners were virtually forgotten. After it was over, as Chapter 6 shows in more detail, the penitentiary filled with newly freed blacks and began to replicate the techniques of slavery.[12]

Few women were held in Tennessee's penitentiary before the Civil War. The first male prisoners had arrived in 1831; the first woman, sentenced to the institution in 1840, had been preceded by 453 men. According to the convict record book, only thirty-one other women arrived over the next quarter of a century. In outward respects, they received care similar to that of men. Apparently they were not even isolated in a separate section of the prison. In the early 1840s Governor James K. Polk appealed for "suitable apartments" in which to segregate the women, but his recommendation went unheeded for four decades. So egalitarian was the penitentiary in its treatment of the sexes that, after the Civil War, it sent women to labor alongside men in coal mines and on railroads.[13]

But despite surface similarities between the care of female and male prisoners, women held at the Tennessee penitentiary in fact experienced disadvantages. Because of their low commitment rate, the institution's failure to hire a matron, and its post-war policy of assigning some women to work-gangs, the women were nearly (sometimes entirely) alone among the men, isolated not by a policy of segregation (as in the North) but by their small numbers and sex. The issue of privacy was always a problem for the women. Sexual exploitation through rape and forced prostitution was constantly present as a threat, if not an actuality. Thus the women's experience of incarceration must have been one of greater loneliness, vulnerability, anxiety, and humiliation than that of men at the Tennessee penitentiary.[14]

Not until the 1880s did the Nashville institution begin to separate women from the main population of prisoners. At this point it segregated women in an upper story of the entrance building, much as Auburn had isolated women above its kitchen fifty years before. Tennessee's slowness in sequestering women was due to several factors: the minuscule size of its female population until after the Civil War; the war itself, which totally disrupted prison management; and the indifference to prisoner care that formed part of the southern penal tradition. As in other states, once women were segregated, aspects of their care deteriorated. They came to suffer from extreme overcrowding: in 1894, forty-five women were incarcerated in a wing of sixteen cells. In their separate female department, women had no employment or other programs, not even a place to exercise. And until a matron was hired at the century's end, they were almost entirely cut off from prison personnel. These conditions were not worse than those of Tennessee's male prisoners, many of whom experienced forced labor as well as desperate crowding. But isolation from the men meant a change in the sources of misery for women, just as it had in New York and Ohio: earlier, women suffered from superficial egalitarianism; later, from segregation.

STAGES IN THE SEGREGATION OF FEMALE PRISONERS AND SOURCES OF UNEQUAL TREATMENT

As these examples indicate, there were phases in the process by which female prisoners were separated from the main, male populations. Patterns differed from state to state, but broadly speaking, there were three stages in the separation process. During the first, women formed part of the general prison population; they were confined in large rooms or individual cells but not further isolated. During the second, they were removed to separate quarters within or attached to the men's section—to the kitchen attic at Auburn, the annex at the Ohio penitentiary, and the upper floor of the entrance building in Tennessee. In the third stage, women were relocated to an even more isolated building on or near the main prison grounds. New York's Mount Pleasant Female Prison illustrates this third stage, as does the Woman's Building erected in the northwest corner of the yard of the new penitentiary opened by Tennessee in 1898. The evolution of separate quarters for women tended to be most rapid in the Northeast, a bit slower in the Midwest, slower still in the South, and most laggardly of all in the West. (In the late 1970s, a few western states still remained in the second stage, holding their few female felons in small units adjacent to their prisons for men.[15])

After the separation process began, female prisoners tended, in Francis Lieber's phrase, to be "much and unfortunately neglected." Their care paralleled that of men in the same institution, but the superficial resemblances concealed important discrepancies. Women were sometimes treated less severely. However, for each exemption they paid a corresponding price. Less discipline meant less supervision, and hence less protection from one another and male officers. When they lacked individual cells, women could not be classified by seriousness of offense or behavior in prison. In congregate cells they had more opportunity for conversation and companionship than men, but they suffered from lack of privacy. And in nearly every state, separation meant less access to fresh air, exercise yards, and prison staff.[16]

One source of differential treatment was the simple fact that so few women were sentenced to state prisons. In the late eighteenth and nineteenth centuries, women rarely made up more than 10 percent of a prison's population, often far less. Visiting in the early 1830s, William Crawford found only ninety-seven women in the penitentiaries of the seven most populous states and the District of Columbia. Fifteen years later, Dorothea Dix counted a grand total of 167 females in prisons from Maine through Virginia.[17] Beaumont and Tocqueville remarked of female inmates,

> It is because they occupy little space in the prison, that they have been neglected. It is the same with most evils of society, a remedy for which is ardently sought if they are important; if they are not alarming they are overlooked.[18]

Officials resented the extra demands that a few female prisoners placed on their resources. Chaplains and physicians found it bothersome to visit the female department after making their usual rounds. And to hire a matron to supervise a handful of women seemed an unwarranted expense.

Several nineteenth-century penologists addressed the question of why male prisoners so greatly outnumbered female ones. Francis Lieber found the answer in a lower female rate of crime. "In all countries women commit less [sic] crimes than men, but in none is the disproportion of criminals of the two sexes so great as in ours."[19] This lower crime rate Lieber in turn attributed mainly to women's social conditions:

> Women commit fewer crimes from three causes chiefly: (1) because they are, according to their destiny and the consequent place they occupy in civil society, less exposed to temptation or to inducement to crime; their ambition is not so much excited, and they are naturally more satisfied with a dependant [sic] situation; (2) they have not the courage or strength necessary to commit a number of the crimes which largely swell the lists of male convicts, such as burglary, robbery, and forcible murder; (3) according to their position in society they cannot easily commit certain crimes, such as bigamy, forgery, false arrest, abuse of official power, revolt, etc.[20]

William Crawford, on the other hand, suspected that chivalry, together with a need for female services and lack of cell space for women, worked to keep their numbers low:

> Few circumstances . . . impress a visitor more forcibly than the small number of females to be found in the penitentiaries of the United States. . . . I fear, however, that the criminal calendars do not convey a correct idea of the extent of crime among the female population: at least I have been assured that from the general sense which exists of the value of female services, particularly in those parts of the country which have been but recently settled, there prevails a strong indisposition to prosecute, especially if the offender be not a woman of colour. Magistrates are also reluctant to commit women from the circumstance of there not being any suitable prisons for their reception. With the exception of Pennsylvania and Connecticut, there is not a single State in which the treatment of female prisoners is not entirely neglected.[21]

In all likelihood, both Lieber and Crawford were partially correct. Today, too, far fewer women than men are committed to prison, because of lower rates of offending. Women are socialized to be more passive and nurturing than men, and as a result, they commit less crime. The same was true in the past. And in the nineteenth century, judges probably were reluctant to incarcerate women, especially those who seemed to remain within the bounds of respectability. As Sing Sing's chaplain put it in 1841, courts evidently refused "to send any female to the State prison save the *vilest of the vile*."[22]

But it was not only their small numbers that made female convicts seem insignificant. To many officials, women were by definition more troublesome and less able than men. For example, women—the outsiders— were identified as the source of sexual trouble. The proximity of women was thought to drive men to the unhealthy practice of masturbation; the presence of women led to scandals when officers were discovered fostering prostitution or fathering children. One former inmate, a male, complained of Newgate's women that "The utmost vulgarity, obscenity, and wanton-ness, characterizes their language, their habits and their manners[,] . . . agonizing . . . every fibre of delicacy and virtue." Women alone seemed to be at fault in such matters. Enoch Wines and Theodore Dwight, national authorities on prison management, argued for entirely separate prisons for women "on moral grounds, because where the two sexes are confined in the same building or the same enclosure, the very fact of this contiguity has an exciting and bad effect, and leads to endless attempts to communicate, which are not unfrequently, against all probability, successful." Wines and Dwight found, moreover, that "where prisoners of different sexes are con-fined in the same building or enclosure it is often necessary to impede light and ventilation by half closing windows, and by putting doors across pas-sages which would otherwise be left open, thus violating the laws of hygiene and obstructing an important condition of health." Such barriers were usu-ally placed on the smaller, women's units. Thus women bore the burden for separation of the sexes, just as they often bore the blame for sexual disturbances in the first place.[23]

Neglect was also a result of female prisoners' apparent inability to earn their keep. Administrators had little interest in inmates who could not turn a profit. "The product of women's labor in the State prisons," Dix observed, "fails to meet the expenses of their department." Of the female department at Connecticut's Wethersfield prison, Crawford reported: "The directors have stated their conviction that no contract can be made for the profitable employment of this part of the establishment, after paying the expense of its support and management." In an era when prisoners were expected at least to support their institution, and sometimes to contribute significantly to state revenues as well, these were serious charges against female convicts. However, those who complained of the financial liability of female de-partments ignored the fact that women were simply not assigned to, or contracted for, high-profit tasks. Provided with less lucrative work, they were in fact prevented from earning as much as males.[24]

Finally, differential treatment of women stemmed from the common belief that a female criminal was far worse than any male, depraved beyond redemption. (This conviction prevailed until the reformatory movement began.) In 1833 Francis Lieber stressed that "the injury done to society by a criminal woman, is in most cases much greater than that suffered from a male criminal," a phenomenon he attributed to woman's role as guardian of society's morals: beginning from a higher elevation, woman had further to fall. "[A] woman once renouncing honesty and virtue, passes over to the most hideous crimes which women commit, with greater ease than a man proceeds from his first offense to the blackest crimes committed by his sex." Thus, Lieber maintained, "a woman, when she commits a crime, acts more in contradiction to her whole moral organization, i.e., must be more depraved, must have sunk already deeper than a man." Similarly, Mary Carpenter, the English authority on women and crime, wrote that "female convicts are, as a class, even more morally degraded than men." We hear echoes of this belief in the complete corruption of the female criminal in Gerrish Barrett's report that the nine women in Ohio's annex gave more trouble than the penitentiary's five hundred males. A similar conviction informed the first European treatise on female crime, in which Lombroso explained that the female offender outdistanced the male in primitive depravity. At bottom the conception was rooted in the archetype of the Dark Lady—dangerous, strong, erotic, evil—a direct contrast to the obedient, domestic, chaste, and somewhat childlike Fair Lady of popular imagery.[25]

Gender-based perceptions—that female prisoners were the source of sexual mischief; that they could not earn as much as men; that they had gone beyond the pale of redemption—combined with the problem of smaller numbers to create a situation in which women's needs were slighted. The same factors operated to ensure that, once the double standard of care developed in informal practice, it continued and, in some institutions, intensified as the years went by.

MATRONS, LADY VISITORS, AND WOMEN'S PRISON REFORM

Toward the end of the nineteenth century, women themselves led the movement to establish separate prisons for their sex, and women directed these institutions as well. To what degree were women involved in the care and supervision of female convicts earlier in the century? The answer to this question helps complete the picture of treatment of female prisoners in the early period. In addition, it indicates the limits on female supervision in predominantly male institutions, particularly as a means for promoting change.

By the mid-nineteenth century, a number of states had hired matrons to supervise their female convicts. As the female populations expanded, need for matrons became ever more obvious, and one legislature or prison administration after another grudgingly established the office of matron. Quite early, moreover, far-sighted penologists began to formulate a theory about matrons that later played an important ideological role in women's prison reform. According to this theory, matrons were necessary because female prisoners by nature needed special treatment that only other women could provide. This idea appeared, in embryonic form, in Lieber's observation of the early 1830s that

> a matron [is] necessary for the special superintendence of the female prisoners; she is quite indispensable if the Auburn system is applied to women as well as men; she alone can enforce the order of this system, while it is nearly impossible for male keepers. The whole spirit of opposition in womankind is raised against him [sic]. Besides, the moral management of female convicts must differ from that of male criminals. . . .[26]

Over the next three decades this belief was expanded and refined into the notion that female supervisors were not only necessary but also possibly reformative agents. Carefully selected matrons, went the new argument, could provide role models and thus effect positive change in their charges. In the late 1860s, Wines and Dwight endorsed an English authority's belief that

> 'It is especially important . . . that female officers should be distinguished for modesty of demeanor, and the exercise of domestic virtues, and that they should possess that intimate knowledge of household employment, which will enable them to teach the ignorant and neglected female prisoner how to economise her means, so as to guard her from the temptations caused by waste and extravagance.'[27]

Matrons who exhibited characteristics of middle-class homemakers might inspire female criminals to become respectable women.

But although these new conceptions and justifications of the matron's role were in the air, they had little effect on practice before 1870. Matrons in the early prisons and penitentiaries seldom performed more than a custodial function. In many institutions, there was but one matron to supervise the entire female population. Usually she lived in the institution (sometimes in the women's section itself) and was on duty twenty-four hours a day, six and one-half days a week. Little biographical information is available on these early matrons, but they appear often to have been older women, widowed, forced by economic hardship into such unpleasant work. In other instances, they were wives of wardens. In any case, as working-class women they were unlikely to provide the middle-class role models that progressive penologists recommended. Moreover, even if some early matrons had had the energy for reform, they had no authority with which to realize such an ambition. Hired by the warden, they could also be fired by him if they strayed too far from prison tradition. Mary Weed, who ran Philadelphia's Walnut Street Jail between 1793 and 1796, was an exception to this rule. But elsewhere, women involved in prison administration were subordinate to men.[28]

Another route through which women became involved in prison operations before 1870 was lay visiting. Inspired by religious principles, some women passed through the dreary gateways of penitentiaries to succor and uplift female criminals. Most notable among this group were the lady visitors at Philadelphia's Eastern Penitentiary. Eastern was famous in the United States and Europe for its system of perpetual solitary confinement. Inmates were kept in total isolation from one another on the theory that they would thus reflect and repent instead of picking up new criminal habits. Despite the spartan aspects of their care, Eastern's prisoners were well supervised, and they were permitted to have selected visitors. At a time when its female population numbered as low as twenty, the institution hired a matron to care for their needs. Moreover, according to Dorothea Dix, although they were "chiefly employed in making and repairing apparel," the women had "full time for the use of books, and the lessons which are assigned weekly by the ladies who visit the prison to give instruction."[29] These visitors belonged to the Association of Women Friends. Dix reported that the Quaker women made

visits every Monday afternoon throughout the year; and you may see them there seriously and perseveringly engaged in their merciful vocation. Their care extends to the convicts after the expiration of sentences. These ladies read the scriptures, furnish suitable books for the prisoners, give instruction in reading, writing, and arithmetic; and what is of great value, because reaching them through a direct influence, instruct them by conversation, suited to their capacity.[30]

The efforts of the Philadelphian ladies to comfort and educate female inmates echoed, if but faintly, events already underway in England, where about 1815 Elizabeth Fry, another Quaker, had begun similar work. Such efforts were soon mirrored in several New York State developments. At Ossining, New York, two women took over management of the Mount Pleasant Female Prison in the mid-1840s and introduced some of the techniques of reform that later became staples of women's prison discipline. At almost the same time, middle-class women in New York City organized a women's branch of the reformist Prison Association of New York. Under the leadership of yet another Quaker, Abigail Hopper Gibbons, this Female Department of the Prison Association established a halfway house where discharged female prisoners could receive shelter, moral training, and help in finding positions as domestic servants. On both sides of the Atlantic, these early manifestations of concern by women outside the walls foreshadowed the tremendously strong current of reform that eventually swept some women out of men's prisons entirely and into female-run institutions of their own.[31]

But true reform, in the sense of structural change in the care of prisoners, could not be accomplished by these lady visitors, high-status matrons, and prison association members. Such activists supplemented the matron's role and contributed to its redefinition, but at mid-century they did not actually challenge the conditions under which women were confined. Despite prisons' growing willingness to employ matrons and the unquestionably meliorative efforts by outsiders in Philadelphia, Ossining, and New York City, profound change in the condition of female prisoners could not occur until reformers identified what was later recognized as the source of the problem: the fact that women were held in institutions designed for men. Once the problem was defined, the solution seemed obvious—a fourth stage in the process of separation of female from male prisoners, in which the former would be removed to prisons of their own.

THE MOUNT PLEASANT FEMALE PRISON

This fourth stage did not occur until the reformatory movement began in the last quarter of the nineteenth century, but it was anticipated by New York's establishment of the Mount Pleasant Female Prison at Ossining in 1835. The founding of Mount Pleasant was a milestone in the evolution of women's prisons. This institution was the first women's prison in the United States: it was deliberately established by an act of the legislature,[32] in contrast to other women's units of the period, which developed haphazardly as appendages to men's prisons. Although Mount Pleasant was both geographically close to and administratively dependent on the Sing Sing prison for men, it existed apart, with its own buildings and staff. Moreover, during the years in which Mount Pleasant was administered by two innovative women, it became the site for experiments that forecast the great reformatory movement just ahead.

Construction having taken several years, Mount Pleasant was not ready to receive prisoners until 1839. Even before the prison officially opened, women at Bellevue were transferred to Sing Sing, so anxious was New York City to pass them on. They were held in a cellblock of the men's institution until the new prison was ready, at which point they and the women from Auburn were transferred to Mount Pleasant. A New York law of 1841 instructed that, thereafter, all women sentenced to a state prison should be sent to the female department at Sing Sing.[33]

The women's prison was situated on the hill behind Sing Sing, separated from the men's quarters by a roadway and overlooking the Hudson River. According to a description of the late 1860s, it was "a handsome building . . . with a Doric portico of imposing proportions."[34] The inside was modeled on the Auburn plan, with three tiers of twenty-four cells each. In the west end of the building, from which the view was best, the matrons had their quarters. At the east end, within the prison area, stood an elevated platform used for chapel services and lectures. Below it was a nursery. In addition to the main building this prison included a workshop and two large, separate cells for punishment, each cell with its own yard. The men's section of Sing Sing was as yet unenclosed, but a high wall was built around the women's complex to minimize communication between the sexes. More cell space was needed within a few years. The women's prison, however, could not easily be expanded or remodeled. "Poorly designed and difficult to alter," W.D. Lewis has observed, "the Greek temple overlooking the Hudson was an example of penny-wisdom and pound-foolishness."[35]

Ultimate authority for management of Mount Pleasant lay with the board of inspectors of Sing Sing, but daily administration was left to a matron to whom was delegated the same authority over government and discipline as that given the principal keeper of the men's section. Several assistant matrons helped her with these tasks. During most of the years of its operation, the prison's matrons were at best unremarkable, at times disastrous. Two, however, were outstanding: Eliza Farnham, who served as chief matron from 1844 to 1847, and Georgiana Bruce, a former resident of Brook Farm, the Utopian community, who assisted Farnham during her first year. Their experiments with reformational techniques were the most radical and ambitious efforts of the time to improve criminals morally.

Georgiana Bruce's account of the background to Farnham's appointment gives an idea of how tumultuous life could be in an inadequately supervised female department.

[Under the previous matron] there had been a sort of rebellion among the convicts, or among some of the most daring, who had deliberately refused to conform to the rules of the prison, or to perform the duties assigned them. They tyrannized over and maltreated the weaker and more docile of their fellows, and made night hideous by singing blasphemous and obscene songs.

The matron, a respectable, but incompetent person, had finally been attacked and the clothes torn from her body. A well-meaning, tightskulled little chaplain had prayed frantically for the rebels,—prayed to them also. They made a feint of yielding, then turned the prison into a pandemonium again.

. . . The Board, on making a visit to the prison, had been met by shouts of derision and insolent defiance, and they had to make a hasty exit to escape the kids [wooden food tubs] flung at them by the rioters.

By a most fortunate chance Judge Edmunds [Edmonds; board member and prison reformer] heard of Mrs. Farnham, and one interview with her convinced him that he had found the person he was in search of, and she was shortly engaged as a matron. . . .[36]

Farnham was only twenty-eight years old at the time, and Bruce but twenty-five; yet through a combination of firmness and kindness, they rapidly reestablished order at Mount Pleasant. A phrenologist, Farnham believed that if she could stimulate her charges with positive influences, their criminal tendencies would be overcome. To this end she introduced a program of education, instructing the women each morning on "the more interesting persons in the history of our country, in . . . astronomy, in geography, and also in . . . the elements of physiology and physical education." She added novels such as *Oliver Twist* to the prison's library (which at the time of her arrival consisted solely of seventy-five copies of *Call to the Unconverted Sinner*), and she permitted inmates to take books to their cells. "The wayward creatures," Bruce reported, "found by degrees that their prison was turned into a school, and they lost the inclination to make trouble." Farnham was a strict disciplinarian, yet she tried to keep rules to a minimum. She modified the rule of total silence, permitting inmates "to talk in a low tone to each other half an hour every afternoon, providing that they had conformed to the rule of silence during the remainder of the day." In another departure from contemporary practice, she and Bruce attempted to alleviate the grimness of the prison environment by introducing flowers, music, and visitors from the outside. Significantly, Bruce referred to the prison as "our reformatory."[37]

Such innovations, though widely endorsed toward the end of the century, shocked many of Farnham's contemporaries. Conservatives such as Sing Sing's chaplain considered novel-reading irreligious. Moreover, Farnham's relaxation of the silent rule sowed dissension at the neighboring men's prison, where the rule still prevailed. Farnham's opponents publicly attacked her and her reforms. She fought back but eventually lost the struggle, resigning in 1847.

Like most other female convicts of the mid-nineteenth century, those at Mount Pleasant worked long hours at tasks considered appropriate to women—in this case button-making and hat-trimming, as well as sewing clothes for male prisoners. Other than work, their program was minimal, consisting in 1841 of only a Sabbath school taught by lady visitors. By 1843 (the chaotic year preceding Farnham's appointment), even the Sabbath school had been discontinued. With Farnham's arrival began a brief period of programs. Convicts continued to work, but Farnham made time for religious observances and instruction. This enraged her critics, who charged that the women's prison should be earning higher profits. Farnham retorted that women in the female prison, like their counterparts outside the wall, were paid much less than men. But this logic did not appease her profit-minded opponents.[38]

Mount Pleasant seems to have been the first state prison to include a nursery. Babies could occasionally be found in other nineteenth-century custodial institutions: in an act of 1843, for example, the Tennessee legislature instructed the penitentiary to "receive with Pricilla Childress, a convict from the county of Giles, her infant child," and in 1869 New Jersey officials complained that a black woman who had been incarcerated for years had recently given birth to a mulatto child, fathered by a guard. But only the records of Mount Pleasant make reference to separate accommodations for infants. Before special arrangements were made for the care of newborns, infant mortality rates ran high. According to the Prison Association of New York, for instance, before establishment of the Mount Pleasant nursery, every child born at Sing Sing had died. Women's reformatories that opened in the late nineteenth and early twentieth centuries usually allowed women to keep their babies, and because these institutions received mainly young sex delinquents, their infant populations were often sizeable. Babies posed a greater problem for custodial prisons that, like Mount Pleasant, received felons; the serious offenses and lengthy sentences of female felons made prison administrators reluctant to admit infants with their mothers. But Mount Pleasant, because it held the largest population of female convicts in the country and because it was founded explicitly for the care of women, came to terms with the problem posed by infants. The presence of a nursery at Mount Pleasant meant that the difference between the incarceration experiences of men and women was greater at Sing Sing than at other penitentiaries. Moreover, women did not automatically lose their babies or have to devise ways to care for them in single cells. The special needs of female prisoners were being recognized.[39]

Disobedient women were punished less brutally than men at Sing Sing, yet their chastisements were severe. One punishment was gagging, which Dorothea Dix found "shocking and extremely objectionable." Judge Edmonds reported that at Sing Sing, " 'The gag has been sometimes applied, but it has been only among the females that it has been rendered *absolutely* necessary!' " On the other hand, he found, " 'In the women's prison, the lash is never used. There the punishments are confinement to their own cells in the main dormitory, or in separate cells, with reduction of food' " and, of course, gagging.[40] Farnham preferred kindness to punishment as a means to achieve order, but even she could react harshly, meting out long periods of solitary confinement, cropping women's hair, and using the gag and straitjacket. A list of violations and punishments in 1846 included:

— Noise and violence in her room at noon. Shower bath.[41]

— Disobedience and noise in her room. Twelve days in solitary confinement in outer cell.

— Noise in her room at night. Straight [sic] jacket for the night, and bread and water for one week.

— For rushing from her cell when the door was open . . . and repeating it many times . . . a chain six feet in length was made fast to the wall and locked upon her wrist.[42]

Administration of corporal punishment had not yet become a matter about which even reform-minded authorities felt embarrassment.

Overcrowding at Mount Pleasant—or rather New York's refusal to create space for its growing numbers of female convicts—eventually led to the institution's demise. By 1865, with nearly two hundred prisoners, Mount Pleasant was close to double its capacity. That year the legislature ruled that women from the seventh and eighth judicial districts should be sent to local institutions instead of to the women's prison. A law of 1877 ordering transfer of all Mount Pleasant's inmates to a county penitentiary emptied the prison entirely. For more than a decade thereafter, New York held its female state prisoners in local institutions.[43]

As the phenomenon of Mount Pleasant demonstrates, the seeds of the women's reformatory had been sown by mid-century. At Mount Pleasant, women were confined apart from men and supervised by other women. Under Farnham and Bruce, female convicts—for perhaps the first time— were encouraged by prison administrators to reform. And the techniques introduced by Farnham—education, example, sympathy—later became crucial to the reformatory program. But as Mount Pleasant also indicates, these seeds could not survive in the harsh environment of the penitentiary. Education could have little effect in an institution whose main interest was profits; role models and sympathetic understanding were incompatible with straitjackets and bars. Most importantly, no thoroughgoing change in the treatment of women could take place until female prisoners and their matrons were freed from second-class status in institutions that insisted on male authority and precedence.

Until about 1870 the custodial institution was the only type of penal unit for women. It received its fullest articulation at Mount Pleasant, but all other female departments exhibited its traits. The custodial model was a masculine model: derived from men's prisons, it adopted their characteristics—retributive purpose, high-security architecture, a male-dominated authority structure, programs that stressed earnings, and harsh discipline. In comparison to women's reformatories, women's custodial institutions treated inmates like men. But as we have seen, this did not mean that women's care and experience of incarceration were identical to those of males. Probably lonelier and certainly more vulnerable to sexual exploitation, easier to ignore because so few in number, and viewed with distaste by prison officials, women in custodial units were treated as the dregs of the state prisoner population.

CHAPTER 2 ||||||||||||||||||||||||||||||||

Origins of the Women's Reformatory, 1870–1900

About 1870 the penal treatment of women began to undergo revolutionary change. A comprehensive reform movement was set in motion, one that in time challenged nearly every assumption of the penitentiary tradition. This revolution produced a unique model of prison for adults, the women's reformatory. The rehabilitative impulse that fed this revolution also affected men's prisons; the men's prison system, too, established reformatories in the last quarter of the nineteenth century. But men's reformatories did not abandon the custodial model: they were created to punish as well as to rehabilitate and, with their high walls and cellblocks, they repeated the penitentiary design. In short, men's reformatories grafted the new penology of rehabilitation onto the custodial setting.[1] Women's reformatories, in contrast, broke radically with custodialism. Scorning the goal of punishment, leaders of the women's reformatory movement concentrated on rehabilitation. Eschewing traditional architecture, they eliminated walls and cellblocks. These innovators were appalled by prisons that treated women much like men. They devised new programs to meet what they considered the special needs of female prisoners. But the legislation establishing women's reformatories enabled them to incarcerate women for pettier offenses than those for which men could be held, and these laws greatly extended the terms that women were required to spend behind bars. Moreover, reformatory programs, based as they were on a restrictive concept of "true womanhood," imposed on inmates a limiting definition of femininity and required them to conform to a stricter sexual morality than that expected

23

of men.[2] In the process of attempting to rescue and reform fallen women, those who founded women's reformatories established another mode of differential treatment, distinct from but no less oppressive than that of the custodial tradition.

FROM CONCEPTION TO MATURITY:
EVOLUTION OF THE REFORMATORY MODEL

The Revolution Begins

The first steps toward designing a new type of prison exclusively for women were taken in the Midwest. Michigan began the process by founding a prototype of the women's reformatory in the late 1860s. This House of Shelter was not a separate institution, and it survived only a few years; but it introduced a number of the techniques that later became characteristic of true reformatories for women. Not long after the House of Shelter opened, the country's leading penologists gathered in Cincinnati for a historic convention at which they established the ideological platform on which the reformatory movement would be built. In addition, they endorsed the concept of separate prisons for women. Almost simultaneously, a group of Quakers in Indiana opened the first entirely independent, female-staffed women's prison. This institution held felons rather than the misdemeanants who were later identified as the best subjects for reformational treatment. However, it created a context in which, for the first time, reformatory principles could be applied without reference to the demands of male prisoners. Owing to these midwestern developments, the idea that women deserved separate, specialized penal treatment had been within a mere five years both legitimated and put into practice.

At first glance, the Detroit House of Correction seems to have been an unlikely site for far-reaching experiments in the treatment of female prisoners. Established in 1861, the institution was designed to hold Michigan's young male prisoners as well as nearly all of its female ones.[3] It was operated by the city of Detroit but functioned as a state prison, with Michigan reimbursing the city for state convicts' expenses. Despite its name and its original emphasis on female and young male offenders, the Detroit House of Correction was a custodial institution. The separate yards for exercise of women and men, for instance, were each "surrounded by a brick wall sixteen feet high, surmounted with sentinel towers." There was, in brief, nothing remarkable about treatment of women at the institution in its earliest years.[4]

But the Detroit House of Correction was superintended by Zebulon R. Brockway, who from it launched one of the most influential careers in the history of U.S. corrections. Brockway's plan of inducing prisoner cooperation through a system of incentives was already in evidence at the House of Correction in the mid-1860s. There he had begun to use "grading," a method of rewarding obedient prisoners with promotion to better living conditions. As yet, however, he had not introduced the most potent incentive of all, the indeterminate sentence that could grant to well-behaved convicts early release on parole. Significantly, this most radical element of the new penology was first tried out on women.

Specialization in the care of female prisoners began when Brockway established the House of Shelter as an adjunct to his prison. Inspiration had come during a visit to the Lancaster, Massachusetts, school for delinquent girls, where Brockway had observed several reformatory features. One was an approach that divided the girls into small "family" groups in which they received domestic training; another was the employment of female officers considered sufficiently refined to serve as role models. The visit suggested to Brockway "what could be done to save our women prisoners, and on my return to Detroit I asked and readily obtained permission to build what we named the 'house of shelter.' " The shelter opened in 1868.[5]

The following year Michigan enacted the country's first indeterminate sentencing law, the famous "three years law" that empowered Brockway to hold women convicted of prostitution for up to three years. This piece of legislation marked a turning point in American penal policies. It applied to women only, singling them out for special treatment. Moreover, it provided for extended sentencing: the three years law subjected prostitutes to a longer period of confinement than previously on the theory that with retraining, they might be reformed. And the three years law introduced the possibility of parole. It is noteworthy that Michigan refused to apply the bold innovation of indeterminate sentencing to men. Although it was willing to experiment in the case of women, the legislature rejected Brockway's parallel proposal for paroling men sentenced to the House of Correction. Similarly, the total reformatory program was later applied more thoroughly to women than men. This program, like indeterminate sentencing, implied an increase of state authority in the lives of prisoners. Officials were more hesitant to impose on men the most radical forms of control.[6]

The three years law made parole possible, but as yet no one knew what to do with prisoners granted early release—a problem to which the House of Shelter provided an answer. The shelter received women granted parole and held them till their sentences expired. Thus, parole originally meant transfer to a more benign setting rather than release under supervision. At the shelter, parolees resided with several other groups of women. One group consisted of well-behaved "upper grade" women sentenced to the House of Correction; for them, entry into the less punitive shelter served as a reward. Women who voluntarily entered the shelter after their terms at the House of Correction had expired constituted another group; for them the shelter functioned as a halfway house. Finally, the shelter also received wayward girls. To deal with these disparate groups, the shelter developed a program that combined features of relaxed prison discipline with those of the protective "home." This program became typical of the women's reformatory.[7]

At the time the shelter was founded, few prison administrators had any interest in, much less any idea of how to achieve, the reformation of female criminals. But Brockway was convinced that the effort should be made. Before long, he had his prison's inspectors agreeing with him. "The dismissal of a convict woman from her prison gates," wrote the inspectors in 1868, "has been an open dismissal to a life of renewed crime and shame."[8] Brockway freely admitted that he was venturing into new and perhaps perilous territory:

> How much can be done, we confess we do not know. But we are profoundly convinced that little can be done to reclaim fallen women, except through the sisterly care, counsel and sympathy of their own sex.[9]

Maternal care by other, more respectable women was the key idea around which Brockway constructed his program of reform. "It is intended to receive here," the institution's inspectors explained,

> as into a home, women who . . . seem willing to accept a reform of life. It is intended that they should be received here into a family life, where they shall receive intellectual, moral, domestic, and industrial training, under the influence, example and sympathy of refined and virtuous women.[10]

With justification, McKelvey has referred to the shelter as "in a sense the first women's reformatory in America."[11]

Emma A. Hall, hired to be the institution's teacher but later made its matron as well, put the newly forming theories of female rehabilitation into daily operation at the House of Shelter. Emphasizing religious uplift, domesticity, and academic improvement, Hall foreshadowed the generation of reformatory superintendents who followed her. She brought to her work experience as a teacher and a missionary sense of purpose. Brockway spoke with awe of her perseverance under the bleak conditions of the basically custodial prison:

> She had not, nor under the circumstances could she have any social life outside the institution where she lived; no outside entertaining

occasions either private or public. . . . Sole head of the house of shelter, without assistance beyond the service of prisoner women of her charge, she must herself be always present early and late, attending to all the details of the family life.[12]

Willingness to endure the stigma of living with prisoners and dedication to the task of helping less fortunate women also characterized reformers who followed Emma Hall's lead into female corrections. But these later officials usually worked in the more benign context of a true reformatory, and they had other women to support their efforts. In Emma Hall, Brockway indeed found a self-denying, virtuous woman to implement his experiment in reforming female criminals. And in Brockway, female corrections found a powerful superintendent willing to encourage specialized care of incarcerated women.

Under Hall, education assumed a prominent role in the shelter's program. Inmates prepared lessons during their noon work-break and attended school four evenings a week. By 1871, Hall had trained seven inmates to assist with instruction at this school, where prisoners studied reading, writing, and arithmetic. But while education later played an important part in the programs of women's reformatories, it was also stressed by reformatories for men. What most distinguished women's reformatories from men's was the former's emphasis on propriety and decorum—on preparing women to lead the "true good womanly life."[13] Hall pioneered in this type of training. In her words,

the most interesting feature of the house, and I am prone to say the most useful, is the Thursday evening exercise and entertainment. On this evening the whole family dress in their neatest and best attire. All assemble in our parlor, together with some of the longer sentence prisoner women from the house of correction as invited guests, and enjoy themselves in conversation and needlework, awaiting the friend who week by week on Thursday evening, never failing, comes at half past seven o'clock to read aloud an hour entertaining stories and poetry carefully selected and explained. After exchange of salutations between the 'young ladies' and madam the visitor, and after the reading, tea and simple refreshments are served in form and manner the same as in refined society.[14]

Elements of the shelter's Thursday evening programs became hallmarks of the reformatory program: replication of the rituals of genteel society, faith in the reforming power of middle-class role models, and insistence that inmates behave like ladies. Such concerns hardly informed the treatment of men, or even that of women in other custodial institutions. Female corrections was starting to diverge from mainstream prison practice, to define a unique type of treatment.

The House of Shelter closed in 1874, shortly after Brockway and Hall had resigned from the Detroit House of Correction. According to a sour observation by Brockway, the experiment was terminated because overcrowding in the main prison

> made demand for more room . . . so that the house of shelter buildings were required for officers' quarters and offices. There was, too, on the part of my successor as superintendent . . . less appreciation of the importance and practicability of accomplishing reformation with prisoners, notwithstanding the facts and results so clearly manifest.[15]

But although the shelter itself was short-lived, it had inaugurated changes that soon reshaped the penal care of women. In conjunction with the three years law, it had introduced indeterminate sentencing and parole. By promising to rehabilitate, it had justified extended sentencing of female morals offenders. And the shelter had made deliberate efforts to treat female prisoners differently from males by providing training in the way "good" women should behave. Channeled through the conduit of the convention of prison administrators held in 1870 in Cincinnati, the techniques conceived by Brockway and Hall in Detroit flowed into what became a mainstream of female corrections.

The women's reformatory movement was part of a much broader current in prison reform that began not long after the Civil War and produced the penal philosophy known today as the rehabilitation or treatment approach. Disillusioned with older, custodial methods, and half-ashamed by a prison system that aimed no higher than punishment, leading penologists in the late 1860s began a crusade to upgrade both the theory and practice of incarceration. They rejected the older purpose of retribution in favor of a new goal, prisoner reformation. To replace traditional prison practices, they proposed new methods of discipline modeled after a system of incentives and rewards pioneered in Ireland at mid-century. The new penology received its initial—and impressively thorough—articulation at a large gathering of prison administrators and reformers in Cincinnati in 1870. Under the presidency of Rutherford B. Hayes, then governor of Ohio, this first national prison congress endorsed a series of "principles" that guided U.S. penology for the next century. One of the triumvirate who ran the convention and helped formulate its principles was Zebulon Brockway.

Brockway's proselytizing on behalf of the new penology was all the more persuasive because he had already begun putting it into practice at the Detroit House of Correction.[16]

The absolute necessity of prisoner classification formed one of the convention's central themes. Classification itself was not a new idea; it had been of interest to prison administrators since the founding of the first state prisons, for division of inmates into separate groupings provided an obvious means to increase control. But at the 1870 convention, classification was touted as the crucial preliminary step in individualizing the treatment of prisoners; individualized care, in turn, would encourage prisoners to reform. This preoccupation with classification logically led to a call for entirely separate institutions for women. According to the congress's *Declaration of Principles,* "Prisons, as well as prisoners, should be classified or graded so that there shall be . . . separate establishments for women." The *Principles* also held that "both in the official administration of such a [reform-oriented prison] system, and in the voluntary co-operation of citizens therein, the agency of women may be employed with excellent effect." The women's reformatory movement had begun to stir before the Cincinnati meeting. But the congress's endorsement of these principles relating to the classification and employment of women gave the fledgling movement respectability and impetus.[17]

The convention also identified, in broad outline, ideals and techniques that later became basic to the women's reformatory program. Delegates condemned corporal punishments, for example, urging that they be replaced by inducements to good behavior. The meeting's members threw their support behind indeterminate sentencing and state supervision of paroled prisoners. Training in religion, letters, and industry—these, too, were recommended as ways to achieve what Brockway called "the ideal of a true prison system for a state." Most importantly, the delegates advocated increased control over the *minds* of prisoners, the gaining of "the will of the convict . . . so that the prisoner shall choose for himself what his officer chooses for him." These ideals and methods were later incorporated by women's reformatories—much more thoroughly, in fact, than by reformatories for men. But in the process of incorporation they were also transformed, feminized, transmuted into a domestic form unanticipated by those who articulated and endorsed the convention's *Principles.*[18]

Among the Indiana delegation in attendance at the 1870 prison congress were Charles and Rhoda Coffin, a Quaker couple who soon thereafter applied the *Principles* in an all-female setting. Through the Coffins' efforts, the Indiana Reformatory Institution for Women and Girls opened in Indianapolis in 1873. Unlike the Detroit House of Shelter or the earlier Mount

Pleasant Female Prison, the Indiana institution existed apart from a men's prison. In addition to being the first completely independent women's prison, it was also the first to be run by an entirely female staff. Most prison histories recognize the men's reformatory at Elmira, New York, as the first adult reformatory in the country; but that distinction actually belongs to the Indiana women's reformatory, which opened several years earlier.

Pressure for establishment of a separate women's prison in Indiana had built up from several sources. Previously, female felons had been held at the Indiana State Prison at Jeffersonville, where officials had been eager to get rid of them. The prison's warden complained in 1869, "We have all the female convicts of the State, whose labor is altogether unproductive, and who are an expense," and Jeffersonville's physician found female prisoners an "expense and annoyance." Then too, Indiana lacked an institution for delinquent girls; it was thought that by combining the populations of felons and delinquents, the expense of a separate institution for females could be justified. Third and most decisive, "very grave charges" had been brought "against officers and guards" at Jeffersonville "of drunkenness, and . . . prostitution of female convicts, and demoralization generally."[19] When these charges had surfaced in 1866, the Coffins had traveled to Jeffersonville to investigate. "Could I convey to you," Rhoda Coffin wrote,

> some idea of the terrible abuses which have been unveiled in the investigations which my husband and myself have made into the conditions of our prisons . . . , you would at once be convinced of the need of some reform as regards the case of female criminals.[20]

The Coffins had found that guards carried keys to the women's cells. "The results in some instances HAVE BEEN MOST TERRIBLE. . . . [The women] may be forced to minister to the lust of the officers, or, if they refuse, to submit to the infliction of the lash until they do." The Coffins reported the matter to the governor of Indiana, who, in the words of Charles Coffin, "visited the prison himself and entirely substantiated all that we had reported. He brought the subject to the attention of the Prison Committee of the Legislature, and they sent a deputation to visit it and reported back that 'the half had not been told.' " The Coffins' desire to rescue and reform these women accomplished what the distaste of Jeffersonville's officials for female convicts could not have achieved alone. "It resulted," Charles Coffin concluded, "in the establishment of a Women's Prison and Reformatory in Indianapolis, and the removal of the inmates from Jeffersonville to the new prison."[21]

The new institution was situated about two miles from the center of Indianapolis. Observers described its central building as "graceful and imposing" and "not very prisonlike in appearance." This building had two "departments," one for the adult felons, the other for the delinquent girls.

The two were completely separate, however, each having its own kitchen, laundry, and yard.[22]

Responsibility for internal administration was delegated to a superintendent and her assistants. According to law, all these officers were to be women unless the superintendent were married, in which case her husband might also be an administrator.[23] Sarah J. Smith, a Quaker and former matron of Indiana's Home for the Friendless who had participated with the Coffins in earlier efforts at prison reform, became the first superintendent. With her husband, who served as steward, she guided the novel institution through its first ten years. One of Smith's first actions was to journey to Detroit to observe Emma Hall's methods of running the House of Shelter. Like Hall, Smith was intensely religious and deeply devoted to her work. She was also acutely conscious of her responsibility to ensure that the experiment at Indianapolis succeeded:

> This being the only governmental prison known—either in the United States or in Europe, under the entire management of women—we have felt the responsibility of our position and have sought to so discharge the trust assigned to us as to ensure success to the institution and to be an honor to our State, which has thus taken the advanced step of assigning to women the privilege of caring for, elevating and reforming her own sex.[24]

These were heavy burdens, especially as Smith and her colleagues had few precedents to follow in their attempts to develop a distinctive form of penal treatment for women.

Ultimate administrative authority over the new prison was assigned to the three-member Board of Managers, appointed by the governor. Originally, all these managers were men. A conflict soon developed between them and the superintendent, brought to light by Lewis Jordan, a member of the subsidiary Board of Visitors. According to Jordan, writing in 1876, the president of the Board of Managers "to some extent has supplanted the Superintendent in supervising and directing the domestic affairs of the Institution. Upon inquiry, I find that he has made his will paramount in all things." The president had visited the prison frequently and issued orders on his own. Although Smith had not complained to Jordan, "from several sources I have learned that her position has been made quite unpleasant by the continued supervision of the minutiae of the household by the President of the Board." Supporting Smith in the conflict, Jordan recommended that the law be changed to require that all the managers be women. This was accomplished in 1877, at which point Rhoda Coffin joined the board as its president. Thereafter, the two levels of administration were united in their goals and procedures.[25]

In the restrictions it placed on women who might be admitted and in its sentencing structure, the Indiana reformatory adhered to the custodial tradition. Its adult department received only felons, women over fifteen years of age who would formerly have been sent to the state prison. Prisoners were to serve the same terms as if at Jeffersonville, and their sentences were of the traditional, definite type until indeterminate sentencing was introduced at the turn of the century. Several of the prison's records provide glimpses of the first prisoners, the women transferred from Jeffersonville in 1873. These were the women whom the Coffins had discovered being victimized by male guards. Such discoveries notwithstanding, Rhoda Coffin later reported that the prisoners were indignant when, upon arrival in Indianapolis, they found they could no longer trade "certain favors" for liquor and tobacco. According to the prison's first report, "when told they could not use [tobacco] in any form, gloom and sadness settled like a pall upon them which taxed all our ingenuity to dispel. Our superior accommodations sank in utter insignificance, and . . . they wished themselves back to 'old Jeff!' " Another witness described them arriving "with their white tucked skirts and morning wrappers and trunks full of fine clothing." Hardened felons, these first prisoners presented a formidable problem to the Quakers who sought to redeem them.[26]

In its program, the new prison amplified the theme of domestic treatment sounded earlier at the House of Shelter. Like female penologists in other states, Smith and her successors abhorred the trappings of the penitentiary. Inmates under their charge wore "simple, well-fitting dresses, protected by tidy aprons." "Linen covers" were "spread over the clean tables, simple but attractive china" made "the room attractive, and a vase of flowers" was "not considered too good for prison life"—all this on the theory that "refinement" would serve "as a minister in reforming character." The desire to copy home environment influenced discipline as well as decor. Although there was a cell where refractory inmates could be confined, "we have not a weapon of defense in the house," the superintendent reported in 1898, "and they all know it. We cannot govern all alike; their natures must be studied, the flash of the eye; the expression of the face must be noted. We approach very carefully the citadel of the inner life of the subject of reproof and reprimand." Tablecloths and china, reproofs and reprimands—these were logical extensions of the techniques pioneered in Detroit.[27]

In its early days the Indiana reformatory did not offer an educational program, but it did provide an abundance of domestic training. The main activities were laundering, sewing, and knitting. Little machinery was purchased on the theory that "it is best for them to learn these much-needed branches of labor thoroughly by hand, hoping it may help them to get homes when their time expires." The prison aimed at preparing inmates "to occupy the position assigned to them by God, viz., wives, mothers and educators of children." To supply good examples through role models was another important aspect of the prison's reformational program. At the end of its first year the administration announced that its inmates were under the constant influence "of pure womanly examples." No applicant was hired as an officer unless she agreed to conduct religious services.[28]

In the Indiana prison, the reformatory model only partly emerged from its chrysalis: the new institution received only felons; it did not, originally, utilize indeterminate sentencing; and it made no attempt to reform through formal education. But on the other hand, the institution made tremendous advances over the House of Shelter in its total independence from any prison for men and its investment of full authority in female administrators. In the following decades, reformers in a number of states failed to accomplish the political feat that the well-connected Coffins had managed so neatly: persuading key state officials of the need to finance a separate prison for women. That forty years elapsed before another women's reformatory was founded in the Midwest underscores the magnitude of the Indiana accomplishment.

The New Model Takes Shape:
Late Nineteenth-Century Reformatories of the Northeast

Ground for the women's reformatory movement was broken in the Midwest, but shortly after 1870 the thrust of the movement shifted eastward. There, over the remainder of the century, Massachusetts and New York established three more independent prisons for women. Collectively, the three northeastern institutions had a more profound influence on the evolution of the women's reformatory system than any others, for, through successive institutional approximations, they arrived at what reformers throughout the country came to view as the ideal reformatory design. Picking up where the House of Shelter and the Indiana reformatory had left off, these prisons established the "pure" reformatory model that, in the early twentieth century, states throughout the country would attempt to emulate.

The Cottage Plan

One contribution of these northeastern institutions to the reformatory model was the "cottage" plan, an architectural embodiment of the notion that criminal women could be reformed through domestic training. This design was not adopted immediately; the new institutions had to feel their way. The only model for adult prisons available to them was that of the maximum security fortress. In search of a design more suitable to what they considered woman's gentle and domestic nature, leaders of the women's reformatory movement in Massachusetts and New York turned to the cottage plan first utilized at the Lancaster, Massachusetts, reform school for girls in 1856. Lancaster inmates lived in self-contained units built to hold about thirty inmates each. These cottages (which, like the "cottages" built by the wealthy at Newport, in fact looked like substantial homes) were supervised by house parents and managed like families.

This design appealed to those who mapped out the northeastern prisons for women in the late nineteenth century. But the reformers were preparing to deal with adult criminals, not children, and to many of them this was as yet an unfamiliar population. Thus they experimented cautiously with architectural innovation. The reformatory plant evolved slowly from Massachusetts' prison for women to those institutions established later in New York.

The Massachusetts Reformatory Prison, which opened at Sherborn (later incorporated into Framingham) in 1877, most closely resembled the custodial style of prison, consisting of a central building with three hundred cells and two fifty-bed dormitories. Founder Hannah Chickering had projected at least some cottages,[29] but the huge congregate building was erected instead. This structure expressed, architecturally, the older, punitive prison philosophy, and it reflected the fact that the domestic training programs that later became central to life in women's reformatories were still in an embryonic stage. Clearly, the Massachusetts institution (like the one at Indianapolis) was built at a very early point in the transition from prison to reformatory—a circumstance also indicated by its original title, "Reformatory Prison."

The next northeastern reformatory, New York's House of Refuge, opened in 1887 at Hudson. This was the first prison for adults to adopt the cottage plan. However, Hudson also had a central prison building with traditional cells to which new inmates were assigned for a probationary period, an indication of some uneasiness about the new design. This prison building could hold up to 150 inmates, whereas Hudson's cottages had a combined capacity for only 96; the emphasis, that is, still fell on custody. Furthermore, the first cottages did not include living rooms; the notion of the cottage as a family unit was only half-formed as yet. Cottages built at Hudson after it opened, however, did include living rooms, and significantly, in 1897 the State Board of Charities recommended that the cellblocks in the prison building be torn out and this space converted to dormitories.[30] Authorities were beginning to realize that they could break more completely with the custodial tradition.

The last in this series of northeastern reformatories, the Western House of Refuge opened in 1893 at Albion, New York, also consisted of a central building and outlying cottages. But at Albion, the majority of beds were located in the cottages. Moreover, unlike the original cottages at Hudson, those at Albion were, in the words of its first annual report, designed to promote

> the idea of family life, each cottage with its own kitchen, its pleasant dining-room adjoining, which matrons and girls use in common, and the living or sitting room in the second story, where the family assemble in the evening for diversion.[31]

Photographs of the Albion reformatory in its early days reveal a sharp break with the atmosphere of the custodial prison. Though austere, the interior spaces were nonetheless homelike, with flowers and tablecloths, and pictures on the walls.

While they were incorporating the cottage plan, the northeastern reformatories were also moving ever further into the countryside. Many late nineteenth-century reformers subscribed to the belief that rural life was moral life. They reasoned that if offenders were removed from crime-inducing cities, given healthful doses of fresh air, and forced to exercise, they might be cured of the disease of crime.[32] In contrast to the Indiana reformatory, built close to a major town, the Massachusetts Reformatory Prison was located about twenty miles outside Boston. New York's first House of Refuge was situated at Hudson, a village close to the Berkshire mountains of western Massachusetts, its second in the far western area of the state, about halfway between Rochester and Buffalo. Faith in the curative properties of rural surroundings was also reflected in the increasingly large acreage of these institutions: about sixteen acres at Indianapolis, thirty at Sherborn, forty at Hudson, and ninety-seven at Albion.[33] In the early twentieth century, states establishing women's reformatories automatically began by purchasing vast stretches of farmland.

Commitment Standards and Sentencing Practices

The heart of the women's reformatory model lay in its assumptions about commitment. The nineteenth-century northeastern reformatories developed commitment policies that differed greatly from earlier prison practice. They extended the power of state punishment to a population of offenders who previously had been sent to local jails, if incarcerated at all. They instituted indeterminate sentencing schemes that made it possible for states to imprison female misdemeanants and even lesser offenders for periods of years. And they created a category of female state prisoner that had no male counterpart. Men's reformatories held not misdemeanants but felons, the traditional state prisoner population. Men convicted of fornication, drunkenness, and other minor crimes for which women were typically committed to reformatories were simply not sent to state prisons.[34] At most they were punished with brief jail terms, just as women convicted of such offenses had been before the reformatories opened. Women's reformatories, then, were based on acceptance—indeed, willing embrace— of differential standards for the imprisonment of women and men. Reformatory advocates and administrators believed they were doing women a service by providing special care. Women, they argued, deserved extra protection. But the reformers' good intentions do not cancel out the fact that in the course of helping, they gave legal force to a double standard that punished women more severely than men who had committed the same offenses.

Like the standards for the physical design of the ideal reformatory, these commitment standards evolved over time. The first northeastern reformatories varied in the restrictions they placed on prisoners eligible for their care. Venturing as they were into uncharted territory, they experimented with a number of approaches.

The original commitment law of the Massachusetts reformatory permitted it to receive women of all ages, but only those convicted of minor offenses. There was a flood of commitments in the first year—nearly eight hundred women, mainly inebriates and prostitutes; so a provision was added making it possible to exclude repeaters. As time passed, personal and property offenders began to join the population, and early in the twentieth century Massachusetts enacted a law mandating commitment of female felons to the reformatory. But petty morals offenders constituted the overwhelming majority of women received at Sherborn during its first decades of operation.[35]

New York's commitment practices were even more restrictive. Hudson and Albion excluded all but women convicted of petit larceny, habitual drunkenness, and prostitution. (New York's third reformatory, opened in the early twentieth century at Bedford, was more adventuresome, extending its care to women convicted of other misdemeanors and selected felonies as well; but again the emphasis of commitment law and practice fell on petty thieves, inebriates, and prostitutes.) Unlike Massachusetts, New York placed an upper limit on the age of women who might be sent to reformatories, rejecting older inmates as unlikely to reform. The upper and lower ages of those who might be committed to Hudson were continually set lower until, in time, Hudson became a training school for girls. Albion and Bedford settled on a range between sixteen and thirty years of age for their commitments.[36] These two institutions, having defined the most suitable reformatory commitment as a young woman guilty of a minor offense, established the commitment standards that became typical of women's reformatories. When other states founded separate prisons for women in the early twentieth century, they tried (though not always with success) to replicate the commitment practices of—not Indianapolis, Sherborn, or Hudson—but Albion and Bedford.

Another, less visible, aspect of the commitment practices of these northeastern reformatories is equally significant: their exclusion of black women. Published records do not mention this practice, making it difficult to detect. But the reformatories' failure to report on race, while giving details on inmates' ages, marital status, and place of birth, strongly suggests that they accepted white women only. This suspicion is reinforced by Albion's prisoner registries: Albion did not receive a black until after several years of operation; during its first decade, its admissions were 97 percent white. The prison's registries marked out spaces in which clerks were to record all sorts of personal details on incoming inmates, but they left no space for race, indicating that those who designed the registries did not contemplate the possibility of receiving women of color. (When blacks were admitted, the clerk wrote "Negro" at the top of the page.) Black women were admitted to reformatories in the twentieth century, but in small numbers; and they were usually segregated in cottages of their own. As Chapter 6 explains at greater length, the reformatories' racially selective commitment policies, in combination with the tendency of custodial institutions to take in large numbers of black women, meant that the two branches of the women's prison system were split along racial as well as other dimensions. Reformatory officials wished to work with women who were worthy of reform—a viewpoint that, for them and the judges who made the commitments, disqualified most blacks.

Another commitment practice that distinguished reformatories from many custodial institutions was the willingness of the former to allow inmates to keep their babies. All three of the northeastern reformatories made arrangements for the care of infants born in prison or who were nursing at the time their mothers were incarcerated. This policy reflected the prisoners' youth—many were at the point of bearing their first child—and their offenses, which were often crimes against chastity. The Massachusetts reformatory eventually banned babies on the theory that imprisonment "gives a bad record to an innocent child."[37] Hudson and Albion, on the other hand, built separate nursery cottages for their infants, as did a number of twentieth-century reformatories. The presence of babies made incarceration a qualitatively different experience for reformatory women than for custodial prisoners. Infants intensified the domestic atmosphere of the reformatory, and mothers were spared the physiological and psychological trauma of separation from newborn infants.

The early reformatories of the Northeast were among the pioneers in indeterminate sentencing, a phenomenon intimately linked to their founders' desire to hold minor offenders for long periods of retraining. Sherborn, the first founded of the three, went through a period of trial and error as it felt its way toward use of the indeterminate sentence. The law establishing the Massachusetts institution specified a two-year maximum sentence (this for offenders previously liable to a maximum of six months). However, it did not set a minimum term, and many women were released after a stay of less than one year. Short terms seemed to subvert the retraining of offenders; thus changes of 1880 established a one-year minimum sentence for all.[38]

Indeterminate sentencing and the possibility of reformatory care led to differential punishment of men and women, an effect illustrated by two Massachusetts laws of 1880. In that year the legislature ruled that men, and also women sent to local jails, could be held for up to one year on a third conviction of drunkenness. Women sent to the reformatory with the same record, on the other hand, were to be held for a minimum of one year and a maximum of two. Extension of terms for women was justified on grounds of benevolent intention. Reformatory advocates argued that they needed time "to break up, if possible, old habits and associations, and bring the inmates under that moral and religious influence, without which little hope of permanent reformation can be expected." Yet it was through such arguments that a double standard for the treatment of male and female offenders made its way into law.[39]

New York stretched the concept of indeterminate sentencing to its limits. Originally, the minor offenders sent to Hudson or Albion could be held for up to five years. Some courts objected to the disproportionality involved in such long commitments, however. In 1888 the Hudson House of Refuge complained that judges were not sending eligible women to it in the mistaken belief that five-year sentences were too harsh, given the nature of the offenses involved. Judges simply had not grasped the point, according to Hudson's managers, that because the purpose was reformation, long sentences were "indispensable to good results." "[S]urely," the next Hudson report exclaimed, "five years is not too long for the sundering of old and evil associations, the breaking of pernicious habits, the formation of new, and the practice and continuance of such till they become fixed and stable." Despite these protests, in 1899 the maximum term for women committed to Hudson and Albion was lowered to three years. It remained nonetheless true that female minor offenders were still liable to far longer imprisonment than before the reformatories were founded, and that no similar extension of state control occurred in the case of men convicted of petty crimes.[40]

Programs and Discipline

Just as the early northeastern reformatories developed commitment and sentencing practices that came to be regarded as ideal for a women's prison, so did they work out methods for training and disciplining inmates that set the pattern for later reformatories. The three institutions aimed at training prisoners to become upright and competent homemakers. Academic, vocational, and religious training were woven together in programs that emphasized conformity to middle-class concepts of femininity. Of the three, Albion ran the most ambitious educational program, schooling women through the sixth grade level. Like the House of Shelter's Thursday evening soirees, its offerings were laced with gentility. Alice E. Curtin, who headed Albion's school department at the turn of the century, reported that she required written compositions each Friday, gave final exams, and staged graduation ceremonies at which inmates received "certificates of promotion." Albion also sponsored a series of special events. To celebrate the hundredth anniversary of the establishment of the public school system, "Mr. Irving M. Thompson of the Albion School Board gave an informal talk," and he returned again on Arbor Day to "favor" the inmates "with an appropriate address on the uses of trees, their beauty and value." Through such edifying activities, loose girls were to be transformed into respectable women.[41]

Vocational training at the reformatories centered around institutional chores—cleaning, cooking, and sewing—partly out of practical necessity but mostly because administrators believed that reform of female offenders involved making them proficient in domestic tasks. Massachusetts Superintendent Ellen C. Johnson did establish an extensive farm program, and she planted a mulberry orchard in an abortive attempt to start a silk industry. At Albion, too, gardening and farming were important activities in early years. But as time went on, the agricultural emphasis at both institutions declined. Vocational training at New York's nineteenth-century reformatories revolved around the cottages, both institutions priding themselves on their "home-like atmosphere." One Hudson report referred to this as the reformatory's "mainspring."[42]

The northeastern reformatories broke ever further with the traditions of custodialism as they elaborated their characteristic familial mode of discipline. For example, the Massachusetts reformatory permitted conversation only at specified times; Hudson allowed talking in the corridors, where inmates could associate during the day; and Albion seems to have discarded the silent rule entirely. Like the House of Shelter and the Indiana reformatory, the northeastern institutions preferred maternal guidance, the power of good example, and development of inmates' self-control to older penal methods of achieving order.

The reformatories worked out their own, feminized version of the disciplinary techniques advocated by the prison congress of 1870. All three used a grading system to reward good behavior. With promotion to a higher grade came privileges such as transfer from the prison building to a cottage, permission to swing one's arms freely rather than clasping them behind the back while walking, and the opportunity to wear a prettier uniform and add more decorations to one's room. All three also rewarded good behavior with early release from prison. Women were paroled to "good homes," often as domestic servants.

In discussions of prison discipline, there is always a question of how closely administrative rhetoric conformed to reality. Albion, during its early years of operation, seems to have remained faithful to reformatory ideals. Inmates and staff apparently worked together with a good degree of co-operation. Credit for this success was due largely to the first superintendent, Mary K. Boyd. Boyd came to Albion well versed in institutional management, having served for many years as girls' matron at a reform school for juveniles. Persuaded that the female temperament could not abide harsh discipline, Boyd kept rules and punishment to a minimum. Hudson, on the other hand, often reverted to the old-fashioned disciplinary methods that in theory it eschewed. Two years after Hudson opened, the State Board of Charities (SBC) questioned whether solitary confinement was not being overused there. Though convinced that some women had to be kept in cells to preserve "good order . . . and the personal safety of . . . inmates," the SBC hoped such confinement would be used sparingly. Six years later it condemned the use at Hudson of dark cells for punishment, arguing that they were "depressing and unsanitary." According to the SBC, the dark cells were often used to punish trivial offenses, and women were sometimes held in them for weeks with no exercise and little food. But Hudson's lapses were less significant than the SBC's condemnation of them. The SBC assumed that women should be spared stringent rules and punishments. Nineteenth-century reformatories had established this principle, and twentieth-century reformatories tried to follow it.[43]

The experience of incarceration in a reformatory was doubtless far more benign than that of being imprisoned in a custodial institution. An all-female staff greatly reduced the fear of sexual coercion. Reformatories discarded the traditional accoutrements of security, doing away with creneled walls and guard towers, and providing women with semi-personalized rooms rather than cells. Instead of being treated worse than male state prisoners (as was usually the case for women in custodial prisons), reformatory inmates were often treated better. Some of the women who cared for the inmates viewed prison work as a mission, and though these supervisors could be stern and moralistic, many made genuine efforts to help their charges. Reformatory inmates enjoyed fresh air and opportunities for exercise, advantages unknown in many custodial units for women; and few were forced to endure the straitjacket or lash.

It is, however, necessary to recognize that in several important respects, the reformatory regimen was the harsher of the two. First, women's reformatories ignored a fundamental principle of justice, according to which the punishment should fit the crime. Those who lobbied for reformatories maintained that it was quite proper to ignore the rule of proportionality because their aim was not to punish but to treat—to retrain and reform, processes that required time. But in light of the concept of proportionality, up-to-three (or however many) years was a high price to pay for minor offenses. Second, women's reformatories were harsher because they punished women more severely than men who had committed the same offenses. Custodial prisons were more evenhanded: they held men and women convicted of similar crimes.

Finally, reformatories were harsher because they tried to remold prisoners instead of merely punishing them. As Zebulon Brockway observed, "Contrary to a common notion, stricter control is required in a reformatory . . . than in an ordinary convict prison." Michel Foucault, the French prison historian, makes the same point when he writes that the most severe penal institutions are those that impose a variety of disciplines. Like the French training school for boys at Mettray, American reformatories for women combined several "coercive technologies of behavior"—in the American instance, those of the family and school as well as that of the prison. The first two were those that were expected to reform, and of these, familial discipline—which was not imposed in custodial institutions or in men's reformatories—was the most exacting.[44]

THE WOMEN'S REFORMATORY MOVEMENT

By 1900, the revolution was complete: traditional concepts of incarceration had been challenged and the reformatory model brought to the point of full development. Impressive as this accomplishment was, it was no more difficult than the task of founding reformatories in the first place—of creating the contexts in which the experiments had taken place. Establishment of a women's reformatory was usually an arduous process that required mobilization of supporters and organization of legislative lobbies.

Leaders and their Arguments

Those who campaigned for women's reformatories can be separated, for analytical purposes, into three groups. First and most influential were the women who spearheaded state campaigns and those superintendents who became prominent advocates of the reformatory cause. A second group comprised supporters with positions on prison and welfare boards. At first these were nearly all men, but as women recognized their need for political leverage, they found ways to join men on these state boards. The third and most peripheral group consisted of loose confederations of individuals and organizations that, in the various states, helped lobby for separate women's prisons.

Members of the first group—the founders or would-be founders and the proselytizing superintendents—were for the most part middle-class or upper-middle-class women with both a strong desire to involve themselves in socially useful work and the free time to devote to it. Many had been active in other causes such as abolition of slavery, nursing during the Civil War, temperance, and aid to the needy before turning their energies to women's prison reform. For example, Hannah B. Chickering, a founder of the Massachusetts reformatory, had been instrumental in establishing the Temporary Asylum for Discharged Female Prisoners at Dedham. Josephine Shaw Lowell, a prime mover in the establishment of all three of New York's reformatories for women, came from a family deeply involved in antislavery. Having lost a brother and husband during the Civil War, she roused herself from sorrow by helping to establish schools for blacks in the South. Later she became the first female member of New York's State Board of Charities. Lowell's initial undertaking on the SBC was to found an institution for women—in this case, an asylum for "feeble-minded" women at Newark, New York. From their earlier work, women such as Chickering and Lowell had developed the political skills requisite for leadership of the incipient reformatory movement.

Comparison of these leaders with the early nineteenth-century lay visitors and matrons suggests why the later reformers accomplished so much more in terms of real change in the conditions of incarcerated women. Like the Quakers who had visited Philadelphia's Eastern Penitentiary, some of the reformers (Rhoda Coffin, for instance, and Sarah Smith and Hannah Chickering) had strong religious motives for their work. Unlike the lay visitors, however, a number of the reformers became prison officials. And in contrast to the first matrons, the reformers accepted administrative positions not because they needed income but because thay had energy and enthusiasm to devote to a cause. They were, moreover, determined to run their own institutions rather than play subordinate roles to wardens. In contrast to even the most innovative of earlier administrators, Eliza Farnham and Georgiana Bruce, members of the later group had a highly articulated program of reform. In addition, they were willing to fight political battles to realize that program.

In Massachusetts as in other states, mobilization of support for a women's reformatory began with a nucleus of dedicated women who affiliated themselves with a state prison or welfare board. Hannah Chickering, secretary of the Dedham halfway house for discharged female convicts, dominated the Massachusetts movement in its early stages. Chickering's visits to women in jails had brought her face to face with the fact that they were simply not being reformed. "They are soon again arrested, re-committed," she explained sadly, "and this mournful round is trodden again and again, till a wretched death closes the scene for these victims of misfortune, neglect, and sin." Chickering began with the modest proposal that one of the state's jails be turned into an all-female institution. The Greenfield jail was so designated for a brief period, but resistance from the sheriff forced abandonment of that plan. Thereafter Chickering and her associates set their sights higher, on an entirely new institution that would be independent and thus free of male interference. But they recognized that they needed a political base if they were to achieve this aim. Thus they worked to establish a board of commissioners of prisons that would have an advisory board of three women. Chickering became a commissioner on this advisory board when it came into being in the early 1870s, along with Ellen Cheney Johnson, another leader in the Massachusetts movement and later a superintendent of the reformatory. The prison commissioners formed the state body that, in Massachusetts, moved the bill for a women's prison through the legislature and into law. [45] The more peripheral supporters of the movement in Massachusetts included three men active in the national prison reform movement—Zebulon Brockway, Franklin B. Sanborn, and Enoch C. Wines—and a league organized in 1873 to petition legislators to appropriate money for a women's prison. [46]

In New York the movement's leaders were Josephine Shaw Lowell and Abigail Hopper Gibbons, the latter for many years head of the Women's Prison Association of New York. Not surprisingly, in view of Lowell's position as one of its commissioners, the key state body in New York was the State Board of Charities. The outer ring of supporters included Governor Alonzo B. Cornell, who in his annual message of 1881 recommended establishment of a reformatory for women; [47] the Women's Prison Association; and the State Charities Aid Association, a philanthropy with a strong contingent of women, some of them close friends of Lowell.

The women's reformatory movement was not always as successful as the examples of Indiana, Massachusetts, and New York suggest. Three other states experienced a surge of agitation for a women's prison in the late nineteenth century but failed to respond. In New Jersey, a commission appointed in the mid–1880s to study the needs of incarcerated women recommended that a separate institution be built. This suggestion was deflected however, in part by the appointment of a capable matron who brought order to the women's unit at Trenton state prison. [48] In Connecticut, demands for a women's prison were turned aside by the establishment of an institution for a more "hopeful" type of offender, the delinquent girl. Reformers in Rhode Island began calling for a separate prison for women at the very early date of 1869. Using a strategy similar to that concurrently employed in Massachusetts, they succeeded in 1871 in establishing a board of "seven competent women" to inspect institutions in which women were imprisoned. [49] This board tried to enlist Rhode Island's State Board of Charities and Corrections (SBCC) in its cause; but the SBCC consisted solely of men, and they made light of the recommendations of their female advisory board. As one angry woman put it, "You have heard many times that advice is very cheap. Now the women's board is called advisory. They give advice, and the gentlemen [of the SBCC] hear it very politely and ignore it." Thereafter the women focused their energies on getting women "of trained and proven ability in philanthropic methods" appointed to the SBCC itself.[50] Like New Jersey and Connecticut, Rhode Island eventually did establish a separate prison for women. But most of the original members of its reformatory movement died before their goal was realized.

Very similar arguments were put forth in support of women's reformatories in the various states, arguments that often echoed the *Principles* endorsed by the 1870 prison congress. If female prisoners are to be reformed, advocates reasoned, they must be isolated entirely from men and put under the supervision of women. Instead of being relegated to the poorest quarters in the penal institutions, they must be confined under circumstances that might restore their self-respect. They should be provided with academic, vocational, and moral training, and their treatment should be individualized. Female offenders must be held for longer terms than at present, the argument continued, for short terms make reformational work impossible. Further, the reformatory should incorporate classification, grading, and other features of the Irish system of prison discipline. To these arguments of principle, the backers sometimes added a few of practicality: establishment of a women's prison would free cell space for men in jails and houses of correction, and the labor of female prisoners would become more profitable if all were located in one place. On occasion, reformers spoke as though the new institution might also relieve their state prison of its burden of female felons. But in fact, they were mainly interested in petty offenders who, they believed, were more likely to respond positively to retraining.

In New York, a eugenic rationale was added to the usual arguments, mainly through the influence of Josephine Shaw Lowell. About the time she had become a member of the State Board of Charities, Lowell had been deeply affected by *The Jukes,* Richard Dugdale's study of a degenerate family of criminals, drunkards, and mentally diseased persons who, Dugdale implied, were produced by promiscuous women. Lowell was anxious to have New York establish institutions where such women could be prevented from breeding more of their kind. (This belief led to her work to establish the Newark Custodial Asylum for Feebleminded Women, housing a female type considered especially prone to promiscuity.) "[O]ne of the most important and most dangerous causes of the increase of crime, pauperism and insanity," she wrote in 1879, "is the unrestrained liberty allowed to vagrant and degraded women." Lowell argued that reformatories could serve two ends: reformation of fallen women, if possible, eugenic restraint if not. Both ends required longer sentences than "vagrant and degraded women" were currently receiving. Lowell's eugenic reasoning was strongly seconded by her allies in the State Charities Aid Association.[51] In the twentieth century, as we shall see, one of New York's reformatories for women became a testing center for eugenic theory and practice.

The Broader Context

Although lobbyists for women's prison reform were at times frustrated by uncooperative sheriffs, tightfisted legislators, and commissioners who refused to take them seriously, they worked within a cultural context that in many ways supported their efforts. It would be difficult to identify all of the many currents that shaped the character of the women's reformatory movement and its institutions, deeply embedded as these were in pervasive assumptions about differences between the sexes, the origins of social problems, and the rehabilitative potential of institutions. But several factors stand out, calling for particular attention: that type of nineteenth-century meliorism that has been labeled "social feminism"; the closely related social purity movement; evolution in the theory and practice of reforming juvenile delinquents; and the changing image of the female offender.

Social Feminism

During the period 1870–1930, middle-class women participated in a variety of reform movements aimed at improving the lot of "the dependent and defective classes" and other underprivileged or disenfranchised groups. Expanding traditional roles, they moved into areas considered appropriate for women—those involving children, the sick and needy, other women, and public morality. In contrast to "radical feminists" who asked more probing questions about the sexual division of labor and the justice of existing social structures, social feminists began with faith in the existence of a separate woman's sphere and the basic efficacy of the social institutions that they sought to reform. Social feminism flowered most luxuriantly in the Northeast where, owing to more rapid industrialization, middle-class women were more fully freed from household labor. Able to hire servants, purchase machines that lightened household chores, and buy ready-made goods, these women had time to devote to causes. Their economic circumstances encouraged distinctions between the sexes, and between leisured and working-class women as well. The concentration of social feminism in the Northeast does much to explain why, after its start in the Midwest, the women's reformatory movement became most powerful and effective in the Northeast in the late nineteenth century.[52]

The nature of social feminism itself, moreover, helps explain the nature of the women's reformatory. Like other reformers of their day and ours, social feminists involved in prison improvement were not inclined to pose deep challenges to prevailing social arrangements. Their hope was to better prison conditions. Their faith in the intrinsically moral, nurturing, and domestic nature of women (or at least of "true" women) predisposed them to feminize the architecture and routines of institutions that they brought under their control. Armed with belief in inherent differences between the sexes, they naturally sought to establish all-female institutions, prisons uncontaminated by male influence, in which criminal women would receive sympathetic care from members of their own sex.

By drawing on the precepts of social feminism, leaders of the reformatory movement legitimated female involvement in prison administration. This achievement, however, had ironic implications for both their own work and that of later female prison officials. Almost by definition, social feminists clung to and amplified gender stereotypes. Indeed, such stereotypes were the vehicle on which they rode into public life, for, as Jill Conway has pointed out, "Intellectually they had to work within the tradition which saw women as civilizing and moralizing forces in society." However, in the process of establishing educational institutions for females, juvenile courts, settlement houses, women's reformatories, and so on, "they naturally duplicated existing assumptions about the sexes and their roles." As Lois Banner has observed, "The social feminist rationale for the participation of women in reform and in government was . . . anti-feminist in implication" because "it was based on the traditional image of the woman."[53] Similarly, with specific reference to the prison reformers, Estelle Freedman has concluded:

> Like the "separate but equal" racial ideology, . . . social feminist strategy rested on a contradictory definition of equality. . . . [A]t the heart of their program was the principle of innate sexual difference, not sexual equality.[54]

Social feminism cleared the path by which women entered corrections. But it locked female administrators into narrow, sexually stereotyped roles and out of positions in the far more numerous institutions for male offenders. It also encouraged—virtually mandated—them to apply the double standard to their charges.

The Social Purity Movement

One of the many causes to which social feminists devoted their energies was the so-called social purity movement, a national campaign to clean out saloons, stamp out vice, raise standards of sexual morality, and strengthen the American home. The purity crusade began about 1870 with a battle against proposals for regulation of prostitution. Outraged by the suggestion that prostitution should be condoned, feminists and male allies, many of them former abolitionists, organized "as new abolitionists dedicated to the emancipation of the white slave—the prostitute."[55] From there the purity movement swelled to become a multifaceted, loose coalition of groups supporting temperance, moral education, sex education, and municipal government reform, and opposing gambling, immoral literature, and venereal disease. Eugenic and nativist sentiments underpinned the purity campaign as they did many other turn-of-the-century reforms.

The social purity and women's reformatory movements converged over the effort to uplift fallen women. Purity activists encouraged prison reformers to focus on the prostitutes and other loose women who became the reformers' preferred subjects for institutional retraining. The social purifiers found an outlet for their program of moral education, and their concern with protecting women, in the women's prison movement. Those who crossed over from purity efforts to the reformatory movement, furthermore, often brought with them considerable political skills, gained through earlier work in organizing and lobbying.

One of those who moved between social purity and women's prison reform, cross-fertilizing the two movements, was Elizabeth Buffam Chace. A Quaker abolitionist, Chace became, after the Civil War, both a purity worker and a leader of the campaign for a women's reformatory in Rhode Island. Josephine Shaw Lowell, too, was a foe of prostitution and a reformatory advocate. Similarly active on several fronts was Abby Hopper Gibbons. Another Quaker and abolitionist, Gibbons had founded the Isaac Hopper Home for discharged female convicts in New York. As head of the New York Committee for the Suppression of Legalized Vice, she was nationally prominent in the purity crusade. Working closely with Lowell, Gibbons headed the effort to establish the New York reformatory for women at Bedford. To her work on behalf of Bedford she brought a lifetime of experience with political processes, gained in her earlier campaigns. In 1892—when she was over ninety—Gibbons made a dramatic appearance before the New York State legislature to urge enactment of the bill for the Bedford reformatory. According to her friend Alice Sandford, her last words before she died the following year were, "Be sure, Alice, thee makes it a Reformatory and not a Prison." When Bedford finally opened, it fulfilled Gibbons's hope and perpetuated her work by becoming a national leader in methods of reforming the impure woman.[56]

Historians point out that antiprostitution reformers such as Gibbons opposed the double standard of sexual morality. Gibbons and her allies did object, ardently and vociferously, to the arrest of prostitutes while male customers went free, and their efforts were indeed directed toward raising men to the chaste and family-centered sexual ethic upheld by women like themselves. But to emphasize the opposition of purity advocates to the double standard is to obscure the fact that these same people did much to institutionalize the double standard through their work for women's reformatories where prostitutes, public drunkards, and other petty offenders would be subjected to moral retraining. The ethic upheld by the reformers was that of bourgeois women: they did indeed urge men to adopt the same standards; but they did not campaign for prisons where unchaste men, like working-class women with lax morals, would be held for long terms. In the name of reform, opponents of the sexual double standard paradoxically made the criminal justice system an instrument of differential justice that punished women more harshly than men for sexual activity.

Institutions for Juvenile Delinquents

Another influence on the character of the women's reformatory was the system of institutions for juvenile delinquents. Determined to break with the custodial traditions of men's prisons, those who created women's reformatories turned to the juvenile system for a better model. From its inception in 1825, the juvenile system had been based on the *parens patriae* doctrine that justified state intervention in family situations that seemed to encourage delinquency. Under this doctrine, children could be sent to reformatories for status offenses—noncriminal acts (such as waywardness and truancy) considered serious when committed by minors. Intimately connected with *parens patriae* were beliefs about benevolence, prevention, and reform. Removal of children from bad homes to benevolent institutions (so the reasoning ran) would prevent further slippage into vice; and it would provide opportunities to wean children from vices already learned. This philosophy of state-as-parent had inherent appeal for leaders of the women's reformatory movement. They absorbed themes from it into their own ideology, thereby justifying state intervention in cases of moral deviation by adult women.[57]

Reformatory leaders were also attracted by specific features of the juvenile system. That system, as Schlossman has shown, was just beginning to establish itself firmly in the 1850s and 1860s. Its leaders were going through a phase of reconsidering earlier approaches to the cure of delinquency. Rejecting the large congregate buildings and heavy-handed discipline of early nineteenth-century institutions for children, they had begun to domesticate reformatory architecture and programs. One innovation was the cottage plan, first introduced at the Lancaster Industrial School for Girls. (This plan and its familial approach to treatment, as we have seen, profoundly influenced Brockway as he stood on the threshhold of the women's reformatory movement.) In another effort to increase the curative power of the juvenile reformatory, states had begun situating these institutions in rural areas where children would be insulated from urban evils and encouraged to recover their former innocence.[58] The new reformatories for juveniles, moreover, were "anti-institutional institutions." They shed features of the penitentiary in favor of those associated with the common school and the home, introducing academic classes, house parents, and (in girls' reformatories) programs of domestic training. Girls sent to such institutions were often committed for morals offenses. Even before the 1870 prison congress, juvenile reformatories had utilized a form of indeterminate sentence (children could be held till the age of majority) and a type of parole (at Lancaster and other institutions that held them, girls were usually placed as domestic servants toward the end of their terms). Unlike prisons for adult males, the juvenile reform schools were supervised by state boards of charity and institutional boards of managers.[59]

Reformatories for adult women eventually adopted many of these characteristics. Most importantly, the reformatories took on aspects of the protective "home"—a development signified by New York's naming its late nineteenth-century reformatories "refuges." The first two women's reformatories received older women. But later reformatories trained their sights on a population that more closely resembled that of the girls' reform school—young women who had committed status offenses or, at worst, petty theft. This shift in emphasis—really a rejection of the type of women sent to custodial institutions in favor of an entirely new prison population—contributed to a new conception of the nature of "the" female offender.

A New Image for the Female Offender

Women held in state prisons before the establishment of reformatories were popularly regarded as monsters of depravity, far more deeply enmired in corruption than male criminals. Because "true" women were considered the guardians of morality, when a woman transgressed she seemed to threaten the very foundations of society. As noted in Chapter 1, this early view of the female criminal as beyond redemption was related to the archetype of the Dark Lady, a woman of uncommon strength, seductive power, and evil inclination. Just as the reformatory movement began, this image of the criminal woman began to fade from discussions of female criminality. It did not disappear, but it was superseded by a new concept of the female offender as childlike, wayward, and redeemable, a fallen woman who was more sinned against than a sinner herself. If not entirely congruent with the archetype of the Fair Lady, the new image did present the female offender as *potentially* chaste, domestic, and girlish. With reformers' help, this new female offender could regain her place on the pedestal of true womanhood.

Late nineteenth-century beliefs about the nature of women in general helped demote the female criminal from the status of a mature, if wicked, woman to that of an impressionable girl. As social class distinctions hardened within nineteenth-century society, middle-class women became "ladies," delicate and vulnerable creatures. No one expected factory girls or domestic servants to display all the attributes of the lady, but in discussions of "women's nature," traits associated with the lady were generalized to all women. Even the female offender was now depicted as frail and helpless, more a vulnerable child than a hard-hearted enchantress. As the first report of the Hudson House of Refuge put it, "women are weaker and less able to protect themselves." The notion that women were less adult than men was solidly embedded in nineteenth century laws regulating voting, divorce, and property rights. In 1872, for example, the Supreme Court upheld the exclusion of women from the practice of law on the ground that "The natural and proper timidity and delicacy which belongs [sic] to the female sex evidently unfits it for many of the occupations of civil life. . . . The paramount destiny and mission of woman are to fulfill the . . . offices of wife and mother. This is the law of the Creator." According to God, the Supreme Court, and popular opinion, then, women had more in common with children than with adult men. This attitude spilled over into theories about female lawbreakers.[60]

The transformation in the image of the female offender was in large part the work of the reformers themselves. It was they who wrote and lobbied for laws that increasingly restricted reformatory admissions to youthful and minor offenders. A desire to exert their efforts on "hopeful" subjects motivated the reformers. Furthermore, they needed to justify their work: to legitimate their takeover of part of the prison system, they had to prove that criminal women were different from men. According to the Massachusetts Commissioners of Prisons, arguing in 1873 for a women's reformatory,

> women need different management from men; they are more emo-
> tional and more susceptible; they are less likely to be influenced by
> general appeals or force of discipline, and are more open to personal
> treatment and the influence of kindness.[61]

"Emotional" and "susceptible"—this was a far cry from Francis Lieber's picture of the female criminal as a calculating, amoral horror. A report of the Detroit House of Correction made even more explicit the link between the criminal woman's difficult yet malleable nature and the need for female supervisors:

> There are mental peculiarities; there are dark and diverse shades
> of character; there are labyrinths and mazes of moral perversion,
> among female prisoners, that demand the presence and molding in-
> fluence of thoroughly qualified matrons and lady teachers, who,
> by quicker and more exact intuitions, are enabled to treat and con-
> trol more successfully the peculiarities of these erring ones.[62]

The moody, impressionble nature of the "new" female offender qualified her for supervision by other women. Women could lay claim to care of the dependent and delinquent. But hardened adult offenders, including the un-salvageable "masculine" criminal woman of early nineteenth-century thought, were quite another matter.

That the female offender came to be pictured as not only a malleable juvenile but also a sexual delinquent was part and parcel of late nineteenth-century, middle-class attitudes toward sexuality.[63] Social purity workers labored to eradicate prostitution and venereal disease, to foster cohesion in the American family, and to promote higher standards of sexual morality. The impure woman—especially one who willingly engaged in acts of "un-chastity"—posed a direct threat to the self-image of purity crusaders and other women who strove to establish reformatories. As Freedman puts it, the fallen woman "represented, on a basic level, a symbol of women's resistance to the ideal of purity."[64]

Freedman goes on to argue that over the course of the nineteenth century, female reformers became ever more sympathetic to the fallen woman and appreciative of her potential for rehabilitation.[65] It is certainly true that they came to depict her as a victim and then worked vigorously to redeem her. But Freedman's analysis underestimates the challenge presented by the fallen woman to the reformers' self-image. Indeed, if the fallen woman was *not* a victimized "sister" but rather an autonomous, deliberately sexual being, then the *raison d'être* of social feminists—their concept of womanliness and, with it, the justification for their work—was built on air. An unconscious sense of this danger also accounts for the reformers' fixation on the fallen woman and their desire to remake her in their own image.

The new conception of the female criminal and the reformatory model evolved together, feeding into one another. Like sculptures built up in bits and daubs, they both developed through accretion, their features gradually emerging through experiments at the various reformatories. By the end of the nineteenth century, they were fully formed, social creations that no longer needed retooling. Reformers, with the initial, formative stage of their work behind them, were now ready to plunge into the task of establishing separate women's prisons across the country.

CHAPTER 3 ||||||||||||||||||||||||||||||

THE WOMEN'S REFORMATORY MOVEMENT, 1900–1935: FROM SUCCESS TO DECLINE

About 1900, various currents of social concern converged to create a new reform movement that swept over society for the next several decades, restructuring old institutions and introducing new types of public regulation. The Progressive movement was particularly strong in the Northeast and Midwest, where it tackled a broad array of problems from corruption in city government to prison conditions, from denial of women's suffrage to public health and urban slums. Idealistic and moralistic, Progressives proposed to make government responsive to an increasingly urban, industrial, and ethnically mixed society. Like earlier reformers, they desired to purify and uplift, but the Progressive impulse was more secular in nature and more ambitious in scope.

Tremendous optimism characterized Progressive activities on all fronts. According to prison reformers in New Jersey, for instance, the state would actually save money by establishing a women's reformatory. Such an institution, they claimed, would prevent recidivism by "turn[ing] three-quarters of women offenders into self-respecting members of society."[1] Filled with faith in the efficacy of state intervention and in the righteousness of their causes, Progressive reformers militantly extended social controls through Americanization programs for immigrants, constraints on corporate power, establishment of juvenile courts and probation departments, and expansion of psychological testing programs and of public education. Workers in new or rapidly growing professions such as social work and mental health viewed themselves as "social engineers," redesigners of traditional arrangements on a massive scale. Their optimism was fed by confidence in the power of science: with research and rational planning, medical and social science would identify and correct the causes of social ills. In the area of penology, this cult of science manifested itself in enthusiasm for the medical interpretation of crime as a disease. Early in the twentieth century, psychiatrists joined prison staffs to conduct mental tests, make case studies, and individualize treatment; and prison "clinics" and "laboratories" were established to discover scientifically the causes of crime.[2]

Two strains in Progressive thought had a particularly powerful effect on approaches to the female criminal. One was eugenics, the "science" of racial improvement. Some criminals, it appeared to eugenists, were not "made" by faulty environment but "born" through faulty heredity. These "defective delinquents" suffered from an incurable disease—"feeblemindedness"—that rendered them incapable of controlling primitive, criminal urges. The female defective delinquent, because of this innate deficiency, was "denied the power to choose the good" and thus automatically sank into immorality. But—and here the characteristic Progressive hopefulness and reliance on science came in—defective delinquents could be identified by the new science of mental testing. Once identified, they should be segregated for life to prevent them from breeding more of their kind. "Scientific" studies of women such as "Margaret, mother of criminals," and Deborah Kallikak seemed to prove that promiscuous, feebleminded women were the polluted source of generations of criminals, moral imbeciles, and the insane. Through eugenic restraints on such women, crime and other diseases of society might be all but eradicated in the next few decades.[3]

The emergence of prostitution as a national issue in the Progressive period also focused attention on "promiscuous" women. Fueled by elaborate investigations of "the social evil" and "white slavery" in nearly every major city, antiprostitution forces aimed at elimination of loose women, venereal disease, and moral contamination in general. Demanding "that society may be protected" from the immoral woman, one reformatory advocate in Wisconsin inquired, "With her kind drifting up and down the streets of every small town, can you say that your sons and daughters are in no danger? . . ." The antiprostitution movement, led by social purity workers, perpetuated the preoccupation of nineteenth-century prison reformers with the fallen woman. It encouraged establishment of reformatories during the Progressive period and channeled women from the streets into these institutions. With World War I came particular concern that soldiers not be infected by camp-followers. At that point, women's reformatories from Connecticut to Arkansas began receiving women whose only offense was venereal disease. Such women were interned until deemed cured, and their treatment came to play a central role in the program of some women's reformatories.[4]

For the most part middle-class, Protestant, and Yankee to the core, Progressives in some respects were engaged in a defensive action against militant labor, the "new" immigrants pouring into their cities from southern and eastern Europe, and other threats to their class position.[5] Their campaigns did much to defuse unrest and extend the mantle of state control, without addressing fundamental issues such as class inequality and the nature of work in an industrializing society. Nor did Progressives recognize the problems inherent in the institutions they helped found. It is little wonder, then, that some Progressives dedicated themselves to establishing institutions as intrinsically supportive of the status quo as women's prisons. Nor is it surprising that, despite the founders' hopes for miracles of reformation, these prisons became nearly as custodial in operation as nineteenth-century penitentiaries.

FLOWERING OF THE REFORMATORY MOVEMENT

Seventeen women's reformatories came into being during the Progressive period and the years immediately following it. By 1935, such institutions could be found from Maine to California, Nebraska to Arkansas. Several patterns underlay this broad and quite rapid expansion of the women's prison system. First, reformatory building was concentrated in the Northeast and Midwest. As Table 3.1 indicates, these two regions supported thirteen of the new institutions. Only three were established in the South and but one in the West. Second, as Table 3.1 also shows, there was a regional progression in the time at which the reformatories opened. The Northeast, maintaining the lead it had assumed in the late nineteenth century, opened its first reformatory of the new century in 1901. Reformatories of the Midwest were established somewhat later, those of the South later still, and that of California in 1933, at the very end of the reformatory movement. Third, the later the institutions were opened, the more they diverged from the ideal type that the creators of the reformatory model had conceived at the turn of the century. All seventeen of these institutions were reformatories, if that type is defined as a separate and independent prison for women, established through efforts of agitators outside the penal bureaucracy with the aim of rehabilitation. But those founded last—that of Rhode Island (the final reformatory of the Northeast), for instance, and those of the South and West—incorporated so many elements of the custodial model that they barely resembled their archetype. Thus to study the successful development of the reformatory movement is to observe its simultaneous decline.[6]

Leaders, Their Arguments, and Their Tactics

Rescue and *reform*: in the Progressive period as in the nineteenth century, these were the platforms on which backers of separate prisons for women

TABLE 3.1
Women's Reformatories Opened between 1900 and 1935, by Region

	ORIGINAL TITLE	LOCATION	DATE ESTABLISHED	DATE OPENED
Northeast				
N.Y.	State Reformatory for Women	Bedford	1892	1901
N.J.	State Reformatory for Women	Clinton	1910	1913
Me.	State Reformatory for Women	Skowhegan	1915	1916
Conn.	State Farm for Women	Niantic	1917	1918
Pa.	State Industrial Home for Women	Muncy	1913	1920
R.I.	State Reformatory for Women	Cranston	1922	1925
Midwest				
Ohio	Reformatory for Women	Marysville	1911	1916
Iowa	Women's Reformatory	Rockwell City	1915	1918
Kans.	State Industrial Farm for Women	Lansing	1917	1918
Minn.	State Reformatory for Women	Shakopee	1915	1920
Nebr.	State Reformatory for Women	York	1919	1920
Wis.	Industrial Home for Women	Taycheedah	1913	1921
Ill.	State Reformatory for Women	Dwight	1927	1930
South				
Ark.	State Farm for Women	Jacksonville	1919	1920
N.C.	Industrial Farm Colony for Women	Kinston	1927	1929
Va.	State Industrial Farm for Women	Goochland	1930	1932
West				
Calif.	Institution for Women (Female Dept. of San Quentin, 1933–36)	Tehachapi (later moved to Frontera)	1929	1933

Sources: Mainly laws of the states (dates of establishment) and reports of the institutions (dates of opening).
Note: In addition to the institutions listed here, there were two reformatories that survived only briefly; see text, note 6.

campaigned. Some reformatory advocates focused on the need to rescue women from local jails, where female prisoners frequently lived close to males and under conditions of considerable deprivation. According to a 1922 report of the North Carolina State Board of Charities and Public Welfare, in one county jail, "when women are confined they must be kept in the jailer's corridor. There are no toilets in the jailer's corridor, so that the women are compelled to use buckets with no privacy except such as the darkness might afford." The board went on to give examples of sexual molestation of women in the state's jails.[7] A few years later it summarized its arguments in favor of a women's reformatory with the statement that in North Carolina, most

> women offenders . . . are receiving no constructive treatment either physical or moral. Those who are convicted of some offense are usually fined a nominal amount, given a few weeks in jail, or ordered to leave town in a given time. . . . [I]n this way Raleigh contributes to the problem of immorality in Durham; Durham to Greensboro; Greensboro to Winston-Salem, and so on. It is a vicious cycle of crime, changing only in the personnel. The problem still remains untouched.[8]

Maine's State Board of Charities and Corrections also worked for removal of women from local jails. Magistrates often refused to commit women to such unhygienic and hazardous institutions, nol–prossing, suspending, or continuing their cases instead. If the state established a women's reformatory, the board argued, judges would no longer treat women with such leniency and offenders could be rehabilitated.[9]

Other reformers were more concerned with rescuing women from state prisons, an effort in which they were supported by prison officials delighted at the prospect of getting rid of their small but irritating female populations. The superintendent of the Virginia penitentiary, for example, repeatedly recommended establishment of

> [a] separate prison for women. Present conditions are a menace to the discipline and welfare of the inmates of this institution. I do not believe that men and women should be placed in visual contact in prison. It causes moral perversion, sexual diversion and degeneracy.[10]

In California, in particular, reformatory advocates set their sights on removing women from the state prison—in this case San Quentin—where they had been held in inadequate quarters for many decades.

When they argued on the more positive note of reform, lobbyists reiterated the *Principles* of the 1870 prison congress, but they invariably phrased these in terms consonant with the now well-established doctrine that women required specialized treatment. Explaining that female offenders had needs distinct from those of males, backers of the women's prison in Minnesota held that the institution

> should be on the cottage system, in a location that will give every opportunity for the healthful use of the possibilities of farm and garden, as well as the home and domestic crafts that are the delight of normal womanhood. . . . We are beginning to understand more and more that simple labors of home crafts, under kind and sympathetic supervision, . . . in the open country, will do more for the human driftwood of society than any other methods.[11]

In state after state, reformers similarly reasoned that women, due to their domestic and sensitive nature, simply could not be reformed in traditional prison settings.

To these arguments of rescue and reform Progressives added a third—the need to protect society. Prevention of crime was certainly not a new theme, but it figured more prominently in the logic of twentieth-century reformatory supporters than in that of their predecessors. The aim of social protection was usually expressed in a manner that reflected Progressives' preoccupation with prostitution and venereal disease. Throughout the country, campaigns for women's reformatories became a counterpart to campaigns against prostitution. According to one reformatory advocate, "The problem of the woman offender in Illinois is not a criminal problem. It is a sex problem. Eighty-two percent . . . of the arrests of women each year in the State of Illinois are for sex offenses." The solution: "There should be a women's reformatory" to shield society from those who "scatter disease through every community." Alarm about venereal disease was especially important in the establishment of southern reformatories. Virginia's Department of Public Welfare added its weight to pressure for a women's prison because it could find few placements for a group of "diseased prostitutes who are physically and morally dangerous to the communities in which they live." The department had been charged with the care of such women by an act of 1922. "Much more could be done in this work for delinquent women," the board pointed out, "if there were a more adequate staff and facilities for dealing with them." The identification of a similar group in Arkansas nourished the reformatory movement there as well. During World War I, between four hundred and five hundred women convicted of "immorality" were detained for treatment of venereal disease at a clinic in Little Rock. Just after the war, Arkansas established its State Farm for Women, an institution that perpetuated the stress on preventing venereal disease by incarcerating, among others, prostitutes and managers of disorderly houses.[12]

As in the late nineteenth century, it was middle-class women who mobilized the reformatory movement, organizing support groups and letter-writing campaigns, presenting petitions, and pleading their case before legislatures. Now, however, these activists needed to spend far less time acquiring a power base from which to launch their crusades, for many already held positions on state charity boards and in prison reform groups and social purity organizations. As one activist retrospectively observed, women had emancipated themselves "from their reluctance to appear publicly . . . , from their inexperience in cooperative effort and from their lack of influence in the body politic." A prime mover in the New Jersey effort was Caroline B. Alexander (later Wittpenn), a member of the commission that, in 1903 and 1904, recommended establishment of a separate prison for women. She continued to marshal supporters (including her son, the state assemblyman who introduced the bill) until the legislation finally became law in 1910. Wealthy, well-connected, and herself prominent in public office, Alexander provided political and financial support to the reformatory until her death in 1932. In Maine, the movement was spearheaded by a Mrs. L. M. Stevens, president of that state's Women's Christian Temperance Union. Many groups participated in the reformatory effort in Connecticut, but it was the militant, all-female Committee on Delinquent Women of the Connecticut Prison Association that finally led "the women's reformatory into the promised land."[13] (One of the most ardent of the Connecticut agitators, Helen Worthington Rogers, later became a member of the new institution's board of directors.) In California, well-organized club women waged ferocious battle for a women's reformatory, the leader of these lobbyists, Rose B. Wallace, becoming the first chair of the institution's board of trustees. The standard-bearer of the movement in Minnesota was Isabel Higbee, president of that state's Federation of Women's Clubs. In 1915, during the hearing on the bill for a reformatory,

> frail Isabel Higbee . . . was speaking. . . . [S]he was pleading for a more wholesome environment and saner, more humane methods in the state's dealings with women convicted and imprisoned for crime. She finished, groped for her chair, then crumpled to the floor. . . . Men close by sprang to assist her. But she was dead![14]

Moved by her death, the legislature immediately passed the bill founding the Minnesota Reformatory for Women. The process by which similar institutions were started in other states was less dramatic, but in them, too, it was led, pushed, and prodded by already well-established activists who, like Higbee, had turned to women's prison reform.

Reformatory adherents throughout the country looked for guidance and support to superintendents of women's institutions already in operation. Particularly effective on the national scene were Katherine Bement Davis, head of New York's Bedford reformatory and perhaps the most influential prison administrator, male or female, of her day; Jessie D. Hodder, director of the Massachusetts reformatory for women; and Martha P. Falconer, for many years manager of Pennsylvania's reform school for girls at Sleighton Farm. Directors of nationally respected institutions, these superintendents corresponded and traveled widely to proselytize for the reformatory cause. When Ohio's movement began to gather steam, Davis prepared a speech for the October 1910 meeting of the Ohio Conference of Charities and Correction in which she provided her audience with the ideological fuel they needed, spelling out rationales for reformative treatment of women. Davis also gave conference attendants specific guidelines on how to go about establishing a women's reformatory. Within eight months, Ohio's reformatory bill became law. A visit by Martha Falconer to Arkansas stimulated the reformatory movement in that state. In other cases, reformatory advocates traveled to the home bases of well-known superintendents to garner advice and study the institutions firsthand. Backers of the women's reformatory in Wisconsin, for example, sent a delegation to Bedford to "see in what measure that institution would meet the needs of Wisconsin," and members of the New Jersey Women's Reformatory Commission inspected Bedford, Sherborn, and the Massachusetts reform school for girls at Lancaster.[15]

Twentieth-century reformers, like those of the nineteenth century, drew into the movement's orbit a number of organizations and private individuals willing to help lobby. But now these support networks tended to be broader based and larger in membership. At one point the legislature of Rhode Island received petitions for a women's reformatory from hundreds of individuals and ninety-one organizations claiming to represent seven thousand members. Enlisted in the Connecticut effort were several church groups, the Daughters of the American Revolution, the Federation of Women's Clubs, the state's governor, the Hartford Vice Commission, the prison association, various privately run shelters for women, the Social Hygiene Society, superintendents Davis, Falconer, and Hodder, the State Board of Charities and the State Conference of Charities and Correction, suffrage organizations, the Women's Christian Temperance Union, and the Y.W.C.A.[16] Such confederations sometimes had to sustain their efforts for many years and in the face of adamant resistance. Legislators were the usual source of that resistance, but in California the State Board of Prison Directors became the main obstacle. The California reform effort, which began in the 1890s, succeeded in establishing a reformatory in 1929. But the Board of Prison Directors refused to relinquish control over the state's female prisoners. To break the board's legal hold on these women, reformers had to engineer an amendment to the state's constitution. Only after ratification of this amendment in 1936 were they able to deliver control to the reformatory's own trustees.[17]

Through such efforts, women's reformatories were established from coast to coast. Prison historian David Rothman has argued that the Progressive era was characterized by a search for "alternatives" to incarceration, for non-institutional solutions.[18] Whatever the merit of this claim with reference to male offenders, it certainly does not apply to women. Nor does it hold for girls: the system of training schools for female delinquents also developed rapidly in the early twentieth century.[19] Somewhat different factors contributed to the swift expansion of the adult and juvenile systems for females,[20] but in both cases the desire to purify social morality was of paramount importance. Social purity concerns, as we have seen, were expressed in terms of anxiety about female sexual immorality. As Chapter 7 explains in more detail, the Progressive period was one of considerable apprehension about changing gender roles—a period when, it seemed, girls and young women, especially those of the working class, were growing indifferent to the older concepts of womanliness. Conservatives mobilized to establish institutions that would "correct" deviations from traditional roles. "[T]he public response to female delinquency," in the words of Steven Schlossman and Stephanie Wallach, "formed part of a larger cultural reaction, an attempt to revitalize Victorian morality and to punish women—prostitutes and sexually precocious girls alike—who impeded attainment of that goal."[21]

To stanch erosion of Victorian morality was the hope that lay behind reformers' assurances that separate prisons for women would protect society and prevent crime. They spoke of curtailing prostitution, but for Progressives, "prostitution" signified flirtatiousness, having affairs, and bearing illegitimate children as well as selling the body. It "included any form of sexual behavior that violated the moral imperatives of civilized morality."[22] The vehemence of the institutional reaction to sexually active women and girls, even if their behavior amounted to no more than coquetry, is a measure of the threat that they seemed to pose.

REGIONAL DIFFERENCES IN THE PENAL TREATMENT OF WOMEN IN THE EARLY TWENTIETH CENTURY

By the time the reformatory movement came to a close in the early 1930s, regional differences had emerged within the women's prison system. Variations in the impact of the reformatory movement itself created many of these differences. In the Northeast, every state except New Hampshire and

Vermont had established a reformatory.[23] These institutions excluded custodial elements more consistently than the reformatories of other regions. Rhode Island was an exception: it had located its reformatory in a decrepit former house of correction and had failed to institute indeterminate sentencing. But other reformatories of the region did conform closely to the movement's ideals, especially during their first years of operation. Moreover, although several custodial women's prisons (described in the next chapter) were also established in the Northeast, all but that of Vermont had been closed by 1935. Because of the region's widespread adoption of the reformatory model in the early twentieth century, its women's prison system has undergone slight change since then. Already having women's prisons, eastern states have found little reason to establish new ones.

The reformatory movement had a strong but less profound impact in the Midwest. There in the early decades of the twentieth century seven states established reformatories in rapid succession, bringing the total (with Indiana's) to eight. Yet four of the region's twelve states never established a reformatory.[24] The midwestern institutions, moreover, were often less successful in achieving the movement's ideals. Some, like the lackadaisical reformatory at Marysville, Ohio, exhibited little commitment to, or even understanding of, those ideals from the start.[25] Midwestern reformatories were more inclined to accept felons, as well as the usual misdemeanants and status offenders; as a result, they were less consistent in utilizing the reformatory type of indeterminate sentence that had no minimum and a maximum of about three years. In their programs, too, they tended to be weaker than northeastern counterparts. Several had no academic program whatsoever, while others relied on inmate teachers and stressed study of the Bible and hygiene. In addition to their greater readiness to relapse into custodialism, midwestern reformatories differed from those of the Northeast in the way they incorporated the medical approach to treatment of criminals. They seldom expounded at length in annual reports on feeblemindedness, psychopathology, and the need for life sentences for defective delinquents. On the other hand, several midwestern reformatories specialized in treatment of venereal disease, subjecting inmates to frequent vaginal examinations and dosing them with arsphenamine and mercury. Insofar as the midwestern institutions attempted to become "hospitals," in other words, they tended to treat not mental but physical disease.

The South, as already noted, established few reformatories, and those relatively late in the movement.[26] Only that of Arkansas was founded through the agency of social feminists. In North Carolina and Virginia, the other two reformatory states, welfare boards were principal backers, seconded in their demands for separate prisons for women by penitentiary wardens and the National Society of Penal Information.[27] Owing to this minimal infusion of social feminist ideology, southern reformatories were even less successful than those of the Midwest in realizing the reformatory plan. Although all three did provide indeterminate sentences with three-year maximums for misdemeanants, North Carolina alone excluded felons, and only it utilized the cottage plan. During the early years of the reformatories of North Carolina and Virginia (and perhaps that of Arkansas as well; data are simply not available[28]), turnover was in fact quite rapid, suggesting that little effort was made to hold misdemeanants for long terms of retraining. The programs of all three reformatories, moreover, were notably thin. Significantly, the two institutions that most closely resembled northeastern reformatories (those of Arkansas and North Carolina) were eventually closed.[29] Thus, not only was the women's reformatory movement less extensive in the South, but it also produced weak institutions in those states where it did achieve a foothold.

The West's only women's reformatory was also its sole separate female prison for women until the 1960s. Before that time, most western states continued to hold female felons in mainly-male state prisons.

Differences in wealth, population density, and rates of industrialization contributed to the greater success of the reformatory movement in the Northeast and Midwest. States there could afford to operate institutions dedicated to rehabilitation. Southern states, in contrast, were still shattered by the Civil War at the time the reformatory movement matured; and, aside from California, western states were still economically undeveloped. In the more thickly populated and highly industrialized states of the Northeast and Midwest, women were turning to factory work. But the frequent economic crises of the late nineteenth and early twentieth centuries caused widespread unemployment. When women were siphoned out of the industrial labor force by reformatories, more jobs were available for men. For example, one out of every five inmates of New York's Albion reformatory held a blue-collar job before incarceration, but nearly all were paroled to domestic positions. The women's reformatory movement kept women from competing with male workers but not from supplementing their labor. It is hard to imagine such a program taking strong root in areas that were not rich in captial, relatively well populated, and troubled by unemployment. No one in reformatory states consciously thought through these implications; nor were enough women incarcerated in reformatories to have any real effect on labor unrest. But in reformatory states, working-class women were superfluous as factory workers. They were not superfluous as domestic servants, on the other hand; and reformatory states, on account of the size of their middle-class populations, needed the servants whom the institutions trained.[30]

The regional differences in treatment of female prisoners also reflected the greater receptivity of northeastern and midwestern states to proto-Progressive and Progressive reforms. States of these areas were most open to the general prisoner rehabilitation movement that flowed from the Cincinnati prison congress. In them, social feminism prospered, leading to the engagement of middle-class women in prison reform. Where the women's movement flourished, so did women's reformatories. That movement was not nonexistent in the South,[31] but there, owing to racial factors discussed more thoroughly in Chapter 6, feminists were less inclined to be challenged by the plight of fallen women and other female offenders. The social purity movement, too, was most vigorous in the Northeast and Midwest, where it stoked the fires of the reformatory movement with its concern about female sexual immorality.

Finally, broad regional "styles" in incarceration affected both the types of treatment received by women and the rates at which separate women's prisons evolved. In the South, the climate and the plantation tradition worked to establish the penal farm as a substitute for incarceration, and thus to deflect the establishment of independent, congregate institutions for prisoners of either sex. Officials in Massachusetts and other northern states were attracted by the financial advantages of the prison farm, but like an Ohio prison committee of 1908, they decided that "while a State farm might be practical in the South where 85% of the prison population is colored, and where there is no hesitancy about using fire-arms in case any should attempt to escape, and where the winters are so mild that the prisoners can be worked out of doors all winter, . . . in the North a prison farm would not be practical."[32] Northern states had their own tradition, that of reliance on the closed institution. The women's reformatory movement modified this tradition but did not reject it. At the turn of the century, when northeastern and midwestern states established a number of new prisons as spin-offs from their original penitentiaries, women's reformatories became a natural part of the new progression.

It is important to recognize regional differences, whatever their sources. All too often, prison literature generalizes from the northeastern pattern to assume ubiquity of the reformatory model of women's prisons (and, for that matter, ubiquity of northern types of prisons for men). The reformatory model did have an enormous influence on the development of the women's prison system, but it did not affect all regions with equal intensity, thus leaving vacuums that, in some areas, were in time filled by separate women's prisons of the custodial type.

WOMEN'S REFORMATORIES OF THE PROGRESSIVE PERIOD: PROFESSIONALIZATION OF STAFF AND ASSIMILATION OF THE MEDICAL MODEL

If we compare twentieth-century reformatories with their predecessors, it becomes clear that these two sets of institutions differed qualitatively in many ways. Some differences were by-products of Progressivism, others the result of the inevitable decaying effects of time on a movement of institutional reform. Two characteristics that distinguished the twentieth-century institutions from their forerunners stand out: the greater professionalism of their superintendents and their incorporation of medical practices.[33]

The Professionalization of Reformatory Administrators

The Progressive period saw the advent of the first generation of female prison administrators who were professionals—educated, experienced, and confident of their ability to manage institutions. Whereas nineteenth-century officials usually came to women's prisons from backgrounds in volunteer work and with a strong sense of religious obligation, the next group were more likely to have set their sights on paid, professional careers at the start of their adult lives. A number of twentieth-century superintendents had received higher degrees from outstanding institutions. Katherine B. Davis, for instance, had gone on from Vassar College to earn a doctorate at the University of Chicago. Another of the era's best known administrators, Florence Monahan, studied law at Northwestern University, completing the four-year course in three and serving at graduation as valedictorian. Several of the period's superintendents were physicians, and even the relatively weak institutions of the South managed to attract well-educated women: Mary de Wees of the Arkansas reformatory had a college background, and Elsa Ernst, hired to head the reformatory of North Carolina in 1932, had studied psychology at Harvard University. These women not only had superior education to bolster their confidence; many also had received professional training in other penal institutions for women before becoming superintendents. Instead of having to fight to prove their ability, they filled their positions with an ease and sense of earned status uncommon among their predecessors.

Like other "new women" of the early twentieth century, the second generation of superintendents tended to be flexible about gender roles. Many had begun to move beyond social feminism, with its strict demarcation of men's and women's spheres, to broader views of the tasks of which women were capable and a more comfortable working relationship with members of the opposite sex. As James McGovern has put it, Progressive women were "less feminine"—more apt to adopt mannish clothing and hair styles and to enter previously restricted areas of activity.[34] Within reformatories, their more expansive vision of female capacities led them, at least in the early days when the spirit of pioneering still ran strong, to deemphasize needlework and table-serving and to stress farming and other heavy institutional labor. At Bedford and at Clinton Farms (as the New Jersey reformatory was known), inmates graded earth for new buildings and poured concrete for walkways. Katherine Davis was at first determined to train some inmates to compete for nontraditional jobs. "[I]t is not every woman in our mixed throng," she wrote in 1903, thinking perhaps of herself as well as her charges,

> who is adapted by nature or taste to domestic service, sewing or laundry work. In the reformatories for men, no one for a moment seriously considers limiting the trades taught to cooking and tailoring. . . . In the reformatories for women we will never meet with a large measure of success until we . . . provide training in a . . . variety of lines.[35]

Superintendents such as Davis took a similarly bold approach to their own careers: rather than clinging to one position, they moved about among institutions, accepting better positions as these were offered. Florence Monahan headed reformatories in Minnesota and Illinois before becoming superintendent of the California Institution for Women. Helen Hazard held administrative posts at the reformatories of Connecticut and Illinois and later at the first federal prison for women. And Katherine Davis left Bedford in 1913 to become Commissioner of Correction for New York City.

More subtle but equally significant differences between officials of the two periods lay in their attitudes toward inmates. Speeches and conference papers by the professionally successful twentieth-century superintendents indicate a greater sense of social distance between themselves and prisoners. To be sure, women who ran nineteenth-century reformatories could also exhibit moral disdain, and they, too, were highly conscious of social class distinctions between "the girls" and ladies like themselves. But members of the earlier group—humbled, perhaps, by their religious convictions, persuaded that innate femininity linked women of all stations, and themselves lacking status in the male world—were less inclined to view the female criminal as an alien being. Their tone of sympathetic comradeship with fallen women also appears in early reports by Davis and others of her generation. But as management difficulties and routinization wore down these later administrators, condescension and even contempt began to color their commentaries. By 1909 Davis was recommending outdoor work for reformatory inmates on the ground that they were intellectually and emotionally capable of little else. The tendency of twentieth-century superintendents to deal with prisoners as objects was encouraged, as Freedman points out, by the fact that "those trained in social work, law, medicine, and the social sciences approached female prisoners as professional clients or subjects of research." Lack of identification with the inmates was also fed by the popular eugenics movement, which fostered belief in the inherited inferiority of the "lower" classes, and by the self-righteousness of Progressivism itself. Professionalization, the reduction to routine, and class prejudice thus combined to increase the gulf between keeper and kept.[36]

Incorporation of the Medical Model

Although the medical interpretation of crime as a disease was implicit in the principles enunciated by the 1870 prison congress, it was not translated into explicit and widespread practice until the early twentieth century. During the Progressive era physicians, psychologists, and psychiatrists established court and prison clinics to classify offenders scientifically. Reformers and criminal justice workers at all levels began demanding life sentences for offenders diagnosed by the experts as incurable. These developments reflected Progressives' faith in scientific expertise. They also manifested what Rothman has called "the most distinguishing characteristic of Progressivism," its "fundamental trust in the power of the state to do good" and its willingness to have "the state, not the individual, . . . define the social good and take final responsibility for its fulfillment."[37]

One aspect of the infusion of medicine into prison practice was a new interest in venereal disease. The majority of women's reformatories began routinely to administer Wasserman and similar tests to incoming inmates; most attempted to treat the afflicted; and some specialized to such an extent that venereal disease cases and their cure became the center of institutional life. The reformatories of Kansas, Nebraska, and Wisconsin, in particular, concentrated on care of the venereally diseased. One Wisconsin report observed that prisoners often arrived with impaired health, "brought on principally by their own indiscreet, immoral actions," and vaginal examinations constituted not only the main form of that reformatory's admission tests but also, apparently, a regular part of the institutional program. Reports of Kansas officials included a good deal of talk about "cleaning up" inmates, especially those "interned" for treatment of venereal disease. These "internes" were separated from the rest of the population for many activities and had to use separate outhouses. (According to one account, a guard stood outside the toilets to ensure that the infected women used special compartments.)[38] Overwhelming numbers of "treatments" were given to these cases. The Kansas physician's summary for the 1925–26 biennium records that:

> We have performed 138 operations. . . . We have administered 2,319 doses of arsphenamine, 2,227 doses of mercury, and 110 doses of silver arsphenamine, in the treatment of syphilis. We have given 92,648 local treatments to the gonorrhea cases. We sent 1,746 blood specimens to the laboratory for the Wasserman test, and 2,618 smears for microscopic examination.[39]

Similarly, at the Nebraska reformatory, "The major emphasis [was] placed on physical care and on the cure of the large numbers . . . committed for disease."[40]

Another and even more pervasive effect of adopting the medical model was that classification became crucial in reformatory management. Whereas in the nineteenth century classification was a simple matter, with superintendents assigning inmates to cottages largely on the basis of age and "grade," in the twentieth century classification became a matter for experts. Classification committees came into being, staffed by psychologists, psychiatrists, and field workers who investigated inmates' family backgrounds. And now classification decisions were based on the "scientific" results of intelligence testing.

The modern form of the intelligence test was invented in the early twentieth century by the Frenchman Alfred Binet. Binet was well aware of the imperfections of his instrument, especially of the fact that it favored children from well-to-do backgrounds.[41] Those who introduced intelligence testing on this side of the Atlantic, however, were far less cautious. Henry H. Goddard, Lewis M. Terman, Edward Lee Thorndike, and others who dominated the mental testing movement in the United States were eugenists, men with an ideological stake in ferreting out "the unfit." With few pauses to correct the many and glaring inadequacies of their instruments, psychologists plunged into the task of testing delinquents and criminals. Not surprisingly, in view of the primitive nature of the tests and the slipshod methods with which they were administered, huge proportions (usually well over 50 percent) of tested groups proved to be "feebleminded" (or "mentally defective" or "mentally deficient," all three terms having been used synonymously in the teens to denote those today referred to as "mentally retarded"). Reports of their findings flooded the professional and popular literary markets just after 1910, bringing fame to their authors and persuading the public of the scientific accuracy of defective-delinquency theory. Since such large numbers of law-breakers tested as mentally subnormal, it seemed obvious that feeblemindedness was the cause of crime. Science had discovered the source of criminality, and it did not hesitate to recommend a cure for this malady. Because mental deficiency was inherited (so defective-delinquency theorists like Goddard taught), it could be eliminated by eugenic segregation of the feebleminded. With eugenic restraint on breeding by the unfit, crime itself would diminish, perhaps even disappear.[42]

Whether mental testing and defective-delinquency theory affected female prisoners more adversely than males is difficult to say, in the absence of comprehensive data. But is is noteworthy that ever since publication of *The Jukes* by Dugdale, the promiscuous woman had been closely associated with both criminality and hereditary feeblemindedness. Females were the subjects of the majority of mental tests first used to "prove" defective-delinquency theory; throughout the Northeast and Midwest (where the defective-delinquency movement was strongest), immoral women came to be viewed as diseased fountainheads of corruption, polluters of not only their own generation but also, potentially, the next. In light of this attitude, certain arguments for the establishment of women's reformatories—for example, that such institutions would curtail the activities of "sex" offenders who "scatter disease through every community"—take on fuller meaning.[43] To reform some women—the mentally "normal"—was still part of the agenda. But now that agenda expanded to include detection of the feeble-minded. When they could afford to, reformatories hired psychologists to administer mental tests to each new inmate "so that work, classes, and recreation may be provided for her in accordance with her mental capacity." Assignment to inferior programs was the mildest consequence of testing poorly. The worst was transfer to an institution for the feebleminded, a civil commitment that meant the automatic extension of sentence up-to-life. In the early twentieth century, several women's reformatories used this type of transfer to rid themselves of inmates who could not (or, more likely, would not) respond positively to the programs they offered.[44]

New York Reformatory for Women at Bedford
Of all prisons in the country, New York's reformatory for women at Bedford did most to implement the medical approach to criminals. It was the leader that other reformatories, and some men's institutions as well, emulated. Superintendent Katherine B. Davis had long been concerned about "women in the lowest grade" who resisted reform and violated parole conditions after release. With the idea of permanently segregating these troublemakers, in 1910 Davis obtained a grant to begin psychological testing at Bedford. This led to a study in which Dr. Eleanor Rowland found that of thirty-five women examined, thirteen were "decidedly feebleminded" and another six "borderline." As a result, four feebleminded inmates were transferred to the Newark institution for mental defectives and others were isolated on the reformatory grounds.[45]

From Dr. Rowland's research evolved the prototypical prison labo-ratory. Encouraged by Rowland's confirmation of her own suspicion that difficult inmates were in fact feebleminded, Davis asked the New York Foundation late in 1910 to support mental testing on a larger scale. With the $3,000 she was granted, she instituted a clinic at Bedford to conduct scientific studies of inmates and the causes of their criminality. To administer this clinic Davis chose Dr. Jean Weidensall, a psychologist who had worked with William Healy at his court clinic in Chicago and who, before assuming her duties at Bedford, was sent to New Jersey for supplementary training by Henry Goddard. Weidensall's research was designed to sort out the reformable from those who should be sent to institutions for the mentally defective on totally indefinite sentences. She had the professional integrity to resist drawing easy conclusions from intelligence tests, but her report of her findings, *The Mentality of the Criminal Woman,* basically verified defective-delinquency theory.[46]

The next step was establishment at Bedford of an even better-financed clinic, John D. Rockefeller, Jr.,'s Laboratory of Social Hygiene. This laboratory, according to accounts by Davis, came into being through several events. In the spring of 1910, just as Davis was coming to the momentous realization that intelligence tests could be used to classify and hence isolate the feebleminded, Bedford was visited by representatives of the city magistrates and the New York City Charity Organization Society's Committee on Criminal Courts. During their meeting, Davis mentioned that she "believed the day would come when all cases convicted in the courts would be studied by experts before sentence was passed." She was then "asked by a member of the Committee on Criminal Courts to put the suggestions . . . into writing." The upshot was a pamphlet, "A Rational Treatment of Women Convicted in the Courts of New York City," which was privately printed by the COS Committee and found its way into the hands of John D. Rockefeller, Jr.[47]

Rockefeller's interest in defective-delinquency theory stemmed from his abhorrence of prostitution, a vice that he, like many reformers of the period, associated with feeblemindedness, loathsome disease, and need for eugenic legislation and criminal justice reform. In 1909 he was appointed foreman of a grand jury to investigate prostitution in New York City. (His appointment supposedly prompted Rockefeller to remark, "They couldn't have picked anybody who knew less about it."[48]) Several years later he described the manner in which this appointment led to creation of the Bureau of Social Hygiene:

> One of the recommendations made by the jury . . . was that a public commission be appointed to study the social evil. . . . [I] subsequently gave careful consideration to the character of the work which might properly be done by such a commission . . . [and came] to the conclusion that a public commission would labor under a number of disadvantages, such as the fact that it would be short-lived, that its work would be done publicly; that at best it could hardly do more than present recommendations. . . .
>
> So the conviction grew that in order to make a real and lasting improvement in conditions, a permanent organization should be created . . . which would go on, generation after generation, continuously making warfare against the forces of evil. It also ap-

peared that a private organization would have, among other advantages, a certain freedom from publicity. . . .

Therefore, as the initial step, the Bureau of Social Hygiene was formed in the winter of 1911.[49]

Personnel of the new bureau included Katherine B. Davis and, as its chairman, John D. Rockefeller, Jr. Financed mainly out of his own pocket, the bureau became Rockefeller's favorite philanthropy.[50] One of its activities was creation of the Bedford Laboratory of Social Hygiene, a task that presumably appealed to Rockefeller because the majority of the institution's inmates had been convicted of sexually immoral behavior.

The bureau purchased seventy-one acres adjoining the reformatory, and from the state's attorney general it obtained an opinion that operation of the laboratory was "permissible" so long as the state continued to "bear the mere cost of maintenance of the inmates just as if they remained within the present boundaries of the institution grounds." The attorney general's opinion is of interest in that it so clearly indicates the Rockefeller-Davis intention: "Such defective individuals [as would be identified by the laboratory] can then be sent to custodial asylums, such as that at Newark, instead of being set free at the end of a short period of detention, and thus allowed to add to the population of defective and criminally inclined persons."[51] In other words, private funds were to be used to identify candidates for life incarceration, and a private citizen was actually to own part of a state prison. It is no wonder that Rockefeller desired "freedom from publicity."

On the new property Rockefeller built Elizabeth Fry Hall, to which all new inmates were sent for testing and classification. A renovated garage became the testing center, and psychologist Mabel Ruth Fernald was put in charge of the entire operation. By 1916 the laboratory was running three separate departments—one for investigations into heredity and environment by eugenic field workers, one for psychological testing, and one for psychiatric studies.[52]

When the five-year lease on his property expired, Rockefeller refused to reopen the complex until New York promised both to buy it and to use it, in his words, "as a clearing house in connection with a state-wide system for the care of mentally defective women." The bargain was struck. In 1920 the legislature passed New York's first defective-delinquent law: any woman in a state-supported penal institution who was over age sixteen and found "to be mentally defective to an extent to require supervision, control, and care" was to be committed and transferred to a section of Bedford to be known as the Division for Mentally Defective Women. Sentences were to be indefinite, and decisions about parole and discharge were to be made by the superintendent and managers of the reformatory. Inmates transferred to this division soon became an institutional headache. They grew restive when they realized they were not eligible for release at the end of their sentences, and some took matters into their own hands by attempting to escape. So troublesome a group did they prove to be that Bedford got rid of them entirely in 1931. In that year the reformatory at Albion was designated as the state's institution for defective-delinquent females, and thus the plan which Davis (who had long since resigned as superintendent) and Rockefeller had conceived in 1911 for removing the feebleminded from Bedford was finally realized. Meanwhile, Rockefeller kept his part of the bargain. As soon as the defective-delinquent bill became law, he renovated the Laboratory of Social Hygiene so it could be rented by the reformatory until bought by the state. After the legislature appropriated $175,000 for this purchase in 1923, Rockefeller's involvement at Bedford came to an end.[53]

The Laboratory of Social Hygiene did much to bring the field of medicine into crime control, thereby influencing the interpretation of criminal behavior. Once regarded as resulting from inherited feeblemindedness, criminality then came to be seen as an acquired mental, or psychiatric, disease. As a result of this shift, authority for diagnosis of criminality was transferred from intelligence-testers to psychiatrists, an even more prestigious group whose arrival on the scene signaled yet another increase in state control over the criminal. The shift began about 1916 as a result of two developments. First, sophisticated intelligence-testers began to recognize the crudeness of the tests that had seemed to prove that so many criminals were feeble-minded. And second, at Bedford and other institutions, it became apparent that some of the most truculent inmates were not feeble-minded at all. Evidently they suffered from another disease, psychopathy.[54] In 1916 a Psychopathic Hospital was opened on the grounds of the Laboratory of Social Hygiene, explicitly designed to subdue Bedford's most defiant inmates. According to an institutional report, the hospital's "patients" were to

> be selected from that class of cases well known in every institution as . . . the class which gives so much trouble to every officer. . . . They may not be feeble-minded, nor are they insane, but they demand the patience, time and strength of every one. . . . In the outside world they are a menace to the society.[55]

At this point the entire laboratory movement, in courts as well as in prisons, veered toward the psychiatric interpretation and treatment of criminality. While the Bedford laboratory continued to identify the feebleminded and call for their segregation, it now found that the psychopathic, not the feebleminded, were the worst incorrigibles.

The medical model influenced every aspect of the Psychopathic Hospital run at Bedford in 1916 and 1917. Uniformed nurses supervised patients at meals and stood at attention during Rest Period. In a hydrotherapy room that made nearly total immersion possible, "there were given as many as eleven baths a day, varying in time from half an hour to two hours." These efforts to disguise the facts of control were unpersuasive to the patients, however. " 'Unconcealed contempt for . . . anyone representing authority, together with social hatred in general' " seemed to the head nurse to be the outstanding characteristics of the psychopathic woman. Dr. Edith R. Spaulding, the hospital's director, came to doubt that it would again be possible to find "a sufficient number of adequately trained persons . . . willing and able to endure the strain which the treatment of such a group as this entails."[56] Between the lines of her report on the project, Spaulding made it clear that the attempt to cure troublemakers through psychotherapy was a failure. But like others who had closely followed the Bedford experiments, she did not reject the ideology of treatment. Indeed, the effect of the well-publicized Psychopathic Hospital was to validate the treatment ideology.[57]

Without the private financing enjoyed by Bedford, reformatories elsewhere assimilated the medical model more slowly and less thoroughly. They tended to adhere to defective-delinquency theory until the early 1920s, even though the early results of intelligence testing were now widely suspect. Insofar as they absorbed the avant-garde psychiatric understanding of crime, these other reformatories reflected the shift by rather perfunctorily labeling unruly inmates as "psychopaths" and subjecting them (as at Bedford) to hydrotherapy and ice packs. When overcrowding led to a breakdown in discipline at the Connecticut reformatory in the mid-1920s, a report announced, "Many of the women are psychopathic; practically all are disciplinary problems." Maine's reformatory erected a punishment building in the late 1920s after years of agitation for a unit where "psychopathic" women could be transferred. Although the volume of such rhetoric tended to be lower in midwestern reformatories, a Kansas report of 1920 did attribute most disciplinary problems to "nervous, unstable women," maintaining that some should never be released on account of their "inherent weaknesses, viciousness, depravity and defectiveness"; and in the mid-1930s the Wisconsin reformatory complained about "middle-aged psychopathic women of average or superior mentality who are stubborn and at war with their environment, definitely resistive of all efforts to help them."[58] The medical model was being used to place the blame for institutional failures on the inmates. A few reformatories mustered the funds to hire psychiatrists on a part-time basis, but these specialists did little more than help with classification. In no reformatory other than Bedford was an effort made to provide the treatment that, in theory, should have flowed from diagnosis; and in the few reformatories of the South and West, there was almost no interest in the psychiatric theory of crime.

Thus despite Bedford's experiments with psychopaths, the main effect of the medical model on women's reformatories of the Progressive period was to encourage intelligence testing, classification, and the treatment of venereal disease. Yet in themselves, these were weighty developments. All three meant an increase in state power over prisoners; all three contributed toward the eugenic aim of separating sentence from crime, so that in the name of treatment and prevention, prisoners might be held longer than their offenses alone seemed to warrant. And although Bedford's experiments with psychopaths had little impact on other reformatories, they helped persuade the public that crime was a disease and that criminals therefore should be confined until medical experts pronounced them cured.

PROMISE VERSUS PERFORMANCE

The landscape of prison reform is littered with examples of the difficulty of sustaining rehabilitative efforts over time.[59] Reformers' failures to achieve or maintain their goals are the apparently inevitable result of attempting to improve prisoners within coercive settings. Given the inherent conflict between treatment and control, it is not surprising that women's reformatories increasingly deviated from their designers' ideals. Many of the reformatories failed because they were poorly conceived from the start, while others held more promise initially but declined over time.

Through lassitude, underfunding, or a combination of the two, some twentieth-century reformatories simply did not manage to realize fully the reformatory model in the first place. Several failed to adopt the cottage plan—Rhode Island, for instance, established its reformatory with little more than a name change within a former house of correction. Without cottages, institutions could not classify prisoners or provide domestic environments in accordance with the original intent. Some reformatories did not adopt the no-minimum indeterminate sentence; others used it inconsistently. Wisconsin provides a case in point: women committed to its Industrial Home received five different types of sentence. The welter of provisions led to great variety in sentence length and, one surmises, to unrest over inequities, since women convicted of the same offense apparently could receive quite different sentences.[60] In yet other departures from reformatory ideals, few twentieth-century reformatories excluded female felons or women over age thirty, groups that (in theory at least) were not responsive to retraining.

The effects of this slackening in restrictions on commitments were not immediately apparent: until the 1920s, many women's reformatories continued to receive mainly young sex offenders and venereal disease cases. But when, for reasons examined later in this chapter, the proportions of felons and older women began to increase, they squeezed out the young petty offenders for whom the women's reformatory was originally designed. At that point, the aims of rescue and reform had to be abandoned.

Another sign of the corrosive effect of time on reformatory ideals was a decline in quality of programs. Instead of the rich fare of learning, recreation, and moral and vocational training envisioned by the founders, by the late 1920s the majority of inmates had only token programs and makeshift work like rug-hooking to pass the time. Once the institutions were built and the roads laid, inmates with saws and buckets of cement vanished from the scene. Many reformatories continued to operate farms, but employees with machinery took over much of the heavy labor while inmates were increasingly assigned to light harvesting and the tending of flowerbeds.[61] Officers still occasionally led bands of inmates on nature walks, and some reformatories encouraged group activities like glee clubs and dramatic performances, but many lacked the staff to maintain vigorous recreational programs. Less time was devoted to classwork, and education became largely remedial.

A further sign of the corrosive effect of time was a decline in the quality of institutional management. A few officials maintained the Progressive spirit—ubiquitous Florence Monahan, for example, and Connecticut's Elizabeth Munger[62]—but in general those who ran reformatories after 1920 displayed little of the vision and energy of their predecessors. Some of the original superintendents, such as May Caughey in New Jersey and Anna M. Peterson in Connecticut, had resigned after clashes with interfering members of their boards of managers.[63] Others, through overlong tenure, became so routinized that they merely went through the motions of running a "reformatory." This seems to have been one factor hindering development of Ohio's reformatory at Marysville: there both Louise M. Mittendorf, the first superintendent, and her successor Marguerite Kelley Reilley, served long terms, and it is perhaps not coincidental that this was a particularly lifeless institution.[64]

Meager salaries, long hours, and unpleasant working conditions undermined the morale of staff members. According to a report of the late 1920s, at Marysville matrons worked twelve-hour shifts with only two days off each month. Some lived in rooms designed for inmates, and both they and the superintendent received salaries that were "disgracefully low."[65] As Table 3.2 indicates, salaries at Albion usually fell well below those at New York's more prestigious reformatory at Bedford, and salaries at both women's institutions were lower than those at the Elmira men's reformatory.

Petty rules and institutional constraints gave staff members further grounds for complaint. During her reformatory tour of the late 1920s, Eugenia Lekkerkerker uncovered a host of constraints that had a "depressing" effect on personnel,

> such as that the officer must take her meals in the common dining-room and often cannot prepare so much as a cup of tea for herself; that she cannot invite friends to stay overnight or for dinner; that sometimes she cannot receive male callers, or have any relatives live with her, and many other 'cannot's' which do not exist for the outside worker who at least in her free hours can do as she pleases.[66]

Such restrictions did not inspire dedication.

TABLE 3.2
Comparison of Annual Salaries at Three New York State Institutions: the Reformatories for Women at Albion (Western House of Refuge) and Bedford and the Reformatory for Men at Elmira, 1917, 1920, and 1931

	ALBION	BEDFORD	ELMIRA
1917			
Superintendent	$2,000	$3,000	$5,000
Assistant Supt.	1,300	1,800	3,500
Parole Agent	900	900	—
Head, Educ. Dept.	600	1,020	1,800
1920			
Superintendent	$2,500	$3,000	$5,000
Assistant Supt.	1,680	2,000	3,500
Parole Agent	1,020	1,020	1,500
Head, Educ. Dept.	1,020	1,020	1,900
1931			
Superintendent	$3,000	$5,000	$9,000
Assistant Supt.	2,100	2,700	5,000
Parole Agent, Chief	1,492	1,700	—
Head, Educ. Dept.	1,540	1,436	2,500

Sources: New York, *Laws of 1917*, Ch. 181; *Laws of 1920*, Ch. 165; *Laws of 1931*, Ch. 21.

The extent to which institutional management could break down is reflected in a scandal that rocked New York's Western House of Refuge at

Albion in 1920. A legislative committee began investigating after hearing "charges of incompetency, mismanagement and wrong-doing." Three months later, the governor asked John S. Kennedy, commissioner of prisons, to look into charges of cruelty at the refuge. The reports of these investigations showed that the reformatory was troubled by several administrative problems. The board of managers was badly split into two factions. One did almost nothing, while the other took an active role but was too dependent on the wishes of the superintendent. Members of the first faction often did not bother to attend meetings, whereas at the other extreme one of the activists, Monsignor John L. Reilly, was making the institution's parole and discharge decisions practically on his own. Another problem was the superintendent, Flora P. Daniels, who according to all indications was tactless, high-handed, and bullying. Since her appointment in 1916, 145 employees had resigned, a complete turnover in staff. Daniels had, moreover, fired three employees subpoenaed to testify in connection with the legislative investigation, a manifestly retaliatory move. Daniels survived the investigations but the board did not, both the Kennedy report and that of the legislative committee having called for an entirely new set of managers.[67]

After Katherine Davis's departure from Bedford, that institution, too, went through a period of poor management. Four superintendents came and went over the next six years, one of them (Helen A. Cobb) forced out for maltreatment of inmates. Riots and bad publicity led to a nearly complete turnover of the board of managers in 1921; and in that year, apparently on the theory that a male was needed to restore order, the state amended the reformatory's governing legislation to permit Dr. Amos T. Baker to assume the superintendency.[68]

Those who managed the reformatories frequently complained of inadequate resources, and indeed, underfunding was the source of many of the problems that developed within these institutions—initial failures to realize the reformatory plan with cottages and restrictions on commitments; decline in quality of programs; inability to pay decent salaries; and the overcrowding that made it difficult to control, much less provide services to, inmates. To a large extent, however, the reformatory plan itself contributed to the institutions' financial straits. In terms of plant alone, the reformatory was an inefficient and hugely expensive operation, ideally requiring a number of separate cottages (each with its own cooking and dining facilities and staff), a chapel, classrooms, administrative offices, quarters for staff, a farm with buildings for animals and equipment, and so on. No other penal institutions for adults called for so many individual buildings, not to mention so low an inmate-to-staff ratio. States found it difficult to build and sustain such costly institutions, particularly during World War I and years of economic depression.

In some instances, moreover, reformatories were opened so hastily that they had to cope with the financial problems of daily operation and plant development simultaneously. The Connecticut reformatory, for example, began operation under totally impractical, if picturesque, circumstances, consisting of only a few farm buildings scattered among rolling hills and woods. When the first twelve inmates arrived in July of 1918, they took occupancy in a dormitory set up in one of the farmhouses. These women prepared a second farmhouse for the next arrivals, fifteen inmates admitted in August. At that point—two months after opening—the reformatory was filled. Repeated appeals to the legislature eventually produced funds for construction of a recreation building and four cottages. These appropriations came too slowly and too late, however, for the reformatory to be able to fill its original purposes. Reformational programs could not be developed because, aside from the farmhouse rooms, there was no space for classwork, industrial training, or worship. The State Farm's founders had hoped it could handle all the state's criminal and wayward women, including hundreds from local jails. Like other Progressives who established institutions, they had been less than hard-headed in their planning for the future, thus saddling the reformatory, for which they had struggled so arduously, with unmanageable financial and administrative burdens.

Inmates' experiences of incarceration were profoundly affected by their institutions' steady drift toward custodialism. Many early reformatory inmates responded positively to their situation, despite its coercive aspects. Initially multifunctional, the reformatories provided protective and educational services not generally available to young working-class women, some of whom reacted gratefully to opportunities to better themselves or bear illegitimate children away from home. Moreover, in the early days of operation, when administrators and inmates were forced to band together to get their institutions in working order, a spirit of camaraderie often prevailed, especially in those reformatories that began with small populations and minimal resources. Albion's first superintendent, Mary K. Boyd, resisted regimentation and inspired loyalty among prisoners; for years she and others among Albion's first matrons received letters from long-departed inmates who wanted to keep in touch.[69] May Caughey, first superintendent of Clinton Farms, wrote,

Perhaps the first days of this institution were the happiest we have ever had. . . . There was an enormous amount of work to do and very few people to do it. Everyone was so busy getting the house and grounds cleaned up, that we found no necessity for rules of any kind. There was a splendid spirit of responsibility and cooperation which made both officers and girls enjoy any kind of work—for example, when we all pitched in together and scrubbed and shellacked a large floor in one afternoon.[70]

Clinton Farms developed a system of self-government whereby inmates policed themselves and decided punishments for rule infractions.[71] Even at Clinton Farms, however, expansion of the inmate population, together with settling of routines, wore away the spirit of pioneering and cooperation.[72] As the Progressive movement drew to a close, the quality of care within some reformatories deteriorated to the point that inmates staged protests against shoddy treatment. Truculence replaced compliance in their attitude toward administrators.

In nearly every case, after an initial period of small population and harmony between inmates and staff, reformatories became overcrowded and tensions began to rise. The institutions found themselves in an uncontrollable situation. They had overadvertised their own virtues, judges no longer hesitated to commit minor offenders, and prisoners came flooding in. There was no place to put them, much less space or staff for a full-fledged rehabilitative program. As time passed, moreover, parole failures accumulated—embarrassing evidence that the reformatories were failing to deliver on their promises. Unable to admit institutional failure, superintendents pinned the blame on unruly inmates. As we have seen, these administrators seized upon defective-delinquency theory, explaining that they simply could not reform feebleminded women and pleading for opportunities to transfer these irremediables to civil institutions.

Disciplinary Breakdown at Bedford

The most spectacular example of the way in which overcrowding led to disciplinary problems, and disciplinary problems in turn to blaming of inmates, occurred at New York's Bedford reformatory in the teens. Despite lack of bedspace, Superintendent Davis had continued to solicit commitments. When she departed in 1913, the institution was about to explode. Crowding was extreme: in every cottage women were sleeping in corridors, and others were sleeping in the gym. Guards were in short supply. Twenty-five percent of the population had been identified as feebleminded, but few could be sent to the bulging civil asylums for mental defectives. As the 1913 annual report described the situation, "nerves have been strained almost to the breaking point."[73]

The first wave of scandal broke over Bedford in 1915 when an investigation by the State Board of Charities uncovered rampant mismanagement, physically abusive punishments, and "unfortunate attachments formed by the white women for the negroes." Investigators were also alarmed by the high proportion of feeblemindedness. Accepting the findings of the

Rockefeller clinic without question, the investigators stated, "Of the first hundred cases received at 'Elizabeth Fry Hall' twenty per cent. should have had permanent custodial care." The presence of the subnormal inmates, the investigators reported, "hampers the work in every way, it hampers the education and development of the girls; it is also an injury to the subnormal girls, they are out of their element and could be taken care of more cheaply elsewhere." Robert Hebberd, secretary of the State Board of Charities and at the time also chairman of a state commission investigating mental deficiency, personally insisted on the transfer of twenty-two women to state-run civil institutions for mental defectives; a few others were sent to a similar institution operated by New York City. The major effect of this investigation was not improvement of management or relief from overcrowding but endorsement of the theory that reformatory goals were being sabotaged by abnormals.[74]

Between this probe of 1915 and the summoning of troopers to quell riots at Bedford in 1920, blame for institutional disturbances began to shift from the feebleminded to the psychopathic. The change was partly due to the general penological move toward the theory of psychopathy as a cause of crime. But it was also necessitated by the behavior of Bedford's inmates: faced by mental examinations that might send them to civil institutions for indefinite terms on the one hand and staff brutality on the other, the women sustained a rebellion for nearly four years. It was behavior for which feeblemindedness did not provide an adequate explanation. Bedford-based agitation for a defective-delinquent law did not diminish (quite the contrary), but now researchers at the Rockefeller clinic devoted most of their efforts to developing the newer theory of psychopathy that would, they hoped, account for resistance that was articulate, organized, and evidently fearless.[75]

By assaulting an officer, inmate Ruth Carter managed to get herself into court, where the story of wrist-hangings, cold water "dashes," and floggings came out. An investigation by the commissioner of prisons substantiated these charges, but cruelty, sterilizations, and civil commitments continued, provoking more inmate protests. In May of 1920 Bedford's defective-delinquent law was enacted, an event that ignited the final and most vigorous rioting. In July, state police were called in. Although the revolt was subdued, the remaining vestiges of administrative stability disintegrated entirely. Chaos continued until Dr. Amos Baker began to function as superintendent. An ardent eugenist, Baker immediately resuscitated the prison's mental testing program. The combination of renewed mental testing with the now very real possibility of indefinite commitment to the Division for Mentally Defective Women, just a stone's throw away on the reformatory grounds, finally terminated the mutiny, and by the end of 1921 discipline had been restored at Bedford. During the previous six years, however, the nation's most lauded reformatory for women had been brought to its knees by institutional problems, and these problems had been "solved" through a process that made scapegoats of "defective" inmates.[76]

DEMISE OF THE WOMEN'S REFORMATORY

In the early 1930s, felons began to constitute significant proportions of the populations of women's reformatories. Many reformatories had received some felons from the start, but throughout the 1920s they usually managed to hold such commitments to a minimum. They were able to exclude serious offenders because most states also operated a small women's unit at their central state prison, just as they had before the reformatory movement began. These custodial units were crucial to maintenance of the reformatory plan; without them, the all-female institutions could not have continued concentrating on young petty offenders. When, about 1930, many states decided to close these back-up units, transferring their populations to reformatory grounds, the women's reformatory ceased to exist in all but name.

The number of states that made this decision about 1930 is remarkable. In 1929 New Jersey eliminated the women's unit at Trenton State Prison by removing its inmates to Clinton Farms. In a similar but more drastic change in the same year, the Ohio reformatory, which had received felons from its time of opening, was turned into an institution for felons only; petty female offenders, in other words, were now excluded from Ohio's state system. Connecticut transferred women held at the Wethersfield state prison to its reformatory in 1930. (The building in which they now were housed was titled the State Prison for Women, to distinguish it from the State Farm whose grounds it shared; and although it was headed by the State Farm's superintendent, when overseeing inmates at the prison cottage she was called "warden.") In 1933, New York closed the custodial women's prison at Auburn, sending its felons to Bedford.[77] At about the same time it put an end to the venerable reformatory at Albion by redesignating it as an Institution for Mentally Defective Delinquent Women and transferring its nondefective inmates to Bedford. Illinois, Nebraska, and Wisconsin all shut the women's units in their central state prisons in 1933, again by removing felons to reformatories. California's reformatory had received felons from the start, but it legally excluded misdemeanants after 1936, and Virginia transferred all female felons remaining at the state penitentiary to its reformatory in 1939. In state after state, then, the original reformatory population of minor offenders was either severely diluted by felons or pushed out entirely. As felons filled institutions that had been founded as reformatories, misdemeanants were once again sentenced to local jails. The criminal justice system was returning to practices common before the reformatory movement began.

Although the reformatory plan, as originally conceived, faded from existence, it left a legacy that continues to influence women's prisons. On the most obvious level, that heritage is manifest in the separation of female from male prisoners and in physical plants—the spacious and in some cases still isolated tracts dotted with cottages. The reformatory plan also bequeathed its legacy of differential treatment. Most reformatories continued to be headed by women and to hire predominantly female staff.[78] They eschewed training programs that involved heavy, industrial labor, instead gearing vocational programs toward womanly work—food preparation, grooming, sewing, and typing. Female prisoners continued to be encouraged to adopt middle-class standards of propriety, and they continued to be treated as "girls"—childlike creatures in need of firm, parental guidance. Such differential treatment was inevitably treatment inferior to that received by many male state prisoners—less useful in preparing women for competitive jobs, more moralistic, more babying. Like the care offered by the original reformatories but with fewer rehabilitative side effects, it locked women into gender roles. That those persons involved in women's prison reform today find it difficult to overcome the tradition of differential treatment is in part a testimony to the power of the reformatory heritage.

Why did the women's reformatory movement come to an end in the 1930s? The stock market crash of 1929 and ensuing Great Depression played a major role: states simply could no longer afford to operate institutions that held petty offenders for long periods of moral retraining. Wardens of those state prisons that still included female units pressed for removal of women, their arguments gaining force as central prisons grew ever more desperate for space for males. The conclusion seemed inescapable: female departments in the state prisons should be closed and their populations transferred to reformatories. A second factor was the death of the Progressive movement, from which women's prison reform had drawn so much of its energy. Crippled by World War I and the subsequent swing toward conservatism, the reforms of the Progressive period received the *coup de grâce* from the Depression. Simultaneously, the feminist movement underwent rapid deflation. Upon achieving suffrage, women split into a number of factions, few concerned with social meliorism. Finally, the women's reformatory movement ground to a halt because it had achieved its aims. It had sustained itself for sixty years, and in those northeastern and midwestern states where it had flourished, it had for the most part realized its fundamental goal of separate prisons for women.

CHAPTER 4 ||||||||||||||||||||||||||||||

Custodial Prisons For Women, 1870–1935

While the reformatory movement was spreading throughout the country, women's prison units of the custodial type continued to develop separately. These custodial units, too, helped mold the character of the expanding women's prison system. They were more numerous even after the reformatory movement had come to fruition, and they determined the nature of the women's prison system in the South and West. Populated by felons, most custodial units failed to excite the attention of reformers. Some custodial units, to be sure, were eliminated by the reformatory movement: that of Indiana, for instance, was eliminated when establishment of the Reformatory Institution led to closing of the female department at Jeffersonville; others disappeared when, in the 1930s, their inmates were transferred to reformatory grounds. For the most part, however, custodial units were hardly touched by the reformatory movement.[1] They continued along the lines laid down in the early nineteenth century, slowly growing and in some cases developing into fully separate prisons.

WOMEN IN STATE PRISONS:
THE ADJUNCTIVE ARRANGEMENT

There were, in fact, three kinds of state-run custodial institutions for women in operation during the period 1870–1935: units within or attached to mainly male prisons; prison farm camps in the South; and completely independent prisons, separate yet nonreformatory in style. Of the three, the adjunctive arrangement was most common. Nearly every central prison in the Northeast and Midwest maintained a female department until these states opened reformatories, and even thereafter most continued until the 1930s to receive cases considered unsuitable for reformatory discipline. The few states of these two regions that never established reformatories had no alternative but to send female convicts to their central prisons. New Hampshire, for example, held female felons at its State Prison at Concord from at least 1832 until the 1940s.[2] When Paul Garrett and Austin MacCormick inspected Concord on behalf of the National Society of Penal Information in the late 1920s, they reported that accommodations for women consisted of "a wing opposite the cell house for men" that could hold up to fourteen prisoners and included a kitchen and eating area.[3] At no time, apparently, did these quarters fill to capacity; but in other northeastern and midwestern states, female departments were often cramped and crowded. They remained much as they had been in the mid-nineteenth century, generally tucked off in a remote corner of the prison grounds, poorly serviced, with little space for work or recreation.

Conditions for women in the midwestern state of Missouri typified the extreme neglect that women in adjunctive custodial units often endured. Like New Hampshire, Missouri had no reformatory. Unlike New Hampshire, it often had a considerable number of female prisoners, for the federal government, as yet lacking a prison for women, sent them to the Missouri penitentiary. In 1881 the Jefferson City prison held forty women; by 1916, the number had risen to sixty. At the turn of the century, the warden described the "female cell building" as "a disgrace to the State . . . ; it is old and dilapidated, very crowded, with no facilities whatever for caring for the sick." A few years later its women were moved to "the administration building, where they were kept locked in steel cages. . . . Those that were not needed to do the cooking, dining room or dormitory work were assigned to the factories where they worked at sewing machines, doing the same kind of work as the men in the prison." Removed from the center of the prison's activities, the women were all but forgotten by the warden, who left them in the care of an autocratic job foreman and corrupt female trusty. A number of prisoners died from a combination of malnutrition, overwork, and cruel punishments.[4]

In 1926 Missouri again transferred its female convicts, this time to a nearby farm. (This continual relocation of female prisoners occurred frequently in states that held women in units adjacent to their men's prisons; usually women were shifted to ever-larger quarters and, when possible, to buildings outside but close by the main prison's walls.) At the thirty-eight-acre farm, owned by the penitentiary, women lived in a large house said originally to have been the home of a slave owner. Though somewhat removed, the women's branch was "still part of the prison for men and

. . . in no sense a separate institution." When Garrett and MacCormick inspected it in the late 1920s, they observed of the inmates that penitentiary methods "still dominate their treatment. This is the only institution in the country where representatives of this Society have seen women wearing a ball and chain." A decade later, visitors from another group reported that "the Women's Prison attempts nothing beyond keeping its inmates in custody and busy." Until 1934, the silent rule prevailed at meals. Prisoners did a little light farming but otherwise had no program.[5]

Like New Hampshire and Missouri, most states of the southern and western regions had no reformatories. In them, central prisons maintained adjunctive women's units from the time of founding at least into the early twentieth century. (Some of these female departments closed only recently, and others still exist.) These women's units and their populations varied greatly in size. In thinly populated states of the Southwest and far West they often remained small: as of January 1, 1916, the Oklahoma penitentiary at McAlester held only thirty-one women (2 percent of its total population), for instance; in the same year, of 246 inmates at the Idaho State Penitentiary, only two were female. But in other states with thicker populations or higher rates of incarceration, female departments suffered from constantly expanding populations, a situation that led, as in Missouri, to their frequent relocation.[6]

Accommodations for Female Convicts in Tennessee

Tennessee provides a case in point. Immediately after the Civil War, the number of prisoners of both sexes sentenced to the Tennessee state penitentiary increased rapidly. Severe crowding and intermingling of the sexes led to the first step in isolation of the women. In 1881 the penitentiary's inspectors ordered the warden to "see that the male and female prisoners be kept seperate [sic] and apart at all times," and the following year the warden dutifully reported that women were being held in a female department. This was located in the main building, a brick structure that formed the entrance to the prison and also held the warden's office, the hospital, and guards' room. The Female Department lacked cells and was lower in security than the men's section, yet it was at least as crowded and certainly less subject to regulation. Its location caused constant troubles. In his report of 1882 the warden complained that the windows of the Female Department "overlook the Prison yard, in plain view and hearing of the male convicts, which is very demoralizing in its tendency." He urged construction of a wing for women, "entirely out of sight and hearing of the male convicts," and recommended that a matron be hired to manage it.[7]

The warden's first recommendation was fulfilled a decade later with the completion of a women's wing, built within the perimeter wall but separate from the men's quarters. But this solution also proved unsatisfactory. The population of the women's wing was three times greater than its number of cells. There was no employment, no program, no place for exercise. Through idleness, the women grew troublesome; a number escaped. And there was no matron. Early in the 1890s the legislature had established the office of matron, but it refused to fund the position despite the warden's urgent pleas. "[T]here is no matron, for there is no appropriation to pay for the services of the matron," he stormed in his report of 1894. "A matron is absolutely needed. . . . A woman only knows the diseases, distresses and wants of the female sex, and their proper treatment, physically, morally and mentally." Several years passed, however, before the legislature finally financed the post.[8]

The next step in segregation of the female convicts occurred in 1898, when Tennessee replaced its antiquated penitentiary with a new one that included a separate structure for women. The women's building was located in the northwest corner of the penitentiary yard—as far as possible from the men—and surrounded "by a strong, solid fence of wood." It had forty-eight cells, but in contrast to the single cells in the men's section, some of those in the women's building were large enough to hold "several inmates." The new structure made no provision for bathing or cooking. Food was carried to it across the yard and, according to an investigatory committee of 1908, "served almost any way. We think the women are entitled to have their meals served at least as well as they are served in the men's dining room." Although the women's building lacked basic equipment for sanitation and food preparation, it did include a laundry sizeable enough for the occupants to handle the wash for the entire prison.[9]

The program for convicts in the women's building, while an improvement over the nearly total idleness of the previous phase, was still minimal. There were church services on Sundays, usually followed by Sunday school taught by the matron or women from Nashville. On two evenings a week, the matron and convict assistants taught illiterate convicts. As for industry, in the early twentieth century some women worked in the penitentiary's hosiery factory, along with "the lame, young and weaker male" convicts; there, under the contract system, they produced stockings for a New Hampshire firm. The regimen was overtly and unabashedly devoid of rehabilitative considerations.[10]

In 1930 Tennessee once again moved its female prisoners, this time to the Women's Prison erected on penitentiary property about a mile and a half from the main prison. A visiting reformer from the North would probably have mistaken the Women's Prison for a men's institution. Instead of utilizing the cottage plan, it was cruciform in shape and contained cell blocks with tiers four stories high. As in maximum security men's prisons, a corridor separated the cells from barred windows. The care provided by the Women's Prison, according to a report by the Department of Institutions, was "almost purely custodial. Practically nothing is done in the way of treatment and training." There was no teacher and no physician, and the matron enjoyed no administrative independence but rather functioned as a female guard under supervision of the warden. Even the employments of the past—manufacturing hosiery and running the laundry—were now denied to female convicts. The library consisted of "about 200 nondescript volumes, most of them in bad condition." The situation was especially grim for black women: the building consisted of two wings of equal capacity, one designated for each race; but while the white wing was usually underpopulated, the "Negro wing" was "almost constantly overcrowded."[11]

In Tennessee as in other southern states that sent able-bodied males outside prison walls to labor in mines, there were conspicuous differences between the treatment of those men and that of most female prisoners. As we have seen, in the years just after the Civil War a few women were sent to the mines to work beside men; but as Chapter 6 shows in more detail, by 1900 this practice had been discontinued in Tennessee and other southern states, which thereafter kept female prisoners, along with very young, aged, or favored white males, at their central penitentiaries. Even the worst conditions within the walls did not match the horrors of forced labor in the mines or on levee projects, where prisoners were assigned to more strenuous jobs and died at extraordinarily high rates from disease, accidents, and brutality. Men and women within the walls were treated better and relatively evenhandedly. But as women were physically removed from the male population, aspects of their care deteriorated. Like male prisoners they experienced overcrowded, filthy conditions, but the women had fewer job programs and less access to personnel and space for recreation.

―――――――――

Some states turned to the adjunctive arrangement because they held too few women to warrant another solution. Others with larger female populations utilized the adjunctive arrangement because it provided a convenient, inexpensive method for dealing with the administrative problem of segregating women. Many of these states lacked a tradition of concern with penal conditions. In them, prison administrators discovered that they did not need to give much thought to women who were well isolated in separate buildings and supervised by separate, subordinate staffs. The stories of Kate Richards O'Hare and Emma Goldman, political prisoners in the Missouri penitentiary in the early twentieth century, make this clear. William Painter, chief authority at the penitentiary, was an old friend of O'Hare, and he was aware that these vociferous, well-connected women could make trouble for his administration. When O'Hare and Goldman got word through to him, Painter took steps to upgrade conditions in the women's department, installing showers, sending books over from the library in the men's section, and seeing that meals were delivered before they had gone cold. But even these activists found it difficult to attract Painter's attention to hardships in the female department. He was distracted by duties in the men's division and whenever possible left management of the women to their own staff. Once women were pushed out of the way into adjunctive units, they were easily ignored. Through inertia, the adjunctive solution persisted.[12]

A SOUTHERN VARIATION: THE PRISON FARM CAMP

Some southern states broke with the usual pattern by leasing female convicts to farmers or working them on publicly owned prison farms.[13] These "camp" arrangements were ad hoc solutions developed by southern states as they tried to deal with a multitude of penal problems (many of their own making) in the aftermath of the Civil War. In several states the central penitentiary had been destroyed. Even in those where it survived, it was unable to accommodate the enormous numbers of blacks sentenced to hard labor for petty offenses just after the war. Penal servitude rapidly became a substitute for slavery, and prisons adopted techniques of slavery such as the overseer with his lash and the practice of working bands of subjects on farms. In many areas prisoners were rented out to private entrepreneurs under various lease systems. To supplement leasing-out, or replace it as it fell into disfavor, some states purchased large plantations on which they worked convicts themselves, housing them in jerrybuilt camps. As the central penitentiaries were rebuilt and expanded, unproductive "dead-hands" such as women and boys were increasingly sent to them; eventually, that is, women came to be held once again in adjunctive units. In the interim, however, in a number of states female convicts experienced the camp arrangement through being leased to private farmers or forced to work on state-owned plantations.[14]

In Texas, for example, female convicts at the turn of the century were sent to a private farm about seven miles from Huntsville, headquarters of the state's penal system. This farm was owned by a Reverend J. G. Johnson; he provided food and clothing for the women and each year paid the state one-half of his earnings plus a bonus of five hundred dollars. (This variation on leasing-out was the "share" system, under which the state and the person who worked prisoners shared the latter's profits.) The farm was supervised by Johnson's niece, who functioned as matron, and her husband, J. G. Bowden—hence its name of Bowden's Farm. The majority of women held at Bowden's Farm (and in some years there were more than one hundred) were black, most of them serving time for property offenses. The few white women had been convicted mainly of homicide. Black women worked in the fields, while whites served as domestics.[15]

As early as 1900, the superintendent of the Texas penitentiary system recommended that women be removed from Bowden's Farm to a building where they could manufacture clothing for the rest of the state's prisoners. His rationales included control as well as profit:

> [O]n the farm there must be . . . a few men used as trusties. . . . These trusties cannot at all times be kept under the eye of the guards, and therefore we find it impossible to entirely separate the sexes, as the law requires. The negro women are a very low order of beings, mostly from the cities, and as a rule are vicious and troublesome to control, and I think should be kept in a prison specially provided for them.[16]

In 1908 the women were transferred to another camp at Eastham Farm, about twenty miles north of Huntsville. Arguing that "the female convicts should be permanently located on a farm belonging to the State," in 1910 the superintendent recommended "that Camp Goree be converted into a permanent home for the female convicts." Previously used as a state camp for male prisoners, Goree already had a building; and as it was only four miles from Huntsville, it would be convenient for prison officials to administer.[17]

Conditions for women at the Goree Farm, to which they moved in 1910 or 1911, at first resembled those they had experienced earlier at the privately owned farms. The manager's wife served as matron. According to a report of 1911, "the negro women take care of the cotton and corn crop; the white women do sewing, garden work, care for chickens and work around the place in general." Living quarters were primitive. "This camp was in a very dilapidated condition when we [prison commissioners] assumed charge; water had to be hauled; a building with three tiers of bunks, one above the other, all crowded; no hospital, no conveniences whatever." A prison physician found the women's conditions "most unsatisfactory." "There were sixty inmates," he reported in 1911; "all, except the few white and Mexican women, occupied one small building. . . . [T]here were no sanitary facilities whatever, save those provided by nature." Despite renovations, additions, and construction of a sewer system, when Garrett and MacCormick visited Goree in the late 1920s, they found much to criticize. They reported, for instance, that the women lived in wooden buildings that were "crudely designed and constructed" and "a serious fire hazard." These camp quarters were later replaced by more secure structures that became permanent. Today women continue to be held at Goree, which has become one of the largest women's prisons in the country.[18]

It is difficult to ascertain how many states held female prisoners at farm camps (southern post-Civil War penal records are fragmentary and far more concerned with finances than convicts, especially those of the female sex). Perhaps the total came to eight or ten; certainly Louisiana and Georgia were among them. In the late nineteenth century, Louisiana kept female prisoners at the State Penitentiary at Angola, a huge farm about sixty miles north of Baton Rouge. The penitentiary consisted of a central receiving unit and a plantation over which were dispersed a number of camps. As of 1866, it held a total of 228 inmates, of whom only ten were female; all ten were black. By the first decade of the twentieth century, women had been isolated at Camp D; its population, in January of 1908, consisted of sixty females, fifty-two of them black.[19] Women continued to be incarcerated at the Angola plantation until, in 1961, they were transferred to a farm at St. Gabriel, fifteen miles south of Baton Rouge. Today St. Gabriel is an independent women's prison with relatively modern facilities.

During the Civil War, Georgia's original penitentiary burned down, allegedly torched by women intent on escape. Thereafter, female prisoners were leased out. The lessees did not always keep them separate from male convicts: legislative investigators discovered women chained to men and occupying the same bunks. The inquiry also uncovered instances in which lessees had whipped women. And so the state decided to send female convicts to camps where they would be supervised by prison officials. A new penitentiary including a large farm was established in 1898 at Milledgeville, near the state hospital. The plan was for inmates to grow food and provide services for the patients. At first women were held on a part of the prison farm separated from the men's section by a creek. However, because they burned down their building (they seem to have been an incendiary lot), in 1900 they were locked in a wing of a men's building. Subsequently Georgia shifted its female prisoners to a series of inadequate quarters. Recently, like Louisiana, it has created a new and separate prison for women.[20]

The farm solution marked a low point in the penal treatment of both women and men. Whether leased out or worked by the state, convicts sent to the fields toiled extremely long hours at backbreaking tasks. Herman Crow writes in his history of the Texas prison system:

Each day the convicts were moved from their sleeping quarters as early as the guards could safely see to keep them from escaping and returned at dark. Working in the fields under the watchful eyes of mounted guards armed with shotguns and straps, the prisoners were forced to maintain a set pace, regardless of skill or physical condition. For every failure or laggard response to a guard's command, the strap was used, and a pack of hounds was held ready at all times.[21]

The sleeping shacks were unfit for habitation, and the trusties supervised farm workers with malicious cruelty. (According to Crow, for example,

"Trusties who trained dogs would let themselves be treed and then beat the dogs to make them vicious."[22]) Field hands of both sexes were treated less well than farm animals, for unlike the latter, they cost nothing to acquire. It is true that neither women nor men who worked on farms endured the miseries of convicts sent to mines. But, on the other hand, farm conditions fell below those of even southern prisons, where men lived in the central cellblocks, women in adjunctive units, and both were supervised by personnel a shade more professional than trusties.

Southern states' reasons for adopting the farm alternative to incarceration help explain the low quality of care on the farms. Unlike states in the North, those of the South were apathetic about prisoner rehabilitation or even health. Their overriding concern was to exploit prison labor for profit, a concern for which both leasing and state plantations provided a resolution. When, after the Civil War, southern prisons filled with blacks, it seemed natural to transfer to the prison system techniques that had evolved with slavery. The climate encouraged outdoor work, and southern states scattered their convicts over wide areas, making it difficult for officials to monitor prisoner conditions. Few of these officials were inclined to investigate treatment of prisoners in any case. They were for the most part political appointees, and their interest lay with figuring out who would be the next governor. The field hands, supervised by trusties selected from the most hardened of white convicts, were helpless victims of brutal indifference.[23]

INDEPENDENT CUSTODIAL PRISONS FOR WOMEN

Six independent women's custodial prisons were founded during the period 1870–1935, the first since the opening of the Mount Pleasant Female Prison in the mid-nineteenth century. Four of these operated in reformatory states, where they received women regarded as undesirable by the reformatories. The other two were the only female prisons in their states.[24] All were independent institutions, either through geographical separation from men's prisons or through establishment by a specific legislative act. Little effort went into their founding, however. None enjoyed the reformatories' freedom to strike off in directions other than those dictated by traditional, male-centered prison practices. In plant, administration, and type of treatment, they were closer to the adjunctive female units than to reformatories.

Like other custodial units for women, five of the six were started with minimal expenditure and for reasons of administrative convenience rather than reform. New York legislatively established the State Prison for Women in 1893 on the site of an abandoned asylum for insane male criminals. This was adjacent to the Auburn prison where women had been held in the very early nineteenth century. Now, however, the male and female sections were separated "by a high, thick wall, with only a wicket for passage between the two." Two considerations prompted founding the State Prison for Women: New York needed some kind of state accommodation for its female felons, who, as yet barred from its reformatories, were clogging county penitentiaries; and officials were anxious to put the former insane asylum to some use "before damage and deterioration . . . result from . . . non-occupancy."[25]

When Illinois established its independent custodial prison for women, it, too, made use of an older building. Female felons had been imprisoned since the late nineteenth century in the penitentiary at Joliet, where they occupied a building across the street from the men's quarters. The adoption of a new administrative code in 1917 relieved the warden of supervising the women's unit, which became a separate women's prison on July 1, 1919. Erected in 1896, it was designed like a men's prison, with administrative offices in the center, cell blocks to either side, and a walled yard behind. The building was more capacious than most custodial institutions for women, but also "inconvenient, expensive, and not only difficult, but impossible to keep clean; out of date as to plumbing and heating, an unwieldly unit."[26]

In North Carolina, Alabama, and Vermont, the pattern by which an independent prison for women evolved out of a former, mainly male institution was much the same as it had been in New York and Illinois. North Carolina held felons of both sexes at the Raleigh state prison until in 1933 overcrowding forced removal of the women to prison barracks, previously used by men, on the outskirts of town. These barracks were primitive, consisting of two stories of open dormitories with double-decker bunks. Alabama, too, established its female prison by converting a previously male facility, but in this case not the women but the men were moved. From the mid-nineteenth century, both sexes had been incarcerated at the Wetumpka penitentiary. When, upon completion of the new Kilby prison in 1923, "better quarters had been provided for the men," they were transferred out and Wetumpka became female only.[27] Vermont founded its State Prison and House of Correction for Women in 1921 by transferring male misdemeanants out of the former Rutland House of Correction and moving in the female felons held till then at the Windsor State Prison.

In all five of these cases, then (we shall deal with the anomalous sixth in a moment), establishing independent prisons for women involved little more than renaming an already existing institution, usually one considered no longer suitable for men. The physical plants and traditions inherited by the "new" women's prisons forced them into the custodial mold. In these institutions, women received treatment similar to that of men in the corresponding prisons for male felons. But unlike the men's prisons, those for women seldom had a fulltime physician, chaplain, or teacher; and they furnished fewer programs and job opportunities. Their physical plants, moreover, were more outmoded.

Although matrons headed these prisons for women,[28] they took their orders from men who were higher up in the correctional bureaucracy. In New York, for example, the establishing legislation specified, "For the purposes of the government and management . . . such State Prison for Women shall be deemed a department of the Auburn prison."[29] At first glance, the head of the Vermont State Prison and House of Correction for Women seems to have had considerable status, for her title, like that of women who ran reformatories, was superintendent. In 1933, however, the legislature degraded her position to that of matron. (This was a remarkably ungrateful act, for Lena Ross, in charge of the Vermont institution from 1921 until her death in 1936, ran a progressive prison despite almost insuperable odds.[30]) In no case did the matron of a custodial prison have autonomous control over her inmates or in fact have the standing of reformatory superintendents. Little more than guards, these officials sometimes lived alongside the inmates whose dreary routines they supervised.

New York's State Farm for Women at Valatie

At the turn of the century, New York made yet another effort to found an independent prison for women. The attempt foundered—the State Farm at Valatie closed after only three years of operation. It is of special interest, however, in that it was a unique endeavor to develop a new type of custodial prison for older women who were repeat, though petty, offenders.

Before the State Farm was established in 1908, New York had no special institution for misdemeanants over thirty years old; such women continued to be sent to local jails. This population, especially repeat offenders such as inebriates and prostitutes, aroused the concern of the Women's Prison Association of New York (WPANY), the main backer of the State Farm bill. The WPANY had little interest in rehabilitating such women, whom it considered "incapable of reformation." Rather, it wished to keep them off the streets, and that for eugenic reasons. Active in the social purity movement since the late nineteenth century, members of the WPANY believed that women who repeatedly committed petty crimes had a "far-reaching and subversive" influence on the morals of society; that their influence penetrated into homes to destroy family life; and that they lured the young into houses of prostitution. Worst of all, the vast majority of such women were foreigners.[31] In 1906 the WPANY declared,

If promiscuous immigration is to continue, it devolves upon the enlightened, industrious, and moral citizen, from selfish as well as from philanthropic motives, to instruct the morally defective to conform to our ways and exact from them our own high standard of morality and legitimate industry.

"It is for this purpose," the report concluded, "that our bill providing for a State Farm for Women was introduced."[32] The next year the organization elaborated further on the theme of contamination of the American gene pool by degenerate foreigners:

> Do you want immoral women to walk our streets, pollute society, endanger your households, menace the morals of your sons and daughters? . . . Do you think the women here described fit to become mothers of American citizens? Shall foreign powers generate criminals and dump them on our shores?[33]

For such genetic pollutants, the backers of the State Farm bill had in mind a totally indefinite sentence that would force inmates to "remain as long as they live, within the sheltering walls of the institution."[34]

Over the years leading up to enactment of the State Farm bill, WPANY mobilized support in many quarters. The association's report of 1907 announced that the bill had been endorsed by almost every charitable, political, and religious organization in the state, and by boards of magistrates, county judges, court and prison workers, district attorneys, and sheriffs as well. Despite this pressure, the legislature balked several times at approving the bill. Enactment came only after members of WPANY traveled to Albany to enlist the support of people "high in authority from all parts of the State."[35]

The establishing legislation specified that the new institution should be located on fertile land and in a "healthful situation." From the start of their campaign, WPANY members had argued that the best activities for State Farm women would be agricultural. Outdoor work would improve their health, and the vegetables they produced would make the farm self-supporting. Moreover, in a remote area their old criminal ties would be severed.[36] And so 315 acres were purchased near Valatie in Columbia County.

One hundred thousand dollars were appropriated to establish the institution which, according to hopeful projections, would consist of cottages, an infirmary, and workhouses, the whole to have a capacity for five hundred inmates. What in fact materialized must have been disappointing: two cottages with a combined capacity of sixty inmates. Moreover, even when these two cottages had been completed, five years after the prison's founding, they were uninhabitable because no money remained to purchase furnishings. This barrier was overcome by more intense lobbying on the part of WPANY, and inmates did start to arrive in 1914. All had to be held in one cottage, however, as the other was needed for the warden's residence. Although the second cottage was eventually freed for use by inmates, the institution remained poor in space, programs, and personnel.

Ultimate authority over the State Farm was held by the superintendent of state prisons, who was also in charge of New York's prisons for men. (New York's reformatories were supervised by the State Board of Charities, an indication that they, unlike the State Farm, were regarded as eleemosynary institutions.) As at other custodial institutions, there was no intermediate body analagous to the boards of managers that presided over reformatory operations. The WPANY, realizing that a board of managers would provide support for the faltering institution, tried in 1916 to persuade the legislature to authorize one. This effort failed, however, and WPANY itself had to act as the prison's parental body, albeit unofficially.[37]

The founding legislation stipulated that all officers of the State Farm were to be women except in cases where "the nature of the work . . . necessitates employment of men." Administration was deemed one of these cases and John H. Mealey became the State Farm's first warden. Mealey served from 1912 (arriving on the scene before the State Farm opened) to 1916. He had his doubts about the institution and did little to further its cause. For example, while claiming to believe "strongly" in the cottage system, Mealey asked that one large building, "presumably a cellblock," be built to hold three hundred inmates. Such a building, he explained, would reduce costs and improve discipline. Mealey was replaced by Jane L. Armstrong, who had served on the board of managers of the Western House of Refuge at Albion and as a probation officer. She stayed on until the institution's ignominious demise.[38]

According to the establishing legislation, all women over the age of thirty convicted of misdemeanors or lesser offenses who were not insane and had been found guilty at least five times during the preceding two years of any offense whatsoever, might be sent to the State Farm.[39] All sentences were indeterminate with a maximum of three years, the WPANY having failed to realize its goal of totally indefinite sentencing. Courts did not commit women enthusiastically to Valatie. The institution received a total of only 146 inmates. Most were between thirty and sixty years of age at commitment, white, and (perhaps disappointingly to the social purity workers who had lobbied for the State Farm) native-born. The overwhelming majority had been convicted of intoxication.[40] Despite the low number of commitments, the institution's small cottages became crowded. In September of 1917, for instance, the prison held eighty-seven in space intended for sixty. There was little employment for the women—only some farming and sewing. Supervisory staff was almost nonexistent; chaplains and physicians were not hired. The warden lacked funds for books and entertainment. Existence must have been barren for the aging inebriates held at the State Farm, and some tried to improve it: in 1917, seventeen attempted escape, three succeeding.[41]

Several factors contributed to Valatie's dissolution. Not long after it opened, the country went to war; funds and attention were diverted by more pressing concerns. At the same time, Progressive energy for social reform began to subside. Enactment of Prohibition and of immigration restriction laws quieted the fears that inspired the WPANY to found Valatie. Most immediate among causes for the institution's failure was underfunding. Counties would not commit women because they could not afford to transport them to Valatie. At one point, the prison could not release parolees because it lacked funds to return them to their homes. The WPANY assumed both costs for a while, but it could not do so indefinitely.[42]

And so in 1918 the State Farm was turned over to the Department of Health to be used as a treatment center for women with venereal disease. All remaining inmates were summarily paroled. In 1919, the war's end having reduced concern that soldiers might be infected by venereal disease, the institution was returned to the superintendent of state prisons. There was some discussion of designating Valatie as an institution for mentally defective women from Bedford, a proposal that WPANY, predictably, endorsed. This plan did not materialize, however, and in 1920 Valatie again passed out of the hands of the superintendent of state prisons to become a residence for mentally defective children.[43]

The State Farm was a poorly conceived, badly planned, and inadequately financed institution. Basically custodial in intent and design, it attempted to graft features of the reformatory (cottages, rural location, a board of managers, and the three-year indeterminate sentence) onto the custodial model. The attempt was unsuccessful. The original concept of the State Farm as a prison where female misdemeanants could be held indefinitely was, in fact, the *reductio ad absurdum* of Progressive idealism, for it completely disregarded the principle of proportionality and naively assumed that the state could afford to incarcerate relatively harmless offenders for lengthy periods. That other independent custodial institutions founded in the same period survived much longer than Valatie was no doubt a function of the fact that their inmates had been convicted of crimes that seemed to demand state response.

REGIONAL VARIATIONS

The regions of the country varied markedly in the degree to which they relied on the custodial model. Nearly every state maintained a custodial unit for women during the period 1870–1935, but in the Northeast and Midwest the type was not dominant: many more women were sent to reformatories. Except in Michigan, Missouri, and Vermont, custodial institutions in the Northeast and Midwest served as safety valves to the reformatories, back-up units to which serious, older offenders were relegated.

In these regions, moreover, most custodial institutions withered away when, about 1930, their populations were transferred to reformatory grounds.

In the South, on the other hand, custodialism predominated. This region had only a few reformatories, insipid in character, and its other penal units for women tended to be large—in numbers of inmates if not in physical size. They were also unstable: seldom established by a legislative act that might have anchored them to a specific location, they were moved from one unsatisfactory site to another, often to quarters abandoned for men's use. Some southern states developed a variant on the usual custodial solution by leasing female prisoners to local farmers or working them on state penal plantations. In time, women were either reincorporated into the main penitentiary or warehoused nearby, in several instances in a camp that had become permanent.

The South proved to be a hothouse for the worst aspects of custodialism—its disregard for prisoners' health, its dehumanizing environment, its failure to provide programs or protect inmates against violence. When southern female prisoners were not left in total idleness, they were assigned to hard labor, mainly in laundries or clothing factories. At Wetumpka, for example, women manufactured garments for all of Alabama's prisoners in a factory equipped with eighty-one sewing machines; they had demanding production quotas, so high that women collapsed from the severe pace. Southern prison buildings were usually unsanitary, lacking adequate toilet and bathing facilities. Medical attention was available only in the most serious cases, if then, and women with mental disorders were locked in solitary confinement and ignored. The institutions were frequently overcrowded; there was little room for sleeping, much less for recreation. Dormitory design made privacy impossible and fostered both violence and epidemics. The abysmal level to which care of women in southern prisons often sank was described in 1924 by Frank Tannenbaum.

> The condition of the women prisoners is most deplorable. They are usually placed in the oldest part of the prison structure. They are almost always in the direct charge of men guards. They are treated and disciplined as men are. In some of the prisons children are born . . . —either from the male prisoners or just "others." . . . One county warden told me in confidence, "That I neah kill that woman yesterday." . . . One of the most reliable women officials in the South told me that in her State at the State farm for women the dining room contains a sweat box for the women who are punished by being locked up in a narrow place with insufficient room to sit down, and near enough to the table so as to be able to smell the food. Over the table there is an iron bar to which women are handcuffed when they are strapped.[44]

Because of disease and maltreatment, death rates were far higher in southern institutions than those of other regions.

The West was yet another story. Remote from eastern centers of penal reform and preoccupied by settling the frontier, it paid little systematic attention to prison development well into the twentieth century.[45] Only California established a women's reformatory, and that remained the region's sole independent prison for women until the 1960s. Elsewhere western states held their few female felons within or close to their penitentiaries. At the Oregon State Penitentiary at Salem, for instance, women were housed in an upper story of the administration building and supervised by the wife of a deputy warden. The Colorado State Penitentiary at Canon City confined women in a separate structure within the prison until, in 1934, it constructed another building for them outside, but adjacent to, the main prison wall. The Colorado women were now better off in that they had a yard for exercise, but women in both institutions lived under primitive, harsh conditions without the industries and other advantages available to male prisoners. Nevada received women at its State Prison in Carson City after 1869, the year when "a two story building was erected with the upper floor being designed as quarters for females." In some years but one woman resided in this section; in many, none at all. (Infant twins joined the population in the mid-1870s. Their mother was Molly Forsha, convicted of murder, and their father, according to rumor, was the warden.)[46] When Garrett and MacCormick visited the Arizona State Prison at Florence in the mid-1920s, they found that "no satisfactory quarters are provided for the six women prisoners of the state." Returning several years later they discovered that new accommodations had been built for women between the administration building and the front wall—an improvement, but still too close to the men's section.[47]

Aside from California, Washington was the western state that made the best provision for its female convicts. At first it held women within its State Penitentiary at Walla Walla, isolating them in a loft above the mess hall. By 1926, according to Garrett and MacCormick, women were "housed in quarters outside of the prison proper" but close enough to be guarded from a tower on the prison's wall. Up to this point, there was nothing out of the ordinary in their treatment. But in 1930 Washington erected a new women's building, "U-shaped with a wall at the open end forming a recreation courtyard in the center." This structure had ample room, and its semi-separation from the men's prison protected women against sexual exploitation. Although inmates had few jobs or other programs, their large, grassy yard made possible recreational activities unavailable to most other female prisoners of the region.[48]

Despite regional variations, partial justice—punishment that was both more benign and more harsh than that experienced by men—remained the rule in custodial units for female prisoners. Southern systems spared some women from work in mines and on levee and railroad gangs. According to Kate O'Hare, "the females' wing [of the Missouri penitentiary] . . . was much better than some of the older buildings used for the male convicts." O'Hare goes on, however, to exemplify the other sense in which justice for women was partial: their quarters were "far less satisfactory than the one more modern building in the male department."[49] Whether women were held in adjuncts to men's prisons, at prison farms, or in independent custodial institutions, in the period 1870–1935 they were subject to the same liabilities that had been the lot of female state prisoners before the reformatory movement began.

The Implementation of Punishment

Introduction

Part I traced the development of two tracks within the women's prison system, one consisting of the custodial institutions that evolved from men's prisons, the other comprising reformatories that feminized the late nineteenth-century penology of rehabilitation. Part II presents a more detailed view of the two types of women's prisons and their inmates. Based mainly on the prisoner records of five institutions, it begins by looking more closely at some of the issues raised earlier: How did custodial and reformatory prisons differ in terms of their inmates' conviction offenses, sentences, and personal attributes? Part II also addresses (in Chapter 6) the issue of racial discrimination in the two types of prisons; here, as in earlier chapters, a good deal of attention is paid to variations by period and region. The concluding chapter of Part II focuses on the operation of a specific reformatory and deals with issues of social class and social control.

The five institutions whose records form the basis for the following chapters are the Tennessee State Penitentiary, the New York State Prison for Women at Auburn, the Ohio Penitentiary, New York's Western House of Refuge at Albion,[1] and the Ohio Reformatory for Women at Marysville. These institutions provide opportunities for a number of comparisons. Because they were located in different areas of the country, they enable us to inquire about regional variations in conviction offenses, inmate demographics, and so on. Three were custodial institutions (the penitentiaries of Tennessee and Ohio, and New York's State Prison for Women at Auburn) and two were reformatories (Albion and Marysville); thus we can pursue

FIGURE 1
Use of Original Prisoner Records of Five Institutions:
Periods Covered and Sampling Procedures (Female Cases Only) (4606 Total Cases)

	TENNESSEE STATE PEN.	N. Y.— AUBURN ST. PRISON	ALBION REFORMATORY	OHIO PENITENTIARY	OHIO REF FOR WOM
1830	Opened 1831			Opened 1834	
1835					
1840					
1845					
1850	1831–1874[a]				
1855					
1860					
1865					
1870					
1875					
1880					
1885		Women's Prison Opened 1893			
1890	1879–1905[a]		Opened 1894		
1895		1893–1903[b]		1888–4/1910[a]	
1900					
1905					
1910			1894–6/1931[b]		
1915	1912–1922[a]	1912–1922[b]		1912–1916[a]	Opened 19
1920				Women's Annex Closed 1916	1916–192
1925					
1930	1929–1934[a]	1926–1933[b]			1926–3/194
1935		Women's Prison Closed 1933	Closed 1931		
1940					
1945					
	965 cases	669 cases	1583 cases	609 cases	780 cases (624 thru 19

104

our inquiry into differences between the two types of women's prisons. Even within the custodial and reformatory categories, the institutions differed, making further comparisons possible. The penitentiaries of Tennessee and Ohio dated from the early nineteenth century and held both men and women, whereas the custodial prison at Auburn was established late in the nineteenth century and had some independence from the neighboring men's prison. New York's reformatory at Albion conformed closely to the ideals of the reformatory movement; Marysville, on the other hand, demonstrated little interest in those goals. By using these five examples, then, we can refine the general view of the women's prison system that emerged in Part I.

For all five prisons, the principal source of information is prisoner registries—large ledgers in which clerks recorded the name, conviction offense, sentence, and often a great deal of other information on incoming inmates. Figure 1 illustrates the periods covered and sampling methods used for each institution; sources and sampling procedures are described in more detail in Appendix D. These samples give a more complete picture of the conviction offenses, sentences, and other characteristics of women held at a number of state prisons over time than any other source currently available.[2]

Figure 1 (*continued*)
   a) every case
   b) odd-numbered cases
   c) every fifth case
Notes: No women were committed to the Tennessee State Penitentiary until 1840. For the New York State Prison for Women at Auburn, data were collected on every case received May–December 1893 and on all odd-numbered cases thereafter; special detail was necessary in the case of the first receptions because these were women previously convicted (one as early as 1863) who were transferred in groups from the county penitentiaries when Auburn opened. The Albion reformatory (New York Western House of Refuge) opened in 1893 but did not receive its first prisoner until January 1894. The first cases at the Ohio Reformatory for Women included transfers from the Ohio Penitentiary, women committed as early as 1913. Although a few women were mistakenly sent to the Ohio Penitentiary after the transfers took place on September 1, 1916, none were committed there; instead they were sent to the reformatory.

CHAPTER 5 ||||||||||||||||||||||||||||||

Conviction Offenses, Sentences, and Prisoners at Five Institutions

Over the past decade, many states have enacted new determinate and mandatory sentencing laws. These have led criminologists to concentrate a good deal of attention on ways in which changes in incarceration policies affect the composition of prison populations, time actually served, and method of discharge. This chapter reflects this new direction in criminological research; because it deals with conviction offenses and time served and because it ranges broadly in terms of both geography and chronology (covering three regions of the country and the period during which states switched from determinate to indeterminate sentencing), it enables us to observe significant changes in incarceration policies affecting women. These changes generally point toward one conclusion: who goes into prison, and for how long, are more a function of shifting concepts of justice, varying attitudes toward the possibility of rehabilitation, and changing practical considerations than of offense type. This conclusion is reinforced by the next chapter, which examines the influence of yet another factor—race—on the composition of prison populations and sentence length.

CONVICTION OFFENSES

The conviction offenses of prisoners sampled from the five institutions are summarized in Table 5.1. This table confirms an assertion of earlier chapters: women held at custodial institutions (in this case, the Tennessee state penitentiary, the all-female prison at Auburn, New York, and the Ohio penitentiary) were more likely to have been convicted of violent and property crimes than women held at reformatories (the Western House of Refuge at Albion, New York, and the Ohio Reformatory for Women). While public order crimes accounted for but small proportions of the conviction offenses of women held at the custodial prisons, they figured prominently among convictions at the two reformatories. This was especially true in the case of Albion, at which over 80 percent of sampled inmates were incarcerated for public order crimes. That the proportion of public order offenders was smaller at the Ohio Reformatory for Women (52.9 percent), and that this institution's proportions of violent and property offenders were correspondingly larger, is explained by Marysville's less faithful adherence to the reformatory plan. Marysville received felons from the start; indeed, its first commitments included transfers from the Ohio penitentiary, which closed its female department when the reformatory opened. Thereafter Marysville did receive the public order offenders who constituted the bulk of inmates at "purer" reformatories like Albion, but it also took felons who previously would have been sent to the Ohio penitentiary.

TABLE 5.1
Conviction Offenses by Prison: Number and Percentage of Prisoners in Each Offense Category

	TENNESSEE STATE PEN.	N.Y.— AUBURN ST. PRISON	OHIO PENI- TENTIARY	ALBION REFOR- MATORY	OHIO REF'} FOR WOMEN
Violent crimes	398 (41.2%)	242 (36.2%)	201 (33.0%)	19 (1.2%)	173 (22.2%)
Property crimes	514 (53.3%)	358 (53.5%)	315 (51.7%)	217 (13.7%)	178 (22.8%)
Public order crimes	17 (1.8%)	57 (8.5%)	77 (12.6%)	1288 (81.4%)	413 (52.9%)
Other offenses	28 (2.9%)	10 (1.5%)	15 (2.5%)	51 (3.2%)	15 (1.9%)
No informa- tion	8 (.8%)	2 (.3%)	1 (.2%)	8 (.5%)	1 (.1%)
Totals	965 (100%)	669 (100%)	609 (100%)	1583 (100%)	780 (99.9%)

*Does not add to 100 percent because of rounding.
Note: For definitions of offense categories, see Appendix C.

Conviction Offenses at the Custodial Institutions

The breakdowns of Table 5.2 make possible detailed analysis of the conviction offenses of women held at the custodial institutions. Within the violent crime category, homicide was the outstanding offense at all three prisons, but the proportion convicted of murder or manslaughter at the Tennessee penitentiary was higher (nearly 28 percent) than at either Auburn or the Ohio penitentiary (about 15 and 12 percent, respectively). If Tennessee's accessory-to-murder and attempted murder cases are added to those convicted of murder and manslaughter, its total of homicide-related cases jumps to almost 35 percent. No one in the Auburn sample was convicted of being an accessory to murder or of attempted murder, and in Ohio only a few cases had been convicted of attempted murder. The larger proportions of assault convictions in New York and Ohio, compared to Tennessee, suggest that these states may have classified some murder attempts as as-

TABLE 5.2
Custodial Institutions: Offense Breakdowns

	TENNESEE STATE PEN.		N.Y.— AUBURN ST. PRISON		OHIO PENITENTIARY	
Violent Crimes						
Accessory to murder	4	(.4)	—	—	—	—
Attempted murder	65	(6.7)	—	—	21	(3.4)
Murder and manslaughter	268	(27.8)	101	(15.1)	70	(11.5)
Assault	26	(2.7)	53	(7.9)	56	(9.2)
Arson	22	(2.3)	23	(3.4)	11	(1.8)
Robbery	12	(1.2)	52	(7.8)	35	(5.8)
Other	1	(.1)	13	(1.9)	8	(1.3)
Subtotals	398	(41.2)	242	(36.2)	201	(33.0)
Property Crimes						
Burglary	41	(4.2)	35	(5.2)	21	(3.4)
Conc./Rec. stolen prop.	19	(2.0)	22	(3.3)	17	(2.8)
Forg./Counterf./Pass. bad checks	18	(1.9)	19	(2.8)	18	(3.0)
Grand larceny	55	(5.7)	278	(41.6)	65	(10.7)
Larceny	219	(22.7)	—	—	55	(9.0)
Petit larceny	157	(16.3)	1	(.1)	—	—
Other	5	(.5)	3	(.5)	139	(22.8)
Subtotals	514	(53.3)	358	(53.5)	315	(51.7)
Public Order Crimes	17	(1.8)	57	(8.5)	77	(12.6)
Other Offenses	28	(2.9)	10	(1.5)	15	(2.5)
No Information	8	(.8)	2	(.3)	1	(.2)
Totals	965	(100.0)	669	(100.0)	609	(100.0)

Notes: Numbers in parentheses are percentages. For definitions of offense categories, see Appendix C.

saults or allowed women who had in fact attempted to commit murder to plea-bargain for assault. But even if New York and Ohio classified as assaults some cases that were actually attempted murders, their proportions of homicide-related cases still remained lower than Tennessee's. This finding, in combination with the larger overall proportion convicted of crimes of violence in Tennessee, lends support to the claim that the South, over time, had higher levels of violence than other regions.[1]

Supplementary sources shed light on the nature of some of the violent crimes committed by women in Tennessee and New York. In the case of Tennessee, it proved possible to link seven violent offenders in the sample with state Supreme Court records that give details on their cases. In two, the murderer and her victim had a history of family violence, and in at least one of these, the offender apparently acted in self-defense. This was the case of Sallie Griffin, who in 1916 appealed a conviction for premeditated and malicious murder of her husband. She was eighteen or nineteen years old, he had been fifty. According to Sallie's version of the story, they had "had trouble ever since we . . . married," six months before the killing. At the trial physicians had testified that several months before the murder, Sallie was seriously injured by a blow to the ovaries incurred when her husband had kicked her out of bed. (She had refused to have sexual intercourse "by reason of my monthly period.") On another occasion he had hit her on the head with a poker; and otherwise, too, he had "treated his wife cruelly and inhumanly, frequently whipped, cursed and abused her." Sallie's appeal claimed that she should have been convicted merely of voluntary manslaughter, for "just a few minutes before the homicide, the defendant and deceased had a fight, . . . the deceased assaulted the defendant by knocking her through a window, cutting her face and neck; . . . he struck her with a hammer . . . and . . . [told] her that he would knock her brains out." Thinking herself in mortal danger, Sallie had picked up a shotgun and killed him. Eyewitnesses disputed Sallie's claim that she had been threatened with the hammer, however; thus the court refused her motion for retrial and affirmed her sentence of ten to twenty years in the penitentiary.[2]

The other family violence case described in the Tennessee Supreme Court records involved a forty-year-old bootlegger named Kate Nelson, convicted in 1926 of killing her common-law husband, Louis Smith. Smith, according to the court transcript, was known to the police as "an overbearing, violent man." He and Nelson had a long history of fighting before she shot him to death in their kitchen. Convicted of involuntary manslaughter and sentenced to one to two years, Nelson appealed on grounds of self-defense. But as in the case of Sallie Griffin, the court turned down her motion for retrial.[3]

In two other cases heard on appeal by the Tennessee Supreme Court, the crime involved a fight with another woman over a man. Julia Booze was convicted in 1929 of murder, first degree, for killing a woman with whom her husband was having an affair. In 1922, Stella Armstrong was convicted of attempted murder after assaulting one Jennie Manson with a knife. Armstrong suspected that Manson was trying to steal her man, but according to Manson, she had merely been trying to sell him a ticket to her band concert.[4]

Another two of the Tennessee cases involved brawls. In one, two women stabbed a third who had insulted them. In the other, Eva Mai Davis was convicted of voluntary manslaughter after she and some other women got drunk with a group of men and went driving around town. Davis stabbed one of the men with an ice pick, her motive being "that she resented the deceased being with them, he being the odd man in the party." She appealed her conviction on the ground that she was too drunk to know what she was doing. The court was not impressed by this argument.[5]

The final case, heard on appeal in the late nineteenth century, involved a robbery committed by two black women, Fanny Weaks and Spot Scruggs, both twenty-two years old. Their victim was a middle-aged white man who had picked them up in a Nashville restaurant. When he was quite drunk (according to his own testimony), the women suggested that they go down an alley together, at which point they jumped him, taking his wallet and $105. Weaks was sentenced to ten years, Scruggs to five. (This case resembles two others among the Tennessee Supreme Court records; while these involved mere theft, not violence, in them, too, the victims were white men relieved of their money by a team of black prostitutes.)[6]

Because few cases were heard on appeal by the state Supreme Court, it is difficult to glean details on more than the aforementioned instances of violent crime by women in the Tennessee sample. Because of the survival of a Bertillon register in which clerks recorded particulars on each offense, more information is available on women who committed violent crime in New York.[7] Data were collected on every murder and manslaughter case in this volume. (Because the Bertillon register covers admissions between July 1909 and June 1933, the homicide sample overlaps but is not coterminous with the other sample of Auburn prisoners.) The clerks' principal source of information probably was the prisoners themselves, questioned on admission. While prisoners in general may not be a reliable source of information about their offenses, these homicide data are likely to be accurate. The clerks recorded information only briefly (such as "father with axe"), thus minimizing opportunities for exaggeration or exculpation. Then too, the court records that apparently arrived with the prisoners would have constrained them from straying far from the facts.

The Auburn homicide sample produced 148 offenders and 149 victims (one woman having strangled two men). Two-thirds of the victims were adult males. These were identified as husbands in 29 percent of the cases, boyfriends or lovers in 2 percent, and "man" or "boy" in the rest. It seems likely that many of the "men" and "boys" were lovers as well. Although the documents do not so designate them (perhaps because the prisoners did not volunteer the information), the records suggest such a relationship by giving names and other details (such as "her friend Clifford Fuller"). Adult women were the victims in 16 percent of the cases. In another 12 percent, the victims were children identified as the offender's own child in 4 percent of the cases and merely as "child" or "baby" in the rest. Probably some of these other children and babies were the offspring of offenders reluctant to identify them as such.[8]

As for the means of killing, 30 percent of the victims in the Auburn homicide sample were shot with a firearm. Another 26 percent were stabbed.[9] Eight offenders were abortionists whose clients died, and another four killed victims in the course of "illegal operations" that may also have been abortions. Particularly pathetic were the means used by women to rid themselves of unwanted babies—live burial, exposure, throwing the infant out of a window, and, in the case of a fourteen-month-old "love child," "Night— Auto—Threw Body into Lake." In other cases, the method of killing was also unusual: burning a child to death in an oven, the axe-murder of a father, the serving of poisoned candy to a husband.

Although the details varied, the crime patterns of the past form parallels to those found in current studies of women and violent crime, suggesting considerable stability over time in the nature of female offending. Recent evidence indicates that when a woman commits a theft (violent or otherwise), she frequently works in concert with another woman.[10] To judge from the Tennessee court cases and from some registry evidence,[11] this was also true in the past. According to recent studies of women and homicide, when a woman kills, her usual victim is an adult male with whom she has had a close relationship; women seldom kill other women.[12] Auburn's Bertillon registry indicates that this is a longstanding pattern. However, the Tennessee and New York sources also hint at patterns that have not been investigated by other studies of women and homicide.[13] Is it true, as these sources intimate, that children also constitute a small but significant category of victims of female homicide offenders? Such a finding would be logical, given women's involvement in childcare and the stigma attached to bearing illegitimate babies. That it has not emerged in other studies of women and homicide may be a result of failures to analyze victims by age, or of a prosecutorial tendency in other jurisdictions to route homicidal mothers into the mental health system. Second, is it true, as the Tennessee court records suggest, that when women kill other women, these homicides are sometimes triggered by problems concerning their relationships with a man?

With respect to means of killing, too, our data raise several interesting questions. According to other studies, when women use weapons, they tend to use familiar instruments—knives rather than firearms. In his investigation of homicides committed in Philadelphia between 1948 and 1952, Marvin E. Wolfgang found that women had shot their victims in only 20 percent of the cases; 64 percent had killed by stabbing. Yet, according to the Bertillon registry, women used guns more often than stabbing instruments. As William Wilbanks has pointed out, "Although there is a common stereotype of a woman wielding a kitchen knife, the extent of this stereotype's accuracy is unknown." The facts presented here suggest that we should question the stereotype more thoroughly. The abortionists and those convicted of committing "illegal operations" also suggest a new line of inquiry: to what extent, in other jurisdictions in the past, did criminalization of abortion (and, perhaps, prohibitions against midwifery) lead to conviction of women for homicides?[14]

Turning now to the property offenses committed by women held at the three custodial institutions, Table 5.2 indicates close equivalency in overall proportions: at each prison, just over 50 percent of the sampled inmates had been convicted of some form of property crime. At each prison, moreover, small and roughly equal proportions were confined for burglary, concealing or receiving stolen goods, and some form of forgery. Table 5.2 indicates less consistency among the proportions held for the various forms of larceny. In some respects, however, this lack of consistency is more apparent than real.

A much greater proportion of the Auburn offenders had been convicted of grand larceny—almost 42 percent, in comparison to less than 11 percent at the other two prisons. However, the Bertillon register's capsule descriptions of Auburn's grand larceny cases suggest that these were often offenses that might elsewhere have been charged as mere larceny: "Robbing business partner of money" (charge of attempted grand larceny, second degree); "Picking pocket" (grand larceny, second degree); "Taking fur coat from dept. store" and "Taking money from a man's pocket" (both attempted grand larceny, second degree).[15] Moreover, although only 19.7 percent of the Ohio sample had been convicted of grand larceny or larceny, and none of petit larceny, the Ohio prisoners were not less larcenous than counterparts at the other two prisons, a fact that becomes clear when one examines the subcategory of "other" property crimes. This includes 125 cases (20.5 percent of the Ohio penitentiary sample) of pocket picking, an offense not classified by Ohio into any of the larceny subcategories. Thus there probably was a closer equivalency in the actual theft behaviors of women held at Auburn and the Ohio penitentiary than Table 5.2 indicates.

It does seem likely that, just as Table 5.2 suggests, many more women were incarcerated for petty theft in Tennessee than in the other two states. (As Chapter 6 explains in more detail, just after the Civil War southern states passed laws making possible the incarceration of newly freed blacks for the most minor of larcenies.[16]) Nevertheless, the overall proportions of prisoners committed to the three institutions for some form of larceny were quite similar: 44.7 percent in Tennessee (adding the grand larceny, larceny, and petit larceny subcategories), 41.7 percent in New York (adding the same subcategories), and 40.2 percent in Ohio (adding the pocket pickers as well). Allowing for the probability that New York's grand larceny cases were often not too "grand," it seems that relatively minor thefts were the outstanding variety of property crime for women in these three regionally separate states.

For the female prisoners of these three institutions, then, property crimes constituted the most common conviction offense, and these crimes apparently often involved thefts of small amounts. In all probability, these patterns reflected actual patterns of offending; irrespective of whether they were caught and incarcerated, women in the past who committed crimes seem to have committed not violent but, rather, property offenses, often of small consequence. Today, too, according to arrest statistics, larceny-theft is the most common form of female crime. And female property offenders continue to be heavily involved in petty thefts—shoplifting, passing bad checks, and other traditionally female offenses. As in the case of violent crime, there seems to be a good deal of stability over time in patterns of female property offending. And as with violent offenses, gender roles evidently play an important role in shaping these patterns. Women are socialized to nurture rather than to aggress, to provide for their families but not to engage in displays of physical power. Moreover, insofar as women have opportunities to commit property crimes, these opportunities lead to the theft of household items or small amounts of money (as through writing bad checks). As Darrell J. Steffensmeier has observed, men tend to exclude women from criminal subcultures involved in more serious types of property crime. Finally, women have traditionally been trained to "think small," another factor that no doubt helps determine the unambitious nature of their property offenses.[17]

Although public order crimes did not form a significant category of conviction offenses at any of the custodial institutions, the proportion in Tennessee was smaller (about 2 percent) than in New York (8.5 percent) and Ohio (nearly 13 percent). This difference probably stemmed from greater concern in the two northern states with female morals offenders. As Michael S. Hindus discovered in his comparison of the criminal justice systems of South Carolina and Massachusetts in the nineteenth century, the northern state had a long tradition of prosecuting offenses against morality (especially when they were committed by women), whereas South Carolina remained indifferent to such violations.[18] Women confined at Auburn and the Ohio penitentiary for public order crimes had been convicted mainly of abortion, bigamy, incest, sodomy and other deviations from sexual propriety. Southern women probably committed such acts with equal frequency. However, as Chapter 6 illustrates, southern states were loathe to send white women to state prisons, and they tended to ignore offenses against morality committed by blacks. This explains the smaller proportion of public order offenders at the Tennessee penitentiary.

Conviction Offenses at the Reformatories

At the Albion reformatory—the institution that more than any other in the country established the ideals of the women's reformatory movement— few inmates had been convicted of serious crimes. None had been sentenced for murder. Only three had been convicted of manslaughter (Table 5.3), and two of these cases involved manslaughter in the second degree. Half of the twelve assault cases involved third degree assault; similarly, one of the two robbery cases had a charge of third degree. This tendency of Albion women to have been convicted of second or third degree violations carried over into the property crime category: of the eight burglary cases, for instance, seven involved burglary in the third degree; all of the forgery cases involved either second or third degree violations; and twenty-one of the twenty-nine grand larceny cases involved violations in the third degree. The great majority of Albion's property offenders had been convicted of petit larceny. And over four-fifths of the Albion sample had been sentenced for public order crimes.

Serious and petty offenders mixed to a greater extent at the Ohio reformatory. The range of this institution's conviction offenses was extreme—everything from using obscene language to murder. A comparably wide range could occasionally be found at custodial prisons (one case of loitering, for example, turned up in the Tennessee sample), but in them mixing of serious with petty offenders was unusual. At the Ohio reformatory, on the other hand, heterogeneity was the rule. The large proportions in *each* of the three major offense categories of violent, property, and public order crime show how establishment of this institution worked to expand the state's power of social control. Marysville received all cases that previously would have been sent to the penitentiary (most of the violent and property offenders) and, in addition, hundreds of public order offenders who, before its establishment, were seldom confined in a state institution.

At both reformatories, the majority of offenders had been convicted of public order crimes, but there were important differences between the two in the types of conduct that triggered incarceration for offenses in this category. Most of Albion's public order offenders seem to have been captured by the criminal justice system for some type of sexual misconduct. Though this is not immediately apparent in Table 5.3, it becomes clearer when one looks more closely at the subcategory of disorderly conduct. Nearly all of the 782 disorderly conduct cases—736 or 46.5 percent of the entire sample—had been convicted of vagrancy. According to the prisoner

TABLE 5.3
Reformatory Institutions: Offense Breakdowns

	ALBION REFORMATORY	OHIO REFORMATORY FOR WOMEN
Violent Crimes		
Attempted murder	— —	13 (1.7)[a]
Murder and manslaughter	3 (.2)[b]	69 (8.8)
Assault	12 (.8)	21 (2.7)
Arson	— —	9 (1.2)
Robbery	2 (.1)	35 (4.5)
Other	2 (.1)	26 (3.3)
Subtotals	19 (1.2)	173 (22.2)
Property Crimes		
Burglary	8 (.5)	24 (3.1)
Conc./Rec. stolen property	3 (.2)	13 (1.7)
Forgery/Passing bad checks	7 (.4)	46 (5.9)
Grand larceny	29 (1.8)	58 (7.4)
Larceny	2 (.1)	16 (2.0)
Petit larceny	166 (10.5)	11 (1.4)
Other	2 (.1)	10 (1.3)
Subtotals	217 (13.6)	178 (22.8)
Public Order Crimes		
Alcohol–related	90 (5.7)	111 (14.2)
Childcare–related	27 (1.7)	151 (19.4)
Disorderly conduct	782 (49.4)	7 (.9)
Drug–related	2 (.1)	13 (1.7)
Marriage–related	32 (2.0)	18 (2.3)
Sex–related	339 (21.4)	94 (12.0)
Status–type offenses	12 (.8)	7 (.9)
Other	4 (.3)	12 (1.5)
Subtotals	1288 (81.4)	413 (52.9)
Other Offenses	51 (3.2)	15 (1.9)
No Information	8 (.5)	1 (.1)
Totals	1583 (99.9)[c]	780 (99.9)[c]

[a]Numbers in parentheses are percentages.
[b]There were no murder cases at Albion.
[c]Does not add to 100 percent because of rounding.
Note: For definitions of offense categories, see Appendix C.

registries, about half of those sentenced for vagrancy, or roughly one-fourth of the total reformatory sample, were convicted of violating Section 887,

Subdivision 4 of the Code of Criminal Procedure, a combined vagrancy-prostitution charge. In these vagrancy cases, at least, the offense had overtones of sexual promiscuity. It is impossible to arrive at a precise total for Albion's sexual misconduct cases owing to the ambiguous nature of some of the conviction offenses—"public nuisance," for example, and "keeping bad company." But sexual misconduct certainly would include most (if not all) of the 26.7 percent convicted of the combined vagrancy-prostitution charge, the 21.4 percent convicted of obviously sex-related offenses, the 2 percent sentenced for the marriage-related offenses of adultery and bigamy, some of those sentenced for childcare-related and status offenses (such as endangering the morals of a child, and keeping bad company), and others who violated city ordinances and special sections of the New York Penal Law.[19] It seems probable, then, that for at least half of Albion inmates, sexual misconduct was the act that led to incarceration. Few of these sexual deviations would have landed a male in state prison; indeed, many of them would not have been considered as offenses when committed by men.[20] With the establishment of reformatories like Albion, the criminal justice system became a means for state punishment of women who failed to conform to the sexual double standard.

The great extent to which such reformatories became involved in maintaining the double standard, and the extraordinary degree to which the criminal justice system became dedicated to repressing female sexuality at the turn of the century, are made manifest by the fact that most women sent to Albion because of sexual misconduct were *not* prostitutes. This fact is established by details in the registries and case files on women arrested for the Section 887 violation. The 887 charge was sometimes used to punish premarital pregnancies, for example—or a series of them, as with Case No. 1451, who had just borne her third illegitimate baby when county officials decided to send her to the reformatory. Sometimes an 887 charge was brought on the complaint of some member of the woman's family, such as an exasperated mother or embarrassed husband. According to a newspaper clipping attached to the registry entry for Rosetta B., for instance, one month before her commitment this eighteen-year-old's husband had had her arrested for truancy, and the judge had put her on probation. When, a month later, she ran away for an entire weekend, only to be discovered on Monday morning by the police "in a resort on Elm Street," the husband complained again to the judge, who committed Rosetta to three years at Albion under the vagrancy-prostitution statute. Similarly, nineteen-year-old Sarah M., married for one month, was committed on the 887 charge. "Sarah did not know it," reads a note on her record, "but it was her husband who had her sent here." The 887 charge could cover a multitude of peccadillos from cuckolding to keeping bad company; but women convicted under it were not professional prostitutes.

The mildness of the offenses for which most of Albion's sexual miscreants had been apprehended illuminates the nature and effects of the antiprostitution campaigns that engaged so many turn-of-the-century reformers. These crusades against "the social evil" were ostensibly directed against prostitution; but as several studies have shown, "prostitution" was defined to encompass even minor deviations from middle-class standards of female propriety. Actual, paid prostitution seems to have begun to wane about 1900; however, the looseness with which "prostitution" was defined kept the target group large and fueled the alarm. It also meant that large numbers of young, working-class women who were not prostitutes but led sexually autonomous lives were affected by the vice campaigns. Such women constituted the bulk of Albion's sex offenders.[21]

Some Albion inmates *were* professional prostitutes—the 8.5 percent sentenced for prostitution, for example, and the additional .5 percent convicted of keeping a house of ill fame. There were also other women who had engaged casually in acts of sex for money, such as one who had frequented "Jimmy Joe's place on Railroad Ave. where she received men." But most of the sex offenders seem, like Jennie B., merely to have been sexually active: Jennie was sent to the reformatory for five years for having "had unlawful sexual intercourse with young men and remain[ing] at hotels with young men all night particularly on July 4, 1893." In fact, institutions that, like Albion, took themselves seriously as reformatories had little interest in the hardcore professional prostitute; instead they sought impressionable young women who might respond positively to their programs.

For only a small proportion of the women imprisoned at Marysville, in contrast, did premarital sex and other forms of promiscuity lead to conviction. Disorderly conduct charges account for less than 1 percent of the Marysville convictions, in comparison to nearly 50 percent at Albion (where they included the vagrancy-prostitution charge). Only 12 percent of the Ohio reformatory's inmates had been found guilty of obviously sex-related offenses (in comparison to over 21 percent at Albion), and although some offenses in other public order subcategories carry sexual implications ("under immoral influence," for example), it seems clear that Ohio's criminal justice authorities had less interest than those of New York in reforming fallen women. They had less opportunity to indulge such concern, for their state had no institution like Albion devoted to the rehabilitation of loose women.

If not sexual delinquents, in what types of public order offenders *did* the Ohio reformatory specialize? The two subcategories with the largest proportions of cases were those involving alcohol and childcare offenses; in both instances, these proportions were higher than at Albion. The childcare convictions in Ohio mainly involved contributing to delinquency[22] (97 cases or 12.4 percent of the sample) and child neglect (43 cases or 5.5

percent). In the absence of details on specific cases, it is difficult to explain why such childcare offenses figured this prominently in the Marysville sample. On the other hand, it *is* possible to pinpoint a factor in the alcohol-related cases: Prohibition. In Ohio, alcohol offenders were usually convicted not of intoxication but of violating laws prohibiting the manufacture and possession of alcohol. Most were prosecuted during the 1920s. According to the reformatory's report for 1926, for instance, its population had swelled drastically over the preceding two years owing to an influx of liquor law violators—112 in 1925 and 260 more in 1926.[23] Women in New York may also have become bootleggers in the 1920s, but if prosecuted and imprisoned, they were evidently sent to the Bedford reformatory, for they show up in neither the Auburn nor Albion samples.

SENTENCES, TIME SERVED, AND METHOD OF RELEASE

The five prisons under consideration varied in the type of sentence their inmates received. The three custodial institutions held prisoners for fixed terms until their states adopted indeterminate sentencing policies, at which point most prisoners received both a minimum and maximum sentence and had the possibility of early release on parole. With only rare exceptions, felons at the custodial institutions served at least one year, and in cases of first degree murder, their sentences could extend to life. At Albion, all women received a special type of indeterminate sentence with no minimum and, until 1899, a maximum of five years; in 1899, the maximum was lowered to three years. At the Ohio reformatory, most inmates had indeterminate sentences with both minimums and maximums. There the mixed population of misdemeanants and felons resulted in a wide variety of sentence lengths: some prisoners received minimums as low as two months with a maximum of one year, while more serious cases had minimums of one year or more and maximums of up to life.

At all five institutions, a small proportion (ranging from 2 to 8 percent) of the prisoners had been convicted of more than one offense—a second or third count of manslaughter, for instance, if the offender had attacked two or three people; several counts of receiving stolen property if she had been found with a large quantity of stolen goods; or, in the case of one Albion inmate whose first conviction was for prostitution, a second count of saloon-visiting. In some cases, these multiple convictions affected sentencing. Usually offenders with multiple convictions received concurrent sentences, which did not extend release dates, but a few were sentenced to consecutive terms. This happened most frequently in Tennessee: 8 percent of the Tennessee sample had been convicted of more than one offense, and 5.5 percent received consecutive sentences. None of Albion's fifty-seven offenders with multiple convictions suffered any obvious consequence, for by law they could not be held longer than the reformatory's maximum of five (later, three) years. The handing down of multiple convictions was not necessarily an empty judicial gesture, however, since it may have influenced the length of time a woman was held at Albion before parole.

This leads to the question of how much time women actually spent in the various prisons. Table 5.4 shows the average time served in months by institution and period of commitment. The most interesting feature of this table is the decline it shows in average time served at four of the five prisons from 1888 onward. (At the fifth, the Ohio reformatory, there was a minor rise from 24 to 25.8 months between the periods 1916–1921 and 1926–1934, an increase almost certainly due to the reformatory's exclusion of misdemeanants after 1929.) Table 5.4 throws light on a much-argued question: did introduction of indeterminate sentencing increase time served? New York adopted indeterminate sentencing for felons in 1901, Tennessee and Ohio in 1913.[24] In no case did the switch to indeterminate sentencing lead to an increase in time served. Instead, after its introduction, average time served usually continued a decline begun earlier.[25] Table 5.4 suggests a move in all the states toward lighter punishment over the course of the late nineteenth and early twentieth centuries.

The trend began before the introduction of indeterminate sentences, probably as a result of prison officials' increasing willingness to award prisoners "good-time" credits—one day off time-to-be-served in return for a certain number of days of cooperative behavior. (The records of the Tennessee penitentiary make it clear that officials of that institution, at least, were quite ready to award good-time credits even if the inmates had not been particularly cooperative. They would "remove" good-time credits when an inmate acted up, but when she reached the day on which she would have been released if she had accumulated all possible credits, they reinstated the lost credits and sent her packing.) The continuation of this trend after the introduction of indeterminate sentences is probably attributable to the flexibility built into this type of term. Like fixed terms, indeterminate sentences permit legislatures to set high maximums in response to public outrage over notorious crimes. Unlike fixed terms, indeterminate sentences give prison officials and parole boards leeway to reduce time-to-be-served in response to prisoners' good behavior or more practical considerations. The general move toward shorter prison terms may also reflect changing concepts of proportionality. During the late nineteenth and early twentieth centuries, criminal justice officials, and perhaps even the public at large, may have become more lenient in their attitudes toward the punishment of felons.

Average time served was longest at the Tennessee penitentiary and Auburn prison (40.7 and 39.6 months, respectively), the custodial institutions with the largest proportions of violent and smallest proportions of

TABLE 5.4
Average Time Served in Months, by Prison and Period of Commitment

	AVERAGE NUMBER OF MONTHS	NUMBER OF CASES (PERCENT OF SAMPLE)
Tennessee Penitentiary: Total	40.7	596 (61.8%)
1831 through 1859	33.3	20
1860 through 1887	33.0	20
1888 through 1892	56.2	13
1893 through 1903	52.9	97
1904 through 1905	43.5	24
1912 through 1922	41.7	189
1929 through 1934	35.4	233
Auburn Prison: Total	39.6	484 (72.3%)
1888 through 1892*	54.4	45
1893 through 1903	37.5	225
1912 through 1922	36.2	156
1926 through 1933	31.1	54
Ohio Penitentiary: Total	28.0	552 (90.6%)
1888 through 1892	29.9	92
1893 through 1903	29.1	210
1904 through 4/1910	28.1	160
1912 through 1916	23.2	90
Albion Reformatory: Total	33.8	1369 (86.5%)
1894 through 1903	40.3	214
1904 through 1911	36.8	332
1912 through 1922	31.9	438
1923 through 1925	30.8	108
1926 through 6/1931	28.9	276
Ohio Reformatory for Women: Total	25.3	606 (97.1%)
1916 through 1921	24.0	170
1926 through 1934	25.8	436

*The forty-five Auburn cases committed from 1888 through 1892 had previously
been committed to county penitentiaries and included a high proportion of long-
termers.
Note: There is wide dispersion around the means.

public order offenders. Yet time served was not necessarily longer at custodial than reformatory institutions: at the Ohio penitentiary, the average
was 28 months, whereas at Albion it was 33.8 months. Moreover, average
time served was greater at Albion, which excluded felons, than at the Ohio
reformatory, which held them along with misdemeanants. That Albion
held women for comparatively lengthy terms despite the mild nature of

their offenses was doubtless a result of its moral fervor: perhaps more thoroughly than any other reformatory, this institution dedicated itself to remolding the character of the fallen woman, a process which, its founders had maintained, required time. But Ohio's reformatory, as shown in Chapter 3, was relatively indifferent to rehabilitation.

Several questions arise about periods in which, according to Table 5.4, average terms served were unusually long. First, why did women committed to the Tennessee penitentiary from 1888 through 1903 spend an average of over 50 months in prison, whereas earlier convicts served an average of about 33 months and later ones an average of no more than 43.5 months? The length of average time served in the 1888–1903 period is also remarkable because this was not a period in which dramatically high proportions of women were committed for violent crimes. It may be that in the earliest periods, when the prison still had no separate quarters for women, officials got rid of their few female convicts as rapidly as they could. After the Civil War, in the absence of slavery, the penitentiary began to function as a tool for the social control of blacks, whom it began to receive in large numbers; and at the turn of the century, racial tensions ran high in the South in general.[26] Moreover, Tennessee opened a new penitentiary with a separate female department in 1898. Now that the institution had (temporarily) more adequate quarters for women, and a laundry in which to work them, it had less reason to hurry them out. Such pragmatic factors may account for the lengthy periods of incarceration of women committed from 1888 through 1903.

A similarly lengthy average time served (54.4 months) occurred at the Auburn prison for women committed from 1888 through 1892. These offenders were sentenced before Auburn opened and held in county penitentiaries until transferred to the new female prison. Their sentences were long enough to keep them in the system for some time; these women were not representative.

Women sentenced to the Albion reformatory from 1894 through 1903 spent much more time in prison (40.3 months, on the average) than those committed in later years because, until the statutory change of 1899 lowered the maximum sentence, women could be held for up to five years. More puzzling is the fact that for women committed from 1904 through 1911, the average time served was 36.8 months—longer than the then legally permissible limit of three years. This discrepancy evidently was caused by a practice of meting out a second three-year sentence to some parole violators, whose double terms increased the average. The subsequent and continuous decline at Albion in average time served probably reflects both crowding and routinization, though it is notable that even women committed in the late 1920s received on the average but 7.1 months of parole. The reformatory continued to hold them for retraining for most of their

36-month sentences—another illustration of how an institution's enthusiasm for rehabilitation could affect time served.

Analysis of the method by which women were discharged from the five prisons illustrates the steady move toward indeterminacy, a progression that generally correlated with a decrease in time served. Analysis of method of discharge also shows how release could be affected by institutional idiosyncracies, including dedication (or lack of it) to the rehabilitative ideal.

Sampling from Tennessee's penitentiary records commenced from an earlier date—1831, when the institution opened—than from the other four prisons. In the earliest period (1831–1859), there were only two forms of release from this penitentiary, "definite" (i.e., some final type of discharge)[27] and death. In the next period (1860–1877), a few prisoners received some form of indeterminate release, and thereafter, the proportions with indeterminate releases grew steadily while those with definite releases declined until, in the final period (1929–1934), 87.5 percent had an indeterminate release and only 8.9 percent had a definite release. This gradual shift reflects the introduction of good-time credits and, later, of parole. It is noteworthy that of the 148 cases turned out of the Tennessee penitentiary on definite release, nearly all (142) were pardoned, while the remainder received from the governor a "special commutation" analogous to pardon. In Tennessee as in other states, before award of good-time credits and parole became common, pardons were frequently used as a means to clear out prisons. Even under fixed sentencing rules, women did not necessarily serve their full sentences; but times served were not as low as under indeterminacy.

At the Auburn prison, opened in the late nineteenth century, only 3 percent of the prisoners were dismissed through definite release. Even before this institution began granting paroles in 1901, its prisoners could earn "commutation" by accumulating good-time credits. Thus the proportion receiving indeterminate release from Auburn was higher than in Tennessee (nearly 80 percent in comparison to about 47 percent). The Ohio penitentiary opened early in the nineteenth century, but because the sample excluded women committed before 1888, data on release from this prison also reflect the late nineteenth-century move toward indeterminacy. As at Auburn, about four-fifths of the sample were released before expiration of maximum term through earning good-time credits or (later) through parole.

The rehabilitative ideology did affect these custodial institutions, leading to indeterminate sentencing and parole; but its influence was greater on institutions that also took seriously other recommendations of the 1870 prison congress, such as that recommendation calling for individualizing treatment. Albion commenced operation with an innovative indeterminate sentencing law that practically guaranteed most women early release on parole. But 10 percent of the sample were discharged through some means *other* than parole or expiration of sentence, indicating the lengths to which this institution went to individualize the release decision. Some cases in the "other" release category were deported; some were discharged because they were seriously ill (usually with tuberculosis or influenza); some (48 cases, or 3 percent) were transferred to institutions for the feebleminded. (The significance of feeblemindedness transfers is discussed in Chapter 3.) Even the death discharges were "individualized": when Case No. 15 died, for example, the president of the board of managers paid for the funeral, the physician purchased flowers, and the rest of the staff did what they could to provide a respectable burial.

Release decisions at the Ohio reformatory were more perfunctory. Only 56 percent of the cases received an indeterminate release from this institution, in marked contrast to Albion and most other reformatories, which regarded indeterminate sentencing and parole as central to rehabilitation. That a large proportion (36 percent) received a definite release reflects in part Marysville's tendency to hold prisoners for the maximum time possible and then grant them absolute discharge; 204 of the cases (26.2 percent of the entire sample) received absolute discharge when they left the Ohio reformatory. (Marysville may have been predisposed to absolute discharge because some prisoners had short terms of, for example, two months to one year; parole supervision may not have seemed beneficial or worth the trouble in such cases.) Still others who obtained definite release (70 cases, or almost 9 percent of the total) did so through paying fines. The legislation establishing the reformatory had excluded women jailed in default of payment of fine, and this clause was repeated in an act of 1925. However, the latter act also made it possible for a woman to be sent to Marysville if default of payment would cause her to be imprisoned for thirty days or more *and* if she were to receive a credit of $1.50 for each day of imprisonment.[28] Definite releases became especially common at Marysville after 1925 because of this practice of permitting inmates to work off fines and then leave without parole. The Ohio reformatory illustrates how characteristics of a specific institution—in this instance, lack of interest in rehabilitation and the presence of short-termers and of debtors who could work off fines—could affect methods of discharge.

At each prison, some women died before release. The numbers who died were small at the two reformatories and at the Ohio penitentiary—under 1 percent of the total samples. But death rates were higher at the Tennessee penitentiary (3.7 percent) and at Auburn (3.3 percent); in both instances, most of the deaths occurred before the turn of the century. At Auburn those who died, it seems, were usually older women serving very long or life sentences. But in Tennessee, the deaths frequently involved young women who became ill after only a few months in the unsanitary, disease-ridden penitentiary. In this case, too, an institutional characteristic— here, insalubrity—influenced method of discharge.

A small proportion of inmates released from each institution returned, mainly for parole violations. Returns were uncommon at the three custodial prisons, more frequent at the reformatories. The usual practice was to re-parole recommitments or to hold them till expiration of sentence. Albion also occasionally transferred recommitted prisoners to institutions for the feebleminded.

Owing to the thoroughness of Albion's records, details are available on the processes that led to recommitment of offenders to that institution. Unsurprisingly, in view of its loyalty to the goal of rehabilitation, Albion kept parolees under close surveillance. After release, paroled inmates' activities were scrutinized by a wide variety of agents: the institution's parole officer; local police and probation officers; occasionally a community nurse or other municipal official; and the employers to whom inmates were either paroled as live-in servants or from whom they obtained work after release. Return was not always involuntary, moreover; some women recommitted themselves to the institution because they could not get along with an employer or had become ill.

As for the behaviors that led to parole revocation, these were, predictably, the same sorts of sexual misconduct and boisterousness for which women were committed to Albion in the first place. One woman violated parole by running away from a domestic position to join a theatrical troupe, several by filching from employers, many by becoming pregnant. A parolee named Isabel was returned to the reformatory for "going out with a disreputable married man and on several occasions [remaining out] all night." Another woman's parole was revoked because "[h]er conduct was most reprehensible. . . . She made appointments with entire strangers, male, to go auto riding. Stayed out very late nights. Once all night." And No. 1759 was "[r]eturned for obscenity. Lost her head on account of the many carpenters . . . about while the house was being built. This construction was understood to have been completed before we placed her there." It is important to note that some women who violated parole were not returned to Albion. For example, No. 1739 became pregnant after reparole, but, because she married her boyfriend, the institution decided not to intervene. In these cases, decision making was highly individualized.

THE PRISONERS

It is notably difficult to acquire information on the prisoners around whom the prison system grew, those people who inhabited the honeycomb cells and then died or departed with few traces. Several former inmates such as Sarah Victor and Emma Goldman wrote accounts of their experiences, but autobiographers were unusual.[29] The records of investigatory commissions sometimes preserve testimony given by more typical prisoners, and case files survive from some institutions. Other sources, usually more comprehensive, are the institutional registries of prisoners, which include details on important variables such as sex and race. While these details do not present complete portraits, they make possible construction of generalized profiles of prison populations. In what follows, data from the registries of the five institutions under consideration are used to build such profiles in terms of age, marital status, social class, and religious affiliation. Two other characteristics, place of birth and race, are considered in the next chapter.

Women held at custodial institutions were older when they entered prison than were reformatory inmates. About half of those confined at the three custodial prisons were between twenty-one and thirty years old at commitment. At Auburn and the Ohio penitentiary, nearly all the others were between the ages of thirty-one and fifty. In Tennessee, in contrast, more than a third were under age twenty-one at commitment, perhaps because that state, like others in the South, was slow in establishing institutions for juveniles.[30] Albion's governing legislation, designed to ensure that the reformatory would receive tractable women, limited admission to offenders between the ages of fifteen (later raised to sixteen) and thirty. The legislation had the anticipated effect: two-thirds of the Albion sample were between sixteen and twenty years old at commitment and nearly all the others under thirty. (Occasionally judges strayed beyond the limits to commit women under fifteen or over thirty; but in at least some cases, the reformatory returned such illegal commitments to the courts.) Because the Ohio reformatory received felons as well as misdemeanants, its age-of-commitment pattern resembled that of the custodial institutions: nearly half of the Marysville sample entered between the ages of twenty-one and thirty. These data on commitment age at institutions that received felons are compatible with information on women currently held in penal institutions, two-thirds of whom are under thirty years of age. Moreover, today as in the past, female misdemeanants tend to be younger than felons.[31]

Another characteristic of incarcerated women of the past and present is a tendency to be unmarried.[32] At Albion, over 70 percent were single at the time they entered prison. Smaller proportions of the sampled inmates from the other prisons were single (59, 40, and 50 percent at the Tennessee penitentiary, Auburn prison, and Ohio penitentiary, respectively; no information on marital status is available in the records of the Ohio reformatory). The "single" category at the custodial prisons, moreover, included a higher proportion of widows. Yet, although prisoners at the custodial institutions were more likely to be (or to have been) married than those at Albion, the proportions of single women were still high.

Their employment history suggests that most of the prisoners were working-class women.[33] A few had held white-collar jobs as accountants, bookkeepers, clerks, and so on (6 percent or fewer at each institution except the Ohio reformatory, whose records include no information on prior occupation). In relatively industrialized New York, some had held blue-collar jobs: 12 percent of the Auburn sample, 19 percent of that of Albion. Most of these women had worked in factories or mills. At the Ohio penitentiary, Auburn, and Albion, the majority of inmates had previously held "service" positions, mainly as domestic servants; and in Tennessee, 40 percent had been employed in service capacities. Except in Tennessee, most of the prisoners had worked for wages at some point. Fewer than 1 percent of the Auburn prisoners and under 3 percent of those held at the Ohio penitentiary had never been employed. The figure was higher for Albion (about 22 percent), probably because of the youth of its inmates; many may have still been supported by their parents. Only in Tennessee did large numbers (nearly 50 percent) report having never been employed. The never-employed of the Tennessee sample, however, had not been leisured women: as the next chapter explains, most were black, and many seem to have been migrating north in search of employment at the time of arrest. In their employment history, as in their age and marital status, these prisoners of the past resemble incarcerated women today.[34]

Information on religious affiliation appears in the records of the Tennessee penitentiary, the Auburn prison, and the Albion reformatory. The majority of the prisoners were Protestants, but the proportions varied by region. In New York, with its larger numbers of European immigrants, a significant minority were Catholics (40 percent at Auburn, 32 percent at Albion). A greater proportion of the Tennessee prisoners were Protestants; more specifically, many described themselves as Baptists or Methodists. Few women in the New York samples were listed as having no religious affiliation, but nearly 55 percent of the Tennessee prisoners had "none" or a similar notation in the "Religion" column of the registries. This difference may have been in part a by-product of clerical practices: in New York, record-keepers may have "forced" a choice, while those of Tennessee may have been more receptive to inmate declarations of no religious affiliation. But although the New York data may be somewhat misleading, those of Tennessee probably do reflect a situation in which large numbers of prisoners were decidedly nonreligious, at least in terms of formal church membership.

In sum, the female felons held at custodial institutions tended to be twenty-one years or older at the point of imprisonment. Forty percent or more were unmarried, with the proportion of single inmates having been especially high at the Tennessee penitentiary. The majority had worked, mainly as servants, but the proportion of never-employed was much greater among the prisoners of Tennessee. Women held at the Tennessee penitentiary were also less likely to claim a religious affiliation. The misdemeanants and other minor offenders held at the Albion reformatory were younger at commitment and, by virtue of their age, less likely to be married. Nearly one-quarter of them had never been employed (another reflection of their youth); but in contrast to New York women in general (only 27 percent of whom were gainfully employed in 1910), over 75 percent of Albion's inmates had worked, most of them in menial service positions.

Many features in these prisoner profiles suggest that incarcerated women were more at the margins of society than other women. At both the reformatories and custodial institutions, inmates were young adults. They were at the point of moving away from their birth families, but many had not yet married to form a new family. Although most had been employed at some point, their jobs paid poorly and were low in status and security. These characteristics are compatible with the "control" theory of criminal behavior that has gained considerable currency among criminologists over the past decade. According to control theorists, those who commit crime are less tightly tied than nonoffenders to society's rules by intermediate links to family, jobs, church, conventional activities, and the like. The profile of the typical prisoner in Tennessee—who was younger at commitment than her counterparts at Auburn and the Ohio penitentiary, less likely to be married, more likely never to have been employed, and more likely to be unaffiliated with a church—fits particularly well with control theory. That many of these Tennessee prisoners were black and in the process of migrating from their places of birth increased their marginality. The precariousness of their social position may help explain why these women were more likely than were the inmates of the other two custodial institutions to become involved in serious crime.[35]

Control theory provides a useful tool for analyzing several aspects of female crime. It provides a plausible explanation for the apparently greater involvement of disadvantaged women in criminal behavior. Moreover, although control theorists have not paid much attention to sex differences in rates of offending, the theory has considerable potential: across time in this country, women have had markedly lower arrest and incarceration rates than men, a fact that, as Francis Lieber explained a hundred and fifty years ago, is probably due to their social "destiny"—the greater intensity of their ties to family, home, and church.[36] But although the prison registries and other sources tend to support control theory in terms of female crime patterns, that theory does not adequately explain variations in reactions by criminal justice agents toward female offenders. Control theorists argue that lack of ties to the conventional order fosters criminal behavior. That claim may be true; but it may also be true that lack of bonds to family, secure jobs, church, and so on increase some women's vulnerability to the criminal justice system. Marginal women probably did (and continue to) have special incentives for violating criminal laws. But their very marginality may have encouraged criminal justice officials to process them into the prison system.[37]

Irrespective of the specific characteristics that triggered official reactions (and it seems probable that the impact of characteristics such as marital and employment status varied by time and place), it is obvious that labeling processes affected decisions to incarcerate, quite apart from seriousness of offense. Before reformatories existed, female petty offenders did not go to state prisons. In Ohio (to give another example), public order offenders were sent to the reformatory for childcare and alcohol-related crimes more often than for the sexual improprieties that led Albion's inmates to prison. Unless we wish to argue that Ohio's women were less sexually active than those of New York, we must conclude that differences in policy affected the composition of the female prisoner populations in these two states. Similarly, northern custodial institutions were more likely than the Tennessee penitentiary to incarcerate public order offenders—another illustration of the determinative effect of policy or tradition on the decision whether to imprison someone. As we have seen, time served also seems to have been related more to policy than to offense severity. And as the next chapter shows, differing policies toward black and white women further shaped the compositions of prison populations and lengths of sentences.

The impact of policy on the decision to incarcerate becomes even clearer in a long-range view of the varying proportions of women held in state prisons for violent and property offenses over time. Data from the first half of the nineteenth century are fragmentary, but those that have survived show that of all female state prisoners, very few had been sentenced for crimes of violence. The overwhelming majority had been imprisoned for property crimes.[38] Information from the registries of the three custodial prisons under consideration here shows that, by the turn of the century, about one-third of incarcerated female felons were serving time for crimes of violence.[39] Of women in state prisons today, 40 percent were sentenced for violent offenses.[40] Although the *level* of female crime probably has risen since the early nineteenth century, there is no evidence that the *proportion* of all female offenders who commit violent crime has increased.[41] On the other hand, there is ample evidence that incarceration policies have changed since the early nineteenth century: female property offenders who previously would have served time in state prisons have been squeezed out by violent offenders. In like manner, if data were available to prove the point, we would no doubt find that today's violent offenders serve less time than did nineteenth-century women convicted of the same offenses. One of the first prisoners transferred in 1893 to Auburn from a county penitentiary had originally been sentenced to the old prison for women at Sing Sing in 1865, at the age of sixteen; when she arrived at Auburn, she had already served twenty-eight years.[42] It would be difficult to find such a case today. However, with the current move toward determinate and mandatory sentencing, similar examples may shortly appear again with some frequency in the prison system.

CHAPTER 6 |||||||||||||||||||||||||||||||

Race and Racism in State Prisons Holding Women, 1865–1935

Before 1865, black women entered the prisons of the Northeast and Midwest in numbers grossly disproportionate to their representation in the general populations of these regions. Remembering her experience as an administrator at New York's Mount Pleasant Female Prison in the 1840s, Georgiana Bruce Kirby recalled, "Colored people were at that time convicted and given long terms on the flimsiest testimony." William Crawford, another close observer of American penal systems in the antebellum period, also attributed the racial imbalances within prisons of the northern states to devaluation of blacks: "[T]hese oppressed people form . . . the most degraded class of the community. . . . [T]he only wonder is, that there should not be more crime among a population . . . so disadvantageously situated,"—especially, added Crawford, among "coloured females . . . , greatly as they are exposed to temptation from the walks of life in which they are compelled to move." [1] In the South, on the other hand, few blacks of either sex were held in state prisons before the Civil War. Slaves were disciplined by their owners; only free blacks were eligible for public punishment. As Beaumont and Tocqueville noted, "There are no prisons to shut up slaves: imprisonment would cost too much! Death, the whips, exile, cost nothing." Thus in the South as in the North, though with opposite effects, racism played an important part in determining the composition of prison populations in the antebellum period. [2]

Racism continued to influence prisoner populations powerfully after the Civil War. The proportions of blacks, including black women, continuously swelled in the prisons of the Northeast and Midwest, while the previously white prisons of the South became engorged with newly freed blacks. Even the nascent prison system of the West imprisoned blacks in proportions that far outstripped their scanty representation in the general population. This chapter documents this phenomenon for the period 1865–1935, identifying ways in which the extralegal factors of sex and race influenced incarceration rates and prison treatment of black women in particular. It also examines variations in the effects of sex and race by region, period, and type of offense.

RACIAL PATTERNS IN PRISON POPULATIONS: A COMPARISON OF RATES OF BLACK AND WHITE WOMEN

Information collected from internal records of five institutions confirms the picture of a prison system that has, historically, incarcerated disproportionate numbers of black women. The proportion of black women by period of commitment to these five institutions is shown in Table 6.1. In all cases except that of the Albion reformatory, after the Civil War the number of blacks was disproportionately large. Over 70 percent of women committed to the Tennessee penitentiary in the 1860–1887 period were black; this figure rose to over 90 percent at the turn of the century, when racial tensions ran especially high, and declined to only 65 percent by 1926–1934, the final sampling period.[3] Over the period 1860 to 1930, the number of blacks in Tennessee fell from 26 to 18 percent of the total population. The proportion of black women held at New York's State Prison for Women at Auburn rose from 12.5 percent at the start of the sampling period to nearly 40 percent at its close,[4] a period during which the number of blacks in New York increased from 2 to 3 percent of the total population. Similarly, the population of Ohio as a whole rose from 2 to 5 percent black in the period 1890–1930, but the proportion of black women in its penitentiary increased steadily from 26 to nearly 52 percent, and blacks constituted over 25 percent of the population of the Ohio reformatory from the time it opened. Only at New York's Albion reformatory did the proportion of black female prisoners mirror the proportion of blacks in the state's total population.

Unlike the Ohio Reformatory for Women, which received felons as well as misdemeanants and paid little attention to rehabilitation, Albion concentrated on petty offenders who appeared likely to respond positively to its program of retraining. Apparently its first administrators did not conceive of including black women in this category, for Albion's prisoner registries, while leaving space for entries on a large number of variables (including family history of insanity and epilepsy), allocated no space for recording race. (When in later years blacks were admitted, the clerk penciled "colored" at the top of the page.) The sample of every other case received

TABLE 6.1
Proportion Black, by Period Committed, for Five Samples of Female State Prisoners

	TENNESSEE ST. PEN.		N.Y.–AUBURN ST. PRISON		OHIO PENITENTIARY		ALBION REFORMATORY		OHIO REFORMATORY FOR WOMEN	
	TOTAL	BLACK	TOTAL	BLACK	TOTAL	BLACK	TOTAL	BLACK	TOTAL	BLACK
1831–1859	24	3 (12.5%)	—	—	—	—	—	—	—	—
1860–1887	41	29 (70.7%)	8	1 (12.5%)	—	—	—	—	—	—
1888–1892	72	60 (83.3%)	50	4 (8.0%)	96	25 (26.0%)	1	0 (0%)	—	—
1893–1903	262	237 (90.5%)	255	76 (29.8%)	221	87 (39.4%)	217	5 (2.3%)	—	—
1904–1911	54	49 (90.7%)	—	—	163	71 (43.6%)	354	15 (4.2%)	—	—
1912–1922	239	204 (85.4%)	197	53 (26.9%)	104	54 (51.9%)	527	12 (2.3%)	176	45 (25.6%)
1923–1925	—	—	—	—	—	—	128	2 (1.6%)	—	—
1926–1934	259	169 (65.3%)	154	61 (39.6%)	—	—	314	15 (4.8%)	444	153 (34.5%)
Totals	951	751 (79.0%)	664	195 (29.4%)	584	237 (40.6%)	1541	49 (3.2%)	620	198 (31.9%)

Notes: The table excludes cases for which there was no indication of race (for Tennessee, 1.5 percent of the cases; for Auburn, .7 percent; for the Ohio penitentiary, 4.1 percent; for Albion, 2.6 percent; for the Ohio reformatory, 20.5 percent). For exact dates on periods covered for each prison and information on sampling, see Figure 1.

over the course of Albion's existence as a reformatory identified only forty-nine blacks. Belief that black women were not worthy of rehabilitative efforts seems to have held their numbers low at this institution.

Black women were overrepresented in the populations of custodial institutions and "impure" reformatories like that of Ohio owing to three factors: overt racism, covert discrimination, and higher rates of offending by black than white women for some serious crimes. Racism was most obvious in southern criminal justice systems. After the Civil War, in Tennessee and other southern states, prison populations became predominately black. White legislatures sought to reestablish race control by passing laws directed against blacks. Justice officials found they could increase state revenues by leasing convicts to private contractors, who paid by the head. As Christopher Adamson explains, in the South immediately after the war,

> Criminal laws were enacted which increased the number of offenders. Democrats in Missouri secured passage of that state's "pig" law, which defined the theft of property worth more than $10—including cattle and swine—as grand larceny, punishable by up to five years of hard labor. . . . In 1875 a similar law in Georgia made hogstealing a felony. North Carolina courts did not distinguish between petty and grand larceny, so that a person could get three to 10 years for stealing a couple of chickens. . . . These laws increased the size of the prison labor pool. In Mississippi, it increased nearly 300 percent in less than four years, from 272 convicts in 1874 to 1,072 by the end of 1877. Two years after Georgia's new law was enacted, the size of the convict population had more than tripled, from 432 to 1,441. . . .[5]

Black men and women constituted the overwhelming majority of convicts imprisoned under such laws. In Louisiana, prison officials wondered aloud whether the real reason for sending blacks to prison "upon the most trivial charges" was not "the low, mean motive of depriving them of the right[s] of citizenship." After a turn-of-the-century tour of southern penal systems, Frances Kellor documented numerous ways in which states of the region discriminated against blacks, concluding, "In the administration of the law, both consciously and unconsciously, there comes in this prejudice."[6]

Simultaneously, whites were being screened out of southern prisons. Kellor took pains to point out that this screening process affected women as well as men. The black female offender, she wrote, "is first a negro and then a woman—in the whites' estimation"; black women did not benefit from the "chivalry" extended to white females. A North Carolina report of 1922 described one institution as being so horrible that "the judge refuses to send white women to this jail, but negro women are sometimes sent."

And Eugenia Lekkerkerker, writing in 1931, attributed the high incarceration rate of women of color not only to "strong social (and sometimes judicial) prejudice" but also to these women's lack of access to alternatives "such as probation or private protective work" that channeled white women out of prisons. Thus overt racism—including Jim Crow legislation, desire to profit from the lease system at the expense of blacks, outright judicial favoritism in the disposition of whites, and differential provision of alternatives to incarceration—did much to create the immense racial imbalance in southern prisons after the Civil War.[7]

By definition, it is more difficult to document the covert discrimination that, in other regions of the country, worked to incarcerate disproportionately high numbers of black men and women. As Hans von Hentig pointed out in his 1942 monograph on black female criminality, "It is not easy to verify the numerous complaints of colored people that they are unnecessarily maltreated by the police in many communities and that colored girls are not safe in jails and in prisons." But von Hentig went on to observe, "The high release figures of arrested Negroes . . . seem to confirm many of these charges." He further noted that according to the available evidence, black women convicted of felonies received higher fines than white women, and that even when, in misdemeanor cases, the fines were equal, black women fared worse because of their "low economic status." Citing data on the methods by which black and white women were released from prisons, von Hentig concluded, "[T]he law is more strictly enforced against a colored woman, who is less able to secure adequate legal advice or to make use of 'fixing' opportunities." In summary, he referred to whites' fear of blacks: "From this obscure fear it is but one step to the discriminatory practice of many law-enforcing agencies."[8]

From current studies, we know that in some jurisdictions, discretionary decisions by criminal justice personnel continue to ensnare blacks more readily than whites. Some police scrutinize the activities of blacks more closely than those of whites, enforce laws selectively against blacks, and arrest blacks on less evidence. At the court stage, prosecutors are at times more inclined to proceed with cases involving blacks, and blacks find it harder to raise bail, hire lawyers, and be tried by juries that include members of their own race. At sentencing, moreover, some judges are influenced by race. In addition, blacks probably suffer more than whites from the phenomenon of "accumulated disadvantaged status" whereby "initial differential decisions become amplified as one moves through the criminal justice system." All these factors at times contribute to a process that tends to sift whites out of the system while increasing the probability that blacks will be retained and forwarded to prison. Racial biases that persist today no doubt operated more strongly before the Civil Rights movement began challenging differential treatment.[9]

Overt racism and covert discrimination notwithstanding, the disproportionate numbers of black women and men in prisons of the past seem
also to have been a function of higher black rates of offending. Today,
blacks commit personal crimes such as assault, homicide, and robbery at
higher rates than whites.[10] The same was evidently true in the past. Certainly
blacks tended to be convicted of more serious (as well as more trivial)
offenses, and the criminal justice system is constrained to operate with
relative impartiality when violent crimes are at issue. As the 1904 prisoner
census observed with respect to sex, "The number of women imprisoned
for crimes against the person . . . must be presumed to bear a fairly definite
relation to the total of such crimes committed by women. Homicides,
felonious assaults, and robbery, whether perpetrated by men or women,
are uniformly punished, if at all, with a prison sentence." The census com-
mentary did not make enough allowance for filtering, but its basic point
was accurate: rates of incarceration for serious crimes, whether committed
by men or women, blacks or whites, are shaped by actual rates of offending.
Sex and race interact with type of offense to determine the composition of
prison populations.[11]

This explanation of prison racial patterns in terms of real crime rates
is not entirely distinct from the other explanations based on racism. As
Charles Silberman has pointed out, "Violence is something black Americans
learned in this country."

They had many teachers; violence has been an intrinsic part of the
black American experience from the start. Every other immigrant
group came here voluntarily . . . ; Africans came in chains. . . .
Moreover, slavery was maintained by violence; so was the racial
caste system that was erected after Emancipation. . . .[12]

In his history of Louisiana's prison system, Mark T. Carleton shows how
economic hardship combined with discriminatory laws to push blacks into
crime. "Negroes did steal," Carleton writes.

Frequently they committed crimes of violence as well. But few
Louisianians perceived the causes of black criminal behavior . . . ob-
jectively. . . . Like other Southerners living in an age of mounting
tension between whites and blacks, Louisianians demanded more
rather than less proscription of the Negro, and they were either un-
willing or unable to comprehend that the further subordination and
restriction of opportunity they desired to impose . . . were, in the
end, what induced many Negroes to become criminals.[13]

Von Hentig points to many by-products of racism that put black women
in particular at a disadvantage, increasing their likelihood of becoming in-

volved in crime: the weaker health of black women ("Health is economically much more important to the colored woman than to the white woman, notwithstanding the fact that for the age group 15 to 25 years the mortality among colored girls 'is more than two and three-quarters times as high as for young white women' "); the poorer living conditions of black women ("The housing problem, apart from being a psychological factor, affects the [rate of] sex criminality, and the inescapable altercations lead to fighting, aggravated assault, and manslaughter"); and an economic structure that forced black women to work but segregated them into "the lowest occupations," those most vulnerable to displacement by new inventions such as the washing machine and by economic depressions ("Like a maelstrom the modern industrial development attacks their old occupations and robs them legally of their jobs").[14]

Control theory helps explain the higher crime rates of black than white women for some offenses. As noted in Chapter 5, control theory suggests that weakness of ties to family, church, conventional activities, and so on increases the probability of committing crimes. In many respects, black women do seem to have had looser or more disrupted bonds to the conventional social order. As von Hentig observes, many women participated in the great northward migration of blacks that began after the Civil War. Such "mass movements . . . decompose the normal age structure of a population; like an earthquake they disrupt the old established order and give rise to new and uneven age strata." Moreover, black women were more likely than white to be blocked from forming conventional families by imbalances in the ratios of men to women. Among whites in 1930, males outnumbered females, giving white women good opportunity to marry, establish households, and become economically and psychologically secure. But among blacks, women outnumbered men; thus many young black women had "no possibility of legally sanctioned sexual relations and a regularly established household." Then, too, the economic predicament of black women made it difficult for them to lead conventional lives: often unmarried, frequently forced to support themselves even if married, they were trapped into the lowest-paying and least stable jobs—when they could find employment at all. Circumstance, von Hentig suggests, forced some of these women to turn to crime.[15] His arguments constitute an early formulation of control theory; in fact, they still make up the most thoroughgoing effort to apply that theory to black female crime.

Information from the registries of the five specific prisons under consideration lends support to some of von Hentig's hypotheses. Table 6.2, reporting place of birth by race for women held at four of the five prisons in the late nineteenth and early twentieth centuries, indicates that many incarcerated women, by the time of arrest, had traveled far from their birthplaces. Thus they tended to be cut off from their original families, friends, churches, and traditions. This was true for white as well as black

TABLE 6.2
Place of Birth, by Race and Prison, for Four Samples of Female State Prisoners, 1860–1934

PLACE OF BIRTH	TENN. PEN. %B	%W	N.Y.—AUBURN %B	%W	OHIO PEN. %B	%W	N.Y.—ALBION %B	%W
Tennessee	68.0 (n=492)	65.5 (n=108)						
South, excl. Tennessee	28.1 (n=203)	24.2 (n=40)						
New York			19.0 (n=36)	34.1 (n=156)			52.1 (n=25)	73.1 (n=1055)
Northeast, excl. N.Y.			9.5 (n=18)	10.9 (n=50)			10.4 (n=5)	11.6 (n=167)
Ohio					37.8 (n=76)	51.2 (n=152)		
Midwest, excl. Ohio					15.4 (n=31)	10.8 (n=32)		
South (entire)		a	61.4 (n=116)	3.1 (n=14)	34.8 (n=70)	8.4 (n=25)	33.3 (n=16)	1.1 (n=16)
Europe	—	.6 (n=1)	—	44.8 (n=205)	—	14.8 (n=44)	—	6.1 (n=88)
Other	3.9 (n=28)	9.7 (n=16)	10.1 (n=19)	7.2 (n=33)	11.9 (n=24)	14.8 (n=44)	4.2 (n=2)	8.1 (n=117)
Totals	100.0 (n=723)	100.0 (n=165)	100.0 (n=189)	100.1b (n=458)	99.9b (n=201)	100.0 (n=297)	100.0 (n=48)	100.0 (n=1443)

a 695, or 96.1%, of the blacks; 148, or 89.7%, of the whites (total of first two entries).

b Does not add to 100 percent because of rounding.

Notes: The table excludes racial categories other than Black and White and cases for which information on place of birth was not available (for Tennessee, 8 percent of the cases; for Auburn, 3.3 percent; for the Ohio penitentiary, 18.2 percent; for Albion, 5.8 percent). Records of the Ohio Reformatory for Women do not include place-of-birth data. For information on periods covered and sampling, see Figure 1.

women, but—for three of the four prisons—blacks were more likely than whites to have been born out of state and even outside the region where they were convicted. It might be argued that outsiders were viewed with suspicion and hence more readily arrested and incarcerated, irrespective of their actual crime rates. Such a labeling process may well have contributed to the high proportions of incarcerated "outsiders." But it also seems plausible that migration itself led to higher rates of offending. The employment disadvantages of migrating women may have pushed them into theft: having fewer links to prospective employers and lacking local references, they would have had more difficulty than indigenous women in finding jobs, and some may have turned to crime when other sources of income were unavailable. Moreover, stress—recently identified as a source of family violence—may have predisposed some of them to violent crimes.[16] Certainly black women moving north from the deep South found themselves, like immigrant women from Europe, in highly stressful situations, economically precarious and isolated from their original support groups and cultures as they were.[17]

Of black women held at the Tennessee penitentiary, 68 percent had been born in Tennessee; another 28 percent had been born elsewhere in the region, mainly in states farther south. Many had been arrested in counties bordering on the Mississippi River, a major route to the North. These findings suggest that at least one-quarter of Tennessee's black female prisoners were part of the northward migration of blacks that commenced after the Civil War. These women were recently emancipated from slavery and hence poorly educated, ill prepared to find employment in a region that provided few opportunities, often young (as noted in Chapter 5), separated from their families, and on their own. They probably experienced economic and emotional distress that encouraged criminal activity. Information on place of birth by period of commitment (not shown in Table 6.2) indicates that as time went on, decreasing proportions of black women incarcerated at the Tennessee penitentiary were born in Tennessee while increasing proportions were born elsewhere in the South—a finding that strengthens the hypothesis that some were part of the northward migration. Overall, a similar proportion of white women held at the Tennessee penitentiary had also been born in other southern states, suggesting that migration may have affected their crime rates as well. But in the case of whites, the number of prisoners was much smaller.

Evidence that migration may have engendered criminal activity becomes even stronger when one examines the information of Table. 6.2 on place of birth for women incarcerated at Auburn. Of black women held at Auburn, only 19 percent had been born in New York, in comparison to 34 percent of the white women; a very high proportion of the blacks—61.4 percent—had been born in the South, in contrast to about 3 percent of the whites. The high proportion of whites born in Europe (nearly 45 percent) also tends to confirm the thesis that migration led to higher rates of offending. Again, ethnocentrism (including both racism and nativism) probably contributed, but migration-related crime also appears to have played a part in the high percentage of incarcerated women born out of state. That a greater proportion of Auburn's black than white women had been born out of the region (72 in comparison to 55 percent) helps explain their evidently higher rates of crime.

Auburn's place-of-birth patterns generally repeated themselves at the Ohio penitentiary and New York's Albion reformatory. At both, a higher proportion of white women had been born in-state and a far greater proportion of black women had been born in the South. A small yet significant proportion of white women came from Europe. At both prisons, a greater proportion of black than of white women had been born outside the region.

Differences in the marital status of black and white prisoners further suggest that isolation from family (and hence both emotional and economic supports) helps explain the blacks' apparently greater involvement in crime. Of black women in the Tennessee sample, 64 percent were single, in comparison to 36 percent of the white convicts. Albion data are irrelevant in this respect: because this institution focused on young women, about two-thirds of each race were unmarried. No data on marital status were available in the records of the Ohio reformatory. Among female prisoners at the Ohio penitentiary in the late nineteenth and early twentieth centuries, about half of both whites and blacks were single. But at Auburn, a pattern similar to that of Tennessee appeared: a larger proportion of sampled black than white women (54 in comparison to 34 percent) were single. In two of the three institutions for which marital-status data are available and relevant, then, black women were much less likely to be married—perhaps, as von Hentig suggested, because the pool of available men was smaller for them than for white women. This reinforces the picture of black women as lacking ties that might have helped them stay out of trouble and provided economic support. Often single, moving northward, fending for themselves with few resources, they had greater reason to engage in crime than all but immigrant white women.

The information available on women held at these prisons fits better with control theory than other explanations of criminal behavior. However, control theory *on its own* is unable to account for variations in rates of incarceration; it neglects differences in the responses of criminal justice officials, differences that appear independent of rates of offending and seriousness of offense. Marital status is a partial explanation for differences in rates of offending, particularly for serious crimes. But, as Diane Lewis has argued, marital status may also significantly influence a "court's decision whether to imprison a convicted woman"; black women, being "far less likely to be married than white women," thus are more likely to be incarcerated. Similarly, Donald Black, in *The Behavior of Law*, holds, "The single are . . . subject to more law." Factors such as marital status, race, being an outsider to the community, and so on probably affected *both* offense patterns and officials' responses.[18]

RACIAL PATTERNS IN PRISON POPULATIONS: A COMPARISON OF RATES OF BLACK WOMEN AND BLACK MEN

Black women, historically, were imprisoned in smaller numbers than either black or white men, but they often constituted larger proportions within female state prisoner populations than did black men within the male prisoner groups. As Table 6.3 shows, significantly greater proportions of black women than black men appeared in the 1880 prisoner census for the Midwest and South; in the 1904 prisoner census, this pattern appeared in all regions; and it continued to appear in the South in 1923. The phenomenon is, in fact, far more pervasive than Table 6.3 indicates. To give but a few examples· Between 1797 and 1801, 44 percent of the women sentenced to New York's prison were black in comparison to 24 percent of the men. At the Ohio penitentiary in 1840, 49 percent of the female convicts, but only 10 percent of the males, were black. In 1868, of men held at the Tennessee penitentiary, 60 percent were black in contrast to 100 percent of the women. Similar illustrations could be drawn from many prisons throughout the country before and after the 1880–1923 period spanned by Table 6.3.[19]

Several factors help account for this widespread and enduring imbalance among blacks by sex within prison populations. One is differential involvement in crime by sex and race. Black and white women alike seem to have had much lower actual rates of offending than either black or white men in the period 1880–1923; but the white–female–black–female ratios probably were larger than the white–male–black–male ratios.[20]

A second and again partial explanation of the greater proportions of black women, relative to black men, lies with the phenomenon of "victim valuation." Many personal crimes are intraracial—whites tend to victimize other whites, and blacks other blacks.[21] But according to a number of studies, crimes with white victims are prosecuted more vigorously and punished more harshly than those with black victims. When the offender is black and the victim white, punishment may be particularly severe.[22] In the period 1880–1923, black women probably had more contact with whites than did black men, for the former, through domestic service, had access to white homes. According to the 1904 prisoner census, for example, nearly 80 percent of all black female prisoners had previously been servants. Thus,

TABLE 6.3
Racial Composition of State Prison Populations, 1880, 1904, and 1923, by Sex and Region

	TOTAL STATE PRISONERS		MALES		FEMALES		% BLACK, GENERAL POP.
	%W	%B	%W	%B	%W	%B	
1880							
Northeast	91.9	8.1	91.8	8.2	93.0	7.0	1.6
Midwest	87.8	12.2	88.2	11.8	71.0	29.0	2.2
South	27.0	73.0	27.6	72.4	14.2	85.8	36.0
West	82.0	18.0	82.0	18.0	80.0	20.0	.7
1904							
Northeast	87.4	12.6	87.8	12.2	81.8	18.2	1.8
Midwest	77.5	22.5	78.0	22.0	51.6	48.4	1.9
South	26.3	73.7	27.0	73.0	9.8	90.2	32.3
West	90.9	9.1	91.1	8.9	73.9	26.1	.7
1923							
Northeast	84.8	15.2	84.9	15.1	84.6	15.4	2.3
Midwest	80.3	19.7	80.4	19.6	78.0	22.0	2.3
South	39.7	60.3	40.4	59.6	20.4	79.6	26.9
West	92.9	7.1	93.0	7.0	90.0	10.0	.9

Sources: U.S. Department of the Interior, Census Office (Frederick Howard Wines), *Report on the Defective, Dependent, and Delinquent Classes . . . as returned at the Tenth Census (June 1, 1880)* (Washington, D.C.: Government Printing Office, 1888), pp. 520–25; U.S. Department of Commerce and Labor, Bureau of the Census, *Prisoners and Juvenile Delinquents in Institutions, 1904* (Washington, D.C.: Government Printing Office, 1907), pp. 68–87; U.S. Department of Commerce, Bureau of the Census, *Prisoners 1923* (Washington, D.C.: Government Printing Office, 1926), pp. 250–65. Data on the proportions of blacks in general populations were derived from U.S. Department of Commerce, Bureau of the Census, *Historical Statistics of the United States, Colonial Times to 1970. Part I.* (Washington, D.C.: U.S. Government

1923); the few Chinese, Indians, and so on were sometimes counted as "White," at others as "Colored." The 1880 figures include territorial prisoners held in penitentiaries (as distinguished from county and city jails) and leased state prisoners. Leased convicts were not distinguished from other state prisoners in the table from which the 1904 data were derived; prisoners on state (but not county or municipal) road gangs were included in the figures for 1923. The 1880 figures are derived from data on the total number of state prisoners for the year ending June 1, 1880; the 1904 and 1923 figures are derived from data collected for a particular date. The 1880 and 1904 data do not include Delaware's state prisoners, who were indistinguishably mixed with county prisoners. The 1923 data for Michigan include an indeterminable number of relative to black males, they had more opportunity to offend against "valued" victims. This was especially true in the South, where the disproportion between black male and female prisoners was most consistent.[23]

A third explanation of the larger proportion of black women relative to black men in the prison statistics is the screening out of white female offenders, in combination with the factors that tend to retain blacks in the criminal justice system. Judges sometimes refused outright to send white women to penal institutions. But to white officials, incarceration of a black woman was a matter of small consequence; indeed, in the period 1865–1900, southern contractors leased black female prisoners to farm and mine alongside black men. Reports published by the Tennessee penitentiary in the last quarter of the nineteenth century document the screening process. During this period, the overwhelming majority of female prisoners were black. In the relatively few instances in which white women were sentenced to the penitentiary, their conviction offenses were homicide, or less frequently, arson; only in rare cases was a white woman imprisoned for larceny. (Before the Civil War, in contrast, 45 percent of white women held at the Tennessee penitentiary had been convicted of larceny.[24]) Many of the black women also served time for homicide, but larceny—including petit larceny—was their most common conviction offense. Similar screening processes apparently worked in the prison systems of other regions to minimize the numbers of white women and maintain high proportions of blacks.[25]

For white women, then, the factor of sex interacted with that of race to keep their numbers in state prisons low. Black women, on the other hand, were put at a disadvantage by race and gained no benefit from being female (except, perhaps, when execution was a possible outcome[26]). Gender stereotypes may in fact have compounded their disadvantages. Some social scientists have argued that black women are perceived as "masculine" because they are more independent and assertive than white women; their "gender role behavior, . . . social status and . . . crime pattern . . . contradict acceptable feminine behavior, as defined by the dominant society." The argument holds that black women, perceived as more masculine, are more readily convicted and imprisoned than white women. Sex and race thus interact to increase the involvement of black women with the criminal justice system. Certainly criminal women in general have long been viewed as virile; "masculine qualities," wrote Lombroso in 1895, "prevent the female criminal from being more than half a woman." If (as seems probable) black women in general were considered less feminine than white, black female *offenders* were especially likely to have been viewed as masculine and hence undeserving of protection. They fit almost literally with the stereotype of the Dark Lady, strong and threatening in comparison to the submissive Fair Lady of popular imagery.[27]

RACIAL DIFFERENCES AMONG WOMEN
IN CONVICTION OFFENSES AND SENTENCES

Table 6.4 shows conviction offense types by race for the five prisons whose records were examined in detail. At the three custodial institutions, in the late nineteenth and early twentieth centuries, about 50 percent of women of both races had been convicted of property crimes. Many of Tennessee's black property offenders had committed less serious offenses than their white counterparts, and of course they were incarcerated in far greater numbers. However, the proportions of property offenders who were black and who were white (row totals) closely reflected the proportions of black and white women in the prisons' populations as a whole. There were no marked differences at the custodial prisons, then, between the races in terms

TABLE 6.4
Conviction Offense Type, by Race and Prison, for Five Samples of Female State Prisoners, 1860–1934

	TENN. PEN.		N.Y.—AUBURN		OHIO PEN.		N.Y.—ALBION		OHIO R.W.	
	B	W	B	W	B	W	B	W	B	W
Violent crimes	326	55	95	143	106	89	2	14	112	59
	85.6[a]	14.4	39.9	60.1	54.4	45.6	12.5	87.5	65.5	34.5
	43.7[b]	31.1	48.7	30.6	44.7	25.7	4.1	.9	44.1	11.4
Property crimes	400	100	96	262	122	180	7	203	46	130
	80.0	20.0	26.8	73.2	40.4	59.6	3.3	96.7	26.1	73.9
	53.6	56.5	49.2	56.1	51.5	52.0	14.3	13.8	18.1	25.1
Public order crimes	5	10	2	54	7	65	39	1210	92	318
	33.3	66.7	3.6	96.4	9.7	90.3	3.1	96.9	22.4	77.6
	.7	5.6	1.0	11.6	3.0	18.8	79.6	82.0	36.2	61.4
Other offenses	15	12	2	8	2	12	1	49	4	11
	55.6	44.4	20.0	80.0	14.3	85.7	2.0	98.0	26.7	73.3
	2.0	6.8	1.0	1.7	.8	3.5	2.0	3.3	1.6	2.1
Totals	746	177	195	467	237	346	49	1476	254	518
	80.8	19.2	29.5	70.5	40.7	59.3	3.2	96.8	32.9	67.1
	100.0	100.0	99.9[c]	100.0	100.0	100.0	100.0	100.0	100.0	100.0

[a] Row percent
[b] Column percent
[c] Does not add to 100 percent because of rounding.
Notes: Table excludes cases committed before 1860 and after 1934, missing observations (19 for Tennessee penitentiary, 4 for Auburn, 25 for Ohio penitentiary, 42 for Albion, and 6 for Ohio Reformatory for Women), and "other" race observations (none for Tennessee penitentiary, 3 for Auburn, 1 for Ohio penitentiary, 16 for Albion, and 1 for Ohio Reformatory for Women). For information on periods covered and sampling, see Figure 1.

of proportions of property crime convictions, given the overall racial compositions of the female populations.

At the three custodial prisons, moreover, the second most common type of conviction offense for both black and white women was violent crime. But here greater racial differences emerge.[28] In Tennessee nearly 44 percent of the black women had been convicted of violent crimes, in comparison to about 31 percent of the white women. At Auburn and the Ohio penitentiary, 48.7 and 44.7 percent of black women served time for crimes of violence, in comparison to 30.6 and 25.7 percent of the white women, respectively. Racial biases against blacks and efforts to screen out whites swelled the proportions of blacks, but these proportions probably also reflected a greater involvement of black women in violent crime. Some black women born in the South may have been affected by the generally higher level of violence in that region.[29] Some black women (as indicated by case examples in Chapter 5) may have been responding defensively against men who were themselves prone to violence. And some were perhaps predisposed to violent reactions owing to the stress generated by their dislocation, isolation, and economic marginality. All three factors may have operated simultaneously at times to make black women more likely to engage in crimes of violence.

Offenses against public order constituted only a small proportion of conviction offenses for women of both races in the custodial prisons. However, here the pattern for violent crimes reversed itself, greater proportions of whites than of blacks having been convicted of public order offenses: in Tennessee, nearly 6 percent of the whites, .7 percent of the blacks; at Auburn, 11.6 percent of the whites, 1 percent of the blacks; and at the Ohio penitentiary, 18.8 percent of the whites, 3 percent of the blacks. These differences appear to have stemmed in part from inverse racism: public order crimes such as abortion, aiding and abetting carnal knowledge of a minor, and bigamy evidently were regarded as more serious when committed by white women. Blacks may have been equally involved in such activities, but because they were not expected to behave like ladies, their public order offenses were more easily ignored. In addition, as noted in Chapter 5, the differences reflect regional traditions. In his comparative study of the operation of the criminal justice system in Massachusetts and South Carolina, Michael Hindus found that Massachusetts in the nineteenth century continued to conform to its long tradition of concern with morality by prosecuting large numbers of public order offenders, especially when they were female. South Carolina, on the other hand, remained indifferent to morals offenders.[30] The 1904 prisoner census came to much the same conclusion about the effects of regional traditions when it pointed out that regional variations in the proportions of women imprisoned for offenses against propriety.

146   The Implementation of Punishment

have little bearing on the comparative prevalence of [such] crimes
. . . among women of the different sections, but [rather reflect] . . .
chiefly the variations in the standards of punishing female offenders
by imprisonment. Violations by women of the laws concerning
chastity are not confined to any particular section, yet . . . it is
chiefly in the North Atlantic states . . . that females are found in
prison for such violations.[31]

Conviction offense patterns were less consistent at the two reformatories than at the custodial institutions. At Albion, large proportions of both
black and white women were convicted of the public order offenses with
which this institution mainly concerned itself. Small and nearly equal proportions were sentenced for property crimes and even smaller proportions
for crimes of violence. At Marysville, property crime did not constitute a
particularly important conviction offense category for either race. However,
a large proportion of black women were convicted of violent crimes, whereas
a large proportion of white women were convicted of offenses against public
order. Thus it appears that the "custodial" population at Marysville was
mainly black, the "reformatory" population largely white.

Marysville mirrored the national picture. Table 6.5, comparing the
racial composition of custodial and reformatory institutions for women in
1923, shows that prisoners in the former were predominantly black whereas
those of the latter were mainly white. Were it possible to distinguish further
between "pure" reformatories like Albion and those that (like Marysville)
received felons as well as misdemeanants, the percentage of whites in "pure"
reformatories would be even higher. Such institutions set their sights on

TABLE 6.5
Racial Composition of Female State Prisoner Populations, 1923, by Type
of Institution

CUSTODIAL PRISONS		REFORMATORY PRISONS	
White	Black	White	Black
479	871	979	132
(35.5%)	(64.5%)	(88.1%)	(11.9%)

Source: U.S. Department of Commerce, Bureau of the Census, Prisoners 1923 (Washington,
D.C.: Government Printing Office, 1926), pp. 250–65.
Notes: Counted as reformatories were the separate institutions for women in Arkansas,
California (the short-lived State Industrial Farm for Women), Connecticut, Indiana, Iowa,
Kansas, Maine, Massachusetts, Minnesota, Nebraska, New Jersey, New York (both Albion
and Bedford), Ohio, Pennsylvania, and Wisconsin. All other institutions, including state
road departments, were counted as custodial prisons. Some federal prisoners may have been
included in the figures for Michigan's Detroit House of Correction, for which the census
made no distinction between female state and federal prisoners.

petty offenders who seemed to merit their rehabilitative efforts. They did not exclude blacks entirely, but their interest in redeeming white women balanced the criminal justice system's usual tendency to incarcerate disproportionate numbers of blacks.[32]

In sorting out the effects of race on conviction offenses by region, it is helpful to distinguish between varying intensities of prosecution, using "prosecution" to refer to both arrest and court policies. What might be termed *reactive prosecution* occurs when the criminal justice system responds only to offenses it cannot ignore, and it results in low numbers of cases. Because of reactive prosecution, some white women—but relatively few— were included in the populations of southern prisons in the period 1865–1935; their offenses were so serious that officials had to respond, however reluctantly. *Proactive prosecution* occurs when officials seek out and vigorously process offenders; it is associated with minor offenses and produces large numbers of cases. In the South after the Civil War, for instance, blacks were arrested in large numbers and severely sanctioned for larcenies. Similarly, white women were proactively prosecuted for morals offenses in the North and Midwest. On occasion the justice system also displays a third type of reaction (or, rather, nonreaction): *benign neglect*. As a result of benign neglect, few white women and even fewer black women were prosecuted for public order offenses in the South. Through benign neglect, black women in the North and Midwest tended to escape the negative effects of reformatory benevolence, and in the South after the Civil War, white women were seldom imprisoned for larceny. Operating simultaneously, the three types of responses helped to produce different regional patterns in the conviction offenses of black and white women in the period 1865–1935 and to fill custodial institutions with black women, reformatories with whites.

Just as black women sometimes benefited from varying intensities of prosecution, so, too, did they sometimes fare better than white women at sentencing. Insofar as racial discrimination influenced the sentences of women held at the five prisons under consideration, it adversely affected white rather than black women. Table 6.6 reports the average minimum and maximum sentences by offense type and race. Some of the racial differences are small, and some may be due to sampling error. Nonetheless, for violent crimes, white women had somewhat higher minimum sentences. For property crimes, whites had higher maximum sentences (an average of about 48 months in contrast to 41.7 months for blacks); for public order crimes, whites had higher minimum sentences.

Important differences between the prisons, which are masked by Table 6.6, also indicate that, generally, white women fared worse at sentencing. At the Tennessee penitentiary, black women received longer minimum and maximum terms, on the average, than did white women—just what one might have expected, given the nature of the southern prison system after

TABLE 6.6
Average Minimum and Maximum Sentence, by Offense Type and Race,
for Combined Samples of Female State Prisoners

	AVERAGE MINIMUM SENTENCE IN MONTHS (NO. OF CASES)		AVERAGE MAXIMUM SENTENCE IN MONTHS (NO. OF CASES)	
Violent Crimes	44.7	*(398)*	95.8	*(877)*
Black	41.5	(269)	96.2	(563)
White	50.1	(127)	95.9	(310)
Other	132.0	(2)	39.0	(4)
Property Crimes	20.2	*(397)*	45.2	*(1490)*
Black	21.3	(179)	41.7	(659)
White	19.2	(218)	48.1	(830)
Other	—	—	36.0	(1)
Public Order Crimes	9.4	*(150)*	37.8	*(1513)*
Black	5.6	(11)	35.1	(63)
White	9.7	(138)	37.9	(1437)
Other	15.0	(1)	2.5	(13)
Other Offenses	15.6	*(21)*	38.5	*(110)*
Black	12.0	(3)	39.5	(21)
White	16.2	(18)	38.3	(89)
Other	—	—	—	—
Total	28.5	(966)	53.3	(3990)

Notes: The number of cases on which the minimums are based is smaller than that on which the maximums are based because many prisoners had definite sentences with no minimums, others indeterminate sentences with no minimums. The total number on which the maximums are based excludes 544 missing observations and 72 cases with life sentences. Also note that there is wide dispersion around the means. For information on periods covered and sampling, see Figure 1.

the Civil War. At Auburn, on the other hand, the only significant racial differences appeared in the average minimum for violent crime, which was higher for white women (68.6 months) than for black (58.9 months). At the Ohio reformatory, whites had longer minimums for violent crime and longer maximums for property crime. Thus the information on average minimum and maximum sentences by race indicates discrimination, but mainly in favor of blacks.[33] This generalization does not hold for Tennessee, but at the other four prisons, where differences appear, usually white women had longer terms. Whites fared particularly poorly with respect to their longer sentences for public order crimes.

These findings are consistent with the conclusions of a recent review of research on racial bias in criminal sentencing covering the period 1930–

1978. In regard to imposition of the death penalty, Kleck found discrimination against blacks in the South only. Moreover,

> [r]egarding noncapital sentencing, the evidence is largely contrary to a hypothesis of general or widespread overt discrimination against black defendants, although there is evidence of discrimination for a minority of specific jurisdictions, judges, crime types, etc.[34]

The evidence presented here similarly indicates harsher sentencing of blacks convicted in the South of serious crime. Elsewhere, white women often received longer minimums, maximums, or both.

More severe sentencing of whites should not be greeted as evidence against racism. As Kleck points out, blacks may have been sentenced more leniently for personal crimes because their victims, who tended to be other blacks, were not highly valued by the whites who administered the justice system. These officials may have deemed black-on-black offenses "less serious . . . , representing less loss or threat to community than crimes with white victims." Then too, more lenient sentencing of blacks may have resulted from "white paternalism," the "view among whites of blacks as child-like creatures who were not as responsible for their actions as whites were, and who therefore could not be held [as] accountable to the law."[35] Here Kleck is discussing effects of race only. When sex is also taken into consideration, another aspect of paternalism emerges that probably contributed to harsher sentencing of white female public order offenders: the perception that white women were more deserving of the benefits of reformatory training.

RACIAL DIFFERENCES AMONG WOMEN IN PRISON TREATMENT

In nearly every state in the period 1865–1935, as Part I showed, treatment of female prisoners of both races was in many respects inferior to that of males. It is also important to recognize that the quality of prison treatment could be affected as much by race as by sex. As a rule, the higher the proportion of blacks in a prison population, the lower the level of care, but white women were treated better than black women even in predominantly black institutions.

The South

No region of the country has a clean record when it comes to racial discrimination within prisons, but such a generalization glosses over the frightful treatment of black men and women in the South. After the Civil War, when southern prison systems became distended with recently freed blacks, the lease system came into full force; lessees began working convicts literally to death. Because blacks were now worthless as property, few lessees bothered to provide even minimal care. The maimed and dead were constantly replaced by states that profited from every new convict they supplied. Sellin's study, *Slavery and the Penal System,* rightly concludes that the lease system was "a form of chattel slavery even worse than that from which blacks had been freed."[36]

Some southern states leased women as well as men. According to the 1880 census, Florida and Georgia, then lacking central penitentiaries, gave lessees control of all their female convicts. Alabama, Louisiana, Mississippi, North Carolina, Tennessee, and Texas retained some women at their main prisons but leased out others. Nearly always, the latter were black. Of 40 white women held by these states in 1880, only one was leased, whereas of 220 black women, 81 (about 37 percent) were leased out. Clearly, the burden of leasing fell heavier on black women, just as it did on black men; race was at least as influential as sex in the decision to lease.[37] In Tennessee after the Civil War, leased women joined men in the mines and on railroad gangs.[38] The transcript of a Georgia investigation of 1870 shows how little some lessees discriminated in their treatment of men and women.

Q. [Assemblyman Virgil Hillyer]—Were there any women working on the Brunswick Railroad?

A. [prisoner witness]—Yes, I think there were 19 or 20. They belonged both to the chain-gang and the Penitentiary.

. . .

Q.—Did you see any of them whipped?

A.—Yes.

Q.—Were they whipped on the bare skin?

A.—Yes; I saw their bare skin myself.

Q.—On what part of the body were they whipped?

A.—On the butt.

Q.—Were they whipped in the presence of the men?

A.—Yes.

. . .

Q.—How many licks did they receive?

A.—About 20.

. . .

Q.—Were they kept in separate stockades?

A.—In the same stockade, but in separate rooms.

Q.—Out on the works, were they required to wait on the calls of nature in the presence of the men?

A.—Yes; they were required to do their business right in the cuts where they worked, the same as the men did. It was taken out in the wheelbarrows and carts.

Q. [Mr. Turner, another assemblyman]—Were the white and colored women mixed together?

A.—There were no white women there. One started there, and I heard Mr. Alexander [the lessee] say he turned her loose. He was talking to the guard; I was working in the cut. He said his wife was a white woman, and he could not stand it to see a white woman worked in such places.[39]

Elsewhere women sometimes cooked and washed for leased male prisoners; they, too, lived in the same camps, had no matrons, and were punished as brutally as the men.[40]

Leasing and "state slavery" on prison work gangs eventually led to somewhat better treatment of women (including black women) than men in southern prison systems.[41] Lessees preferred males, from whom they could extract more work. Women chained to men often became pregnant and hence inefficient. And lessees and work gang bosses did not want to hire juvenile prisoners or sick and aged males. So southern states were forced to begin holding such "dead-hands" at their central prisons or to buy plantations on which to work them. In the 1870s, North Carolina purchased land near Raleigh on which it erected buildings for the female and feeble. By 1890 Alabama was keeping women, children, and the sick at its Wetumpka prison, from which they were leased out but only for day labor. Virginia and Georgia shortly followed suit by purchasing prison farms, and in 1914 Florida opened its prison at Raiford for those shunned by lessees. Black women were retained longer than white women by lessees and chain gang bosses, but in time they, too, joined white women at central prisons or prison farms. At these state-supervised institutions, work was somewhat less arduous, death rates were lower (though still higher than in northern prisons), and punishments less cruel than under the lease system.

At the penitentiaries and plantations, black and white women were segregated in housing and blacks assigned to less pleasant tasks. Florida, for instance, held white and black women in separate buildings at Raiford; the laundry was attached to that for blacks. Georgia discovered that black women made excellent field hands because they were "accustomed to this work"; it assigned white women to housekeeping and sewing. Similarly in Texas, where at the turn of the century women were sent to local farms on the "share" system, black women labored in the fields while white women sewed, gardened, and cared for the chickens. Quarters for black women were usually inferior. In Maryland in the early 1930s, for example, black women were housed on one floor of the women's wing at the House of Correction "in cells with open-grate fronts and screen tops," whereas white women resided in a less restrictive dorm on the floor above. Tennessee at the same time held female prisoners at the Women's Prison near its main penitentiary; black and white women were segregated in wings of equal capacity, but the quarters for blacks were much more crowded.[42]

Southern reformatories for women were institutions for whites only. North Carolina's Industrial Farm Colony, opened in 1929, was established to rescue white women from jails with black warders. It apparently remained an all-white institution until, in 1945, it was turned into a training school for black girls. Virginia's State Industrial Farm for Women received only whites from its opening in 1932 until 1939, when pressure to remove women from the penitentiary resulted in construction at the farm of special buildings for blacks. The only other southern reformatory for women, that of Arkansas, also excluded blacks.[43]

Outside the South

Whether racial segregation occurred in the reformatories of the North and Midwest was usually determined by the number of blacks in the population. So few black women were committed to Albion and the reformatories of Maine and Nebraska, for instance, that segregation was impracticable. But in reformatories with sizeable numbers of blacks, segregation was usually the rule.

New Jersey's State Reformatory for Women, opened at Clinton in 1913, held black women in separate cottages. No black women were received the first year, for the original farm buildings precluded separation by race. But that year the legislature appropriated money for the first cottage, designated in advance for blacks. "[W]e realize their treatment will involve many difficulties," the superintendent noted in her initial report, but "we feel that theirs is the greater need." Stowe, the "colored cottage," opened in 1915—"at some distance from the other buildings now in use." According to that year's report, "We run Stowe Cottage . . . almost like a separate institution," with its own school and black officer.[44]

Somewhat self-consciously, superintendent May Caughey offered several rationales for segregation at the New Jersey reformatory. She considered "the problem of dealing with colored delinquents . . . more difficult than that of dealing with white delinquents" since the former were childish and underdeveloped. If mingled with whites, moreover, the black women would merely tag along and therefore fail to cultivate their initiative. Then too, "We feel the colored women are much happier by themselves." With respect to the feelings of black women about segregation, no information is available for Clinton other than Caughey's statement. But in her 1931 study of women's reformatories, Eugenia Lekkerkerker mentioned a case in which "colored girls had revolted against being placed in a separate cottage under colored officers, because they felt . . . discriminated against by this arrangement."[45]

Caughey's third annual report recognized that black women had fewer privileges than whites, but it promised to grant more when they "work into the spirit of the place." These privileges included access to the low security Honor Cottage and membership in the student government, which meted out punishments for rule infractions. Self-government was instituted at Stowe Cottage in 1919, and in 1928 the reformatory integrated its school classes.[46]

Other reformatories that practiced racial segregation include the Illinois State Reformatory, which in the mid-1930s had four cottages for blacks and four for whites. Although housed separately, inmates joined together on work assignments. The Ohio Reformatory for Women and Pennsylvania's State Industrial Home at Muncy similarly segregated the races by cottage. Rhode Island's reformatory had no cottages, but it did have large numbers of black inmates in the late 1920s, when it received federal as well as state prisoners. Most of the black federal prisoners had been convicted of drug violations under the Harrison Act,[47] and according to a Rhode Island report, many had "loathsome diseases in the highly infectious stage." Originally, blacks were assigned to one dormitory in the old wing, whites to another. But by 1928, "colored Federal prisoners" were housed in "excellent single private rooms, each with running water and toilet, and all attractively furnished . . . while the white women inmates . . . are all in the dormitories." Whether because of their "loathsome diseases" or federal insistence, in this case black women evidently gained an advantage through segregation.[48]

New York's reformatory at Bedford was unusual in that superintendent Katherine B. Davis refused to segregate women by race even though the institution received many blacks. But in 1916, after Davis's departure, segregation began as a result of well-publicized internal turmoil. Most of the trouble, as noted in Chapter 3, stemmed from poor administration and overcrowding. However, it was blamed on "the unfortunate attachments formed by the white women for the negroes." Elsewhere, too, according to Lekkerkerker, cottage segregation was practiced owing to "the fact that a peculiar attraction has been found to exist between colored and white women in confinement which intensifies . . . the danger . . . of homosexual involvements." (This "peculiar attraction," noted by many studies of the period on homosexual activity within women's prisons, suggests that administrators' attitudes toward race were often not shared by inmates.)[49]

Racial biases also affected programs. Aside from a few black cottage matrons, staff members at custodial and reformatory institutions were white, and they designed programs with white interests and values in mind. May Caughey's ideal for Clinton, for instance, was to train inmates "that they may know and follow the Truth, which alone can make them free"—an aspiration on which black women may have reflected with some feelings of irony. Visitors from outside—WCTU members, club women, representatives of religious organizations—were white and probably inclined to minister to white rather than black inmates. Recreational activities were segregated and black women encouraged to conform to racial stereotypes. At New York's State Prison for Women at Auburn in 1913, Ward V put on a play called "The Colored Suffragettes." Pennsylvania's reformatory had a music club, "formed of colored girls who sing negro spirituals and folk songs." And a "colored female glee club" performed at the Ohio penitentiary in the late nineteenth century (" 'They are just too cute for anything,' is the common remark [from] visitors"). At reformatories with integrated but tracked educational programs, blacks were more likely to be classified as "low grade," especially after the advent of "intelligence" testing. In custodial prisons, whites tended to get office jobs and other soft assignments while blacks were relegated to the laundries. Furthermore, in institutions in which some but not all jobs paid wages, white women were more readily assigned to the paying positions. Nearly all aspects of treatment, then, were shaped by attitudes that devalued blacks.[50]

———————

The tendency of American prisons, past and present, to incarcerate disproportionately large numbers of blacks and treat them as inferiors has been documented by dozens, perhaps hundreds, of studies. But because these studies have seldom made distinctions by sex as well as race, they have frequently glanced over differences between black male and female prisoners and equally important differences between black and white women. These differences indicate several ways in which the observations made in Part I about partial justice for women must be modified.

Comparison of the treatment of black men and women in southern prisons in the late nineteenth and early twentieth centuries has revealed an exception to the rule that female prisoners generally did not fare as well as male prisoners. By the turn of the century, black female convicts were being brought together at state-run farms and prisons. Black men continued to be leased out. Leasing having been the more savage of the two types of treatment, in this instance women fared better. The distinction, however, should not be used to obscure the extreme inhumanity with which southern whites reacted to black prisoners of both sexes. Nor should we overlook the fact that earlier—immediately after the Civil War—the rule of inferior treatment of women did hold. At that time, many southern states handled their black male and female prisoners with outward equality—sending both down in mines, leasing both, permitting lessees to punish them similarly. In this earlier period, apparent evenhandedness did create worse circumstances for the women, who were outnumbered and more vulnerable sexually. It was only later, after centralization of the female prisoner populations began, that care of women rose somewhat above the men's level.

Comparison of the incarceration rates and in-prison treatment of black women and white women demonstrates that partiality was extended mainly to whites. Chivalry filtered them out of the prison system, helping to create the even greater racial imbalances among female than male prisoner populations. And partiality toward whites contributed to development of a bifurcated system, one track custodial and predominantly black, the other reformatory and reserved mainly for whites. As always, however, racism harmed the favored as well as the castigated group. It created a system that imprisoned more white than black public order offenders. As an apparent result of both devaluation of black victims and white paternalism, black women outside of the South were sometimes sentenced more lightly than their white counterparts. And, as the next chapter demonstrates in more detail, the predominantly white inmates of reformatories were subjected to especially repressive forms of "treatment." Thus white more than black women experienced the effects—good and ill—of partiality.

Clearly, the process by which racism affected criminal justice was far more complex than a simple matter of labeling black but not white women as offenders. True, labeling was part of that process—as when southern prisons drew in black women for petty larcenies while excluding all but the most serious white female lawbreakers. But, as in the case of all southern and many northern reformatories, the designation "prisoner" might be applied more readily to whites than blacks. In these instances, incarceration had a symbolic meaning, signifying that white women were more worthy of redemptive efforts. Moreover, racism affected criminal justice well before official labeling occurred. It apparently influenced actual rates of offending for serious crimes by pushing black women to the margins of society, where they found it exceedingly difficult to establish roots, support themselves, and attain a modicum of security. Before conviction, racism gave rise to different intensities of prosecution of black and white women for various offenses; and after the conviction or official labeling stage, it could lead to differences in sentence length and in-prison treatment. Racism thus shaped both crime rates and administrative policies. These interacted to produce a criminal justice system that reinforced the racial caste system and amplified the misfortunes of black women.

CHAPTER 7 ||||||||||||||||||||||||||||||||||

The Realization of Partial Justice:
A Case Study of
The Social Control of Women

Over the last several decades, historians and sociologists have devoted increasing attention to the phenomenon of social control—the mechanisms by which powerful groups consciously or unconsciously attempt to restrain and to induce conformity, even assent, among less powerful but nonetheless threatening segments of society. Laws, institutions such as schools and prisons, medical policies, informal gestures of approbation or displeasure, even forms of language—all may constitute forms of social control. (*Social control* in this sense should not be confused with criminological control theory, referred to earlier, which offers an explanation for law-violating behaviors;[1] through a complicated and terminologically unfortunate series of developments in social science, similar terms have been adopted to label different concepts.) The control achieved may be merely external, as when people are forced to do things against their wills; or it may be internal, so thoroughly absorbed by its subjects that they come to monitor and correct their own deviations from prescription. In recent years, research in social control has moved in two directions particularly germane to the study of women's prisons. First, it has come to focus sharply on the political implications of coercion. As David Rothman puts it, "A social control orientation . . . suggest[s] that [institutional] innovations were likely to confer benefits somewhere, and so the question becomes, where? If the prison did not serve the prisoner, then whom did it serve?" In other words, historians and sociologists no longer assume that the narratives of social controllers (who often speak sincerely of the benefits they expect to confer on prisoners

157

and the like) tell the whole story; the picture has been broadened to include the political ramifications of extended controls for both reformers and the subjects of reform. Second, feminist theorists have become sensitive to ways in which social controls are exercised on women *as women,* to encourage conformity to prescribed gender roles.[2]

This chapter analyzes an aspect of the social control of women by focusing on a particular type of prison, the women's reformatory. It explores the conjunction between formal vehicles of social control (in this case the laws establishing reformatories and the institutions themselves) and the internalization of their social control "messages" by the targeted group of inmates. The chapter also deals with social control in terms of social class— the process by which, through establishment and operation of women's reformatories, middle-class crusaders came to impose their definition of womanliness on working-class inmates.[3] Earlier chapters discussed the goals of the reformatory movement as its leaders defined them: to rescue and reform unfortunate women. This chapter, in contrast, is concerned with the movement's political implications. Without denying the benevolence of the reformers' aims, it attempts to look beyond good intentions to the movement's methods of social control and their results.

The women's reformatory, as we have seen, was unique as an institution for adults. Founded by middle- (often upper-middle) class social feminists, reformatories extended government control over working-class women not previously vulnerable to state punishment. In addition, the reformatories institutionalized bourgeois standards for female propriety, making it possible to "correct" women for moral offenses for which adult men were not sent to state penal institutions. And reformatories feminized prison discipline, introducing into state prisons for women a program of rehabilitation predicated on middle-class definitions of ladylike behavior. For these reasons, the women's reformatory served special, female-specific functions with regard to social class and social control.

In this chapter, New York's Western House of Refuge at Albion, operated between 1894 and 1931, is used as a case study. Albion built upon experiments by its forerunners to become the first women's prison to realize completely the reformatory plan in architecture, administrative structure, type of inmates and sentence, and program. It established the model adopted by many women's reformatories opened in the early twentieth century.[4] Additionally, Albion adhered to the goals of the women's reformatory movement more consistently than many sister institutions that succumbed to overcrowding, inadequate financing, and routinization. Although it was atypical in this respect, Albion provides a good case for analyzing the ways in which the reformatory movement extended social control just because it did manage to remain relatively "pure." The detailed nature of Albion's prisoner registries and the survival of case files on individual inmates, moreover, make it possible to follow in some depth the events that brought women to this prison, their institutional treatment, and their reactions to it.[5]

SOCIAL CONTROL FUNCTIONS
OF THE ALBION REFORMATORY

Records of the Albion reformatory indicate that in terms of social control, the institution served two primary functions: sexual and vocational regulation. It attempted the first by training "loose" young women to accept a standard of propriety that dictated chastity until marriage and fidelity thereafter. It tried to achieve the second by training charges in homemaking, a competency they were to utilize either as dutiful daughters or wives within their own families or as servants in the homes of others. In operation, techniques used to achieve these ends were usually indistinguishable. Although they are separated here for analytical purposes, in actuality tactics used to realize the dual goals of sexual and vocational regulation worked together, coalescing and mutually reinforcing one another.

From Sexual Autonomy to Propriety:
Preparation for the "True Good Womanly Life"[6]

To control the sexual activities of "promiscuous" women, the Albion reformatory used several approaches. One was the initial act of incarcerating women who had violated standards of sexual conduct for the "true women."[7] Second was parole revocation if a prisoner showed signs of lapsing back into impropriety while out on conditional release. Third was transfer of intractables to a custodial asylum for "feebleminded" women at Rome, New York, where they could be held indefinitely.

Over the thirty-seven years of its operation as a reformatory, Albion received about 3,150 prisoners. The menial nature of the jobs at which their parents were employed and their own previously high rates of employment at poorly paid, low-skilled jobs indicate that most of these prisoners were working-class women.[8] Three-quarters of them (to summarize previous chapters) were between fifteen and twenty-one years old, the rest under thirty. The vast majority—over 95 percent—were white. Most had been born in New York State (particularly in the rural western area where the institution was located) of native-born parents; one-third were Catholic, while nearly all the rest were Protestant; and most were single. The composition of the population reflected the desire of Albion's officials to work with cases who appeared malleable and deserving. The institution's commitment law authorized it to receive women convicted of petit larceny, habitual drunkenness, common prostitution, frequenting a disorderly house, or any other misdemeanor.[9] Originally, it could hold them for up to five years; later, the maximum number of years was reduced to three. Less than 2 percent of the prisoners were convicted of violent crimes (and these were mainly second or third degree assault) and but another 14 percent of property offenses (mainly petit larceny). The great majority (over 80 percent) had been sentenced for public order offenses—victimless crimes such as public intoxication, waywardness, and vagrancy.

As we saw in Chapter 5, for at least half (and perhaps up to three-quarters) of Albion's inmates, the act that led to incarceration had actually been sexual misconduct. Some of these women were apprehended for prostitution. Most, however, were merely sexually active, engaging in flirtations and affairs for pleasure instead of money. The efforts of Albion and other reformatories to curb sexual independence by women occurred within the wider context of antiprostitution and other social purity campaigns. Members of the middle and upper classes increasingly committed themselves to the cleansing of society. At the same time, however, some working women became indifferent to traditional definitions of virtue. In rapidly growing numbers, they left home to join the paid labor force. By 1910, a record high of 27 percent of all New York State women were gainfully employed. Even more significantly, nearly 80 percent of Albion's inmates had previously worked for wages. As they acquired a degree of independence, working women turned to new amusements. To smoke cigarettes, frequent dance halls, and become involved in sexual relationships did not strike *them* as depravity; but their disinterest in the ideals of "true" womanhood evoked alarm in those dedicated to the battle against vice. Reformers came to consider any deviation from female sexual propriety, even when it did not involve a financial transaction, as a form of "prostitution."[10]

The sexual misconduct for which women were incarcerated at Albion came to the attention of authorities through a variety of routes. Sometimes irate parents reported sexually active daughters to the police; at others, cuckolded husbands complained to court officials. Premarital pregnancies alerted social control agents in many cases. In yet others, discovery of venereal diseases led to commitment. For many women, a sign of sexual impurity in combination with some other suspicious circumstance seems to have precipitated arrest. For example, Anna H., one of Albion's few black inmates, evidently came to the attention of police when her husband was arrested for attempted burglary. Anna was examined, found to have venereal disease, and sentenced to Albion for vagrancy. There was no question of her fidelity to her husband: reformatory officials accepted Anna's statement that it was he who had infected her, and they later refused to release her on the theory that she would return to him ("the combination is a very bad one"). But Anna had been living apart from her husband, supporting herself as a waitress, and this irregular arrangement may have increased officials' consternation.[11]

Ostensibly, venereal disease was also the ground on which Lillian R., a Coney Islander of orthodox Jewish background, was originally committed; but in her case, too, unseemly independence and bad associates may have contributed to authorities' concern. Having quit school after the seventh grade to help her widowed mother support a large family, Lillian had been variously employed as a messenger, box factory worker, and forewoman in an artificial flower shop. At the age of sixteen she ran off with a soldier for a week and contracted venereal disease. She and her mother decided (according to her record) that "it would not be right for her to remain in her home with the other children. She was . . . put into the Magdalene Home. [She] was there one week when sent to the City Hospital for treatment." At the hospital Lillian was charged with "contracting an infectious disease in the practice of debauchery" and sentenced to the Bedford reformatory, from which she was later transferred to Albion.[12]

Some women committed to Albion for sexual misbehavior had in fact been sexually victimized. Such was the case with Anna B., who at the age of fourteen had been charged with ungovernability and sent to the Salvation Army Home in Buffalo, where she bore her first child. Not long after she returned home, her father was sentenced to prison for rape. Anna's case file strongly suggests that she was the victim. While her father was still on trial, Anna was sent to Pennsylvania to live with a grandmother. Within a month, she became pregnant by the sixty-year-old man for whom her grandmother kept house. Anna returned home, where she went to work in a restaurant. Convicted of "running around" when she was seven months into this second pregnancy, Anna seems actually to have been exploited twice by much older men.[13]

Although a handful of cases were, like Anna B., "led astray," most of Albion's inmates appear to have been rebels of some sort—against the double standard of sexual morality; against their families or husbands; or against public regulations such as that prohibiting disorderly conduct. But perhaps "rebels" is not the most accurate term: in officials' view, they defied conventions, but many of these young women may have been acting in accordance with other standards that they themselves considered legitimate. Despite their youth, the majority were independent at the point when police officers plucked them from saloons, hotel rooms, and street corners to be sent to the reformatory. Four-fifths of them held jobs. Although over 70 percent had not yet married, they were no longer under their parents' control. Whether reacting defiantly against conventional concepts of morality or simply behaving in ways they regarded as acceptable, most clearly had not internalized a view of themselves as "proper" women, demure and asexual. It was this situation that the reformatory, with its goal of imposing and teaching sexual control, sought to remedy.

If incarceration and training within the institution did not teach the prisoner to conform, the reformatory employed another means: parole revocation. Most of Albion's inmates were released on parole before their sentences expired. During the period of parole their behavior was scrutinized by the institution's parole officers, community officials, and employers. As noted in Chapter 5, when parole was revoked, the violation was frequently sexual in nature.

Some women had parole revoked for overt returns to vice. Such was the case with inmate No. 1899, recalled to Albion after "an officer of Endicott N.Y. arrested her in a questionable resort." Similarly, inmate No. 1913 was forced to return when, after marrying during parole, she was reported by her husband "for misconduct with men." Women who became pregnant during parole were returned to the institution—unless they quickly married someone "respectable." At other times revocation was triggered not by blatant signs of immorality but rather by indications that a lapse was imminent. One woman was returned to the reformatory because she "became infatuated with a married man named L_____ . Mrs. L_____ wrote us" and, after investigating, reformatory officials decided to recall her. Another parolee was revoked for associating with the father of her child ("they were not married and Washington is a most disreputable character"), and No. 1313 barely escaped revocation when "two former inmates report[ed] seeing her frequently at night with different conductors on the Genesee St. line."[14]

In cases that appeared hopeless to Albion's administrators, a third step was sometimes taken to ensure against relapse: transfer to the State School at Rome or another of New York's institutions for the feebleminded. Such transfers carried an automatic extension of sentence up to life, for according to popular theory of the time, the feebleminded never improve. At the turn of the century, the feebleminded were considered innately promiscuous, so Albion's authorities easily assumed that women who would not reform were feebleminded "defective delinquents." Because intelligence testing was still in a primitive stage, it was not difficult to confirm "scientifically" a suspicion of feeblemindedness and thus establish the basis for a transfer. These transfers, which occurred in cases of women who were disciplinary problems within the institution as well as in instances of overt sexuality while on parole, constituted the final disposition for forty-eight of the sampled cases, or 3 percent of all first releases. In addition, thirteen women who were returned to the reformatory for parole violation (5.2 percent of those who were released a second time), and two women (5.6 percent of the thirty-six sampled cases who returned twice to the reformatory and then discharged a third time) were transferred to institutions for the feebleminded. Case file documents such as school records and letters written by these supposedly feebleminded women indicate that they were not in fact mentally retarded. They were, however, noncompliant. The lesson of their transfer to civil institutions was probably not lost on those left behind at the reformatory.[15]

From Sauciness to Subservience:
Preparation for Domestic Service

The second central social control function of the Albion reformatory was to train inmates to become competent housekeepers in either their own homes or those where they were placed as domestics. The institution aimed, in the words of its managers, to reform "unfortunate and wayward girls" by giving them "moral and religious training . . . and such training in domestic work as will eventually enable them to find employment, secure good homes and be self-supporting." To the achievement of this end, the managers viewed the cottage system, with its "plan of ordinary domestic life," as crucial. Acquisition of decorum was also considered critical; the institution emphasized gentility in all aspects of its program. Within this institutional facsimile of the genteel home, inmates received both academic and domestic training, with by far the heavier emphasis falling on the latter. Albion seldom educated inmates beyond the sixth grade level, but it provided abundant opportunities for perfection of domestic skills, instructing prisoners in dressmaking, plain and fancy sewing, knitting, crocheting, "cookery," cleaning, and "ventilation." A steam-operated washing machine was purchased for the institution's laundry, but the sight of it made visiting prison commissioner Sarah L. Davenport "sorry," for it was "not educating the women . . . for the homes they will go to when they leave Albion." Thereafter, the laundry was washed by hand.[16] A "finely equipped domestic science department," outfitted with dining room furniture, coal and gas burners, and kitchen utensils, was added in 1912, and from then on inmates received instruction in

> manufacture and source of food supplies, relative cost, and nutritive values; the care of the kitchen, pantry, and dining room; construction and care of the sinks, stoves, (both gas and coal) and refrigerators; table etiquette; the planning and serving of meals; and waitress' duties.[17]

When members of the board of managers met at the reformatory, inmates practiced for future employment by waiting on their table. As Elliott Curie has put it in writing of the Massachusetts reformatory, the institution "trained women to be women."[18]

For middle-class women who lived in its vicinity, Albion provided trained, inexpensive household help. It was the institution's policy "to place our girls in the home of a woman who will take a motherly interest in them."[19] One-quarter of the prisoners were paroled directly to live-in domestic positions. Of the 50 percent paroled to members of their own families, another sizeable proportion also took jobs as domestics. Housekeeping was familiar to Albion's prisoners, many of whom reported their previous occupation as "domestic" or "houseworker." But the reformatory's records suggest that some, at least, had been less than satisfactory servants, given to carelessness, impudence, filching, and running off with young men. The institution tried to turn these and other inmates into competent, submissive domestics.

Attempts by Albion and other reformatories to train domestics took place at a time when the "servant problem" was particularly intense. Difficulties in finding suitable servants became acute after the Civil War and continued to be so well into the twentieth century. As the number of families that could afford servants increased, the interest of working-class women in domestic service declined. The latter came to prefer factory jobs that offered more money, shorter hours, and greater autonomy. Those who had no alternative to domestic service resented the power of the mistress; they also objected to the social restrictions of live-in positions and to expectations of servility. Many reacted to such conditions with impertinence and petty theft. The distaste of working women for domestic service created a predicament for would-be employers. Servants were necessary for the operation of their households, and (equally important) they were a sign of status. Thus in increasing the supply of well-trained domestics, reformatory officials supported the interests of other middle-class women.[20]

Nearly 20 percent of Albion's prisoners had worked before arrest in mills or factories. But as noted earlier, the frequent economic crises of the late nineteenth and early twentieth centuries led to widespread unemployment and serious labor unrest. Insofar as reformatories removed women from the industrial labor force, they made more jobs available for men. In view of these circumstances, the reformatory's refusal to provide training in skills that might "unfit" women for domestic service is especially significant. "No industries are maintained," one Albion report declared, "but every inmate is taught to cook and care for a home. This is the most important thing in the work of the institution. Most of the girls when paroled go into homes where this knowledge is necessary." Thus Albion not only provided rigorous training in housekeeping but also tended to discourage inmates from moving beyond the home and earning higher wages. It reinforced the point that women's place was in the home by paroling most women to family situations where they were needed as paid or unpaid domestic help.[21]

Employers and the institution formed a symbiotic alliance over the discipline of women paroled as servants. The reformatory required women released to domestic positions to sign a form agreeing to

accept the wages agreed upon between the Superintendent . . . and her employer, . . . her wages to be retained by employer, excepting such amount as the latter thinks necessary for [the] girl. . . .

[C]onsult employer as to her amusements, recreation, and social diversions. To form no friendships, not to visit or receive visits from members of her own family unless approved by the Superintendent. Is not to go out nights excepting when accompanied by a responsible person, and to go very seldom at night. To have one afternoon a week. . . .[22]

Paroled women were also required to send monthly reports to the reformatory, and they were further supervised through visits from a parole officer. If despite these controls a domestic became difficult, the reformatory could revoke parole, a threat that no doubt helped employers maintain discipline. These restraints notwithstanding, many women paroled to domestic positions behaved noncompliantly. Revocations were occasioned by "sauciness," "obscenity," failure to work hard enough, and other demonstrations of independence. Inmate No. 13, for example,

went to Rochester to work for Mrs. . . . J _____ and for a time did very nicely but finding some girls of her acquaintance she began to visit them too often and to neglect her work. She came back to the institution in Aug. 1897 and there remained till [sentence] expiration.

Inmate No. 2585 was originally paroled to a Mrs. F _____ of Rochester. But, "Jane was a slow worker and very untidy and shiftless. She was very fond of reading. Returned [to the reformatory] for a change of place. . . ." Next Jane was sent to a Mrs. S _____ of Buffalo. This time, "On Oct. 11 went to a movie and did not return until eleven o'clock when she was expected at nine." When Mrs. S _____ threatened to return her to Albion, Jane fled. She was not recaptured, but others on domestic parole were returned to the institution for laziness, disobedience, and running away.

In return for the institution's help with disciplining difficult domestics, employers supervised prisoners. They were "authorized and requested to open and read all mail sent and received by girl" and further charged "to guard her morals, language and actions, and aid her as much as possible by advice as to her present and future conduct. . . ."[23] In the course of aiding fallen women, employers were also aiding themselves by maintaining the quality of the services they received. The entire arrangement, in fact, seems to have been one from which employers benefited greatly, receiving trained and supervised servants who promised to consult them in all matters and work six and one-half days a week. If the servant became shiftless or impudent, the criminal justice system would step in to do the necessary disciplining.

TECHNIQUES OF SOCIAL CONTROL

Albion developed a variety of techniques to encourage reform. Some have already been identified: the initial act of incarcerating women for sexual misconduct and other petty offenses; intensive training in domesticity and gentility; a policy of parole to domestic positions; community surveillance; parole revocation; and transfer of the most uncooperative to civil institutions where they could be held indefinitely. Implicit in many of these techniques was another: from the moment of arrest, Albion's inmates were reduced to the standing of children. Like juvenile delinquents, many were detained for status offenses—immorality, waywardness, keeping bad company—for which men the same age were not arrested. At the reformatory they were supervised by motherly matrons, and at parole they were usually released to family situations in which they had a dependent position. Indeed, the very concept of an institution dedicated to the rescue and reform of women under the age of thirty, and operated with an extremely high level of discretionary authority, was rooted in a view of women as childlike creatures. Appropriately, like institutions for juvenile delinquents, Albion was titled a "refuge."

Disruption of inmates' ties with their families was another mechanism used by the reformatory to encourage inmates to conform to its values. Some prisoners, to be sure, had already separated from their families; but being independent through one's own choice was not the same as being severed from one's family by others—and at a time of crisis. Familial disruption was a technique to which women were especially susceptible, their roles being so intimately involved with domestic life. Disconnected from their own families, Albion inmates were more likely to identify with the surrogate "families" of their cottages and, on parole, with those to which they were sent as servants.

Disruption of family life is an inevitable by-product of incarceration, but Albion developed policies relating to mail and visitors that intensified the break. Once in custody, women had immense difficulty contacting families and friends. They were permitted to write letters only once every two months, and these were censored. If the superintendent decided that either the contents or the designated recipient was unsuitable, she would file the letter in the inmate's folder—quite probably without notifying the writer and certainly without notifying the intended recipient, both of whom might therefore wait in vain anticipation. Incoming mail was also censored and often filed away undelivered. Visits were permitted, but only four times a year. A further restriction limited the pool of potential visitors to close relatives, and even these might be banned if deemed bad influences. Moreover, some approved visitors doubtless were discouraged from visiting by the institution's geographical isolation. For all these reasons, commitment to the reformatory resulted in nearly total severance of ties to former support groups. Isolated in this fashion, prisoners became more susceptible to the institution's staff and its moral advice.

Another aspect of familial disruption, separation from children, was sometimes traumatically final. When women were committed, their children might be sent to orphanages or put up for adoption. Such removals occurred even in instances when inmates had husbands living at home. Thus not only were young mothers severed from their children; they also had to suffer the knowledge that their families had been dissolved. In such cases, moreover, the children were now being cared for by strangers. To judge from Albion's records, its inmates were not informed of the welfare of institutionalized or adopted children.

Occasionally ultimate disposition of children would be left undecided and used to induce the mother to conform. Of a woman committed for vagrancy, for instance, the registry reports, "Edna made a splendid record while on parole. Mr. Angel, Humane Officer of Courtland County[,] was so well pleased with her that he returned her children to her."[24] Not to please Mr. Angel, it seems, would have resulted in loss of her children. Another example is provided by the case of Martha, a mother of four, sentenced to Albion for public intoxication. Threat of removal of her children kept Martha sober even in times of great stress:

Martha returned [on parole] to her husband who had promised every[thing] in the way of reform but who is the veriest hypocrit [sic]. She continued leading a true good womanly life hoping to be worthy of her children, as the authorities had promised to restore them when they were satisfied that she would hold out.[25]

In instances like these, there was the initial familial disruption occasioned by commitment and then a threat of further disruption—total loss of children—if the prisoner did not comply with the institution's requirements.

Similar methods of control involved babies who stayed with mothers at the institution. If a woman was nursing at commitment, she was allowed to bring the child with her. Those women who gave birth at Albion were permitted to keep infants. But reformatory policy decreed that all babies had to leave when they reached the age of two. Sometimes the institution decided not to parole a woman until after the baby had been sent away. Mary P., for example, bore a child a few days after her arrival at Albion in 1922, and in September 1924, two years having expired, the child was sent to the Delaware County Superintendent of the Poor. Mary was paroled just a month later to work in her father's cigar factory. Mary's parents may have refused to let her bring home an illegitimate child. Whatever the reason, the effect of holding her slightly beyond the mandatory release date for the baby was to cut Mary off from the only family she had had for two years.

She was, moreover, returned to a situation in which she herself was the child.[26]

Some babies brought into or born at the prison were sent to adoption agencies or other institutions before they reached the age of two. How long their mothers might keep them was a matter of administrative discretion, and like all such matters, liable to be used as a mechanism of control. Albion's records do not refer to the practice of using children to coerce institutionalized mothers, but this form of social control is described in a letter from the superintendent of Maine's State Reformatory for Women to a journalist who had requested information on babies in prison. "The conduct of the mothers," the superintendent informed him,

> decides in a measure the time they are allowed to spend with their babies. . . . They dress and undress and feed their own babies after the baby is six months old. They always have the privilege to kiss them goodnight and to spend an hour in the afternoon with them, unless their conduct precludes the loss [sic] of this privilege.[27]

Restricting access to children was probably used as a social control device at Albion and other reformatories as well.

Despite its emphasis on the home as woman's place, Albion developed parole policies that further disrupted some inmates' ties to their former homes. Women who before incarceration lived in stable family situations were frequently paroled not to their own families but to domestic positions in the homes of others. In some instances, the institution deemed the original family unsuitable and wanted to keep the woman away from it as long as possible. In others, officials seem simply to have decided that for a woman to work and save money was the best way for her to pass parole. Often the domestic jobs were in towns distant from the prisoners' families. Women could take infants with them to some domestic live-in positions, but others required them to leave their babies behind.

Many of these dislocating factors were present in the case of Marjorie M., a twenty-year-old of German extraction who, before commitment, lived with her parents and seven siblings in Batavia, where she was employed as a domestic. The mother of a three-year-old and again pregnant, Marjorie was convicted of disorderly conduct in 1917 and sent to Albion. There she gave birth to her second daughter, Helen. Paroled to a domestic position in Rochester, Marjorie sent five dollars of her eight-dollar weekly salary to the home where Helen was boarded. After parole, she found employment as assistant housekeeper at the Rochester Orphan's Asylum, where Helen was now living. Helen died of diphtheria in the winter of 1920. At this point Marjorie, who at the time of arrest had been living with ten members of her immediate family, was left entirely alone.[28]

The reformatory's policies also perpetuated familial disruption in the case of Henrietta S., a Binghamton woman with two children. After serving time at Albion for intoxication, Henrietta was paroled to a domestic position in Lyndonville, where she earned four dollars a week. When her term was up, she returned to her family with $154 she had managed to save from her wages. The institution interpreted the large sum as a sign of success, but Henrietta and her family paid a high psychological price in return: their family life had been interrupted for three years, and while a Mrs. F _____ of Lyndonville had had cheap use of her services, Henrietta's own children had been deprived of her care.[29]

The reformatory's parole policies were not disruptive of family life in all instances, and perhaps some women who *were* returned to parents or husbands would have preferred a less restrictive arrangement. In either case, the institution exercised tremendous control over inmates' social contacts (probably more than any contemporary prison for men), and it used this control to induce conformity. Denying inmates access to mail and visitors, institutionalizing their children or threatening to do so, on occasion probably blocking access to infants within the prison, developing parole policies that frequently prevented contact with families—through such means the prison demonstrated its power and often disrupted the continuity of whatever family life had existed. The effect was to encourage dependency on the institution and increase the likelihood that inmates would internalize the reformatory's teachings about how women like themselves should behave.

"THE BEST PLACE TO CONQUER GIRLS": THE REFORMATORY'S SUCCESS

Many women incarcerated at Albion went on to lead lives that met the institution's criteria for success, marrying and maintaining homes of their own or remaining for long terms in domestic placements. No doubt many former inmates would have become more sedate in their mid-twenties or early thirties even without the moral influence of the prison, just as more serious offenders outgrow crime. But the reformatory does seem to have set some formerly wayward women on the path to propriety—to have served, in the words of one inmate's sister, as "the only and best place to conquer girls."[30] Albion appears, that is, to have achieved its goals in some, perhaps even a majority, of cases.

The reformatory worked through kindness as well as coercion, and therein lay the key to its success. Had it merely punished, it would have antagonized; but Albion also performed extensive nurturing functions, alleviating some of the harsher aspects of poverty. It served as a hospital where the diseased could receive treatment, the malnourished food, the pregnant decent care at delivery. It also functioned as a shelter to which women could turn from incestuous fathers and brutal husbands. The superintendent and other staff offered counseling in careers, marriage, and child-rearing. Moreover, the institution provided training in manners that many working-class women may have considered valuable: refined behavior was widely regarded as a sign of female superiority, particularly by people with authority and status.[31]

To be sure, the reformatory did not bring every case to the desired conclusion. It tended to be least successful with women whose families had resisted their commitment. In the case of Anna H., the black woman sentenced for vagrancy, for instance, the reformatory was bombarded with appeals for release from the inmate's frantic parents and their lawyer, the mayor of Newport, Rhode Island; the latter also elicited requests for Anna's discharge from the offices of New York's State Board of Charities and Governor Alfred E. Smith. When the superintendent refused to heed these appeals, Anna attempted to escape. Lillian R., the inmate originally sentenced to the Bedford reformatory for "debauchery," was similarly unappreciative of institutionalization. At Bedford she participated in the July 1920 riots against cruelty to inmates. Subsequently, Bedford's matrons told her she was to be paroled, but as Lillian explained in a letter to her mother, "I knew that parole talk was all a frameup"; she realized she was really being transferred to Albion, at the other end of the state. "[I]f they were any kind of women they would tell us just where we are going and not say that we were paroled. . . . [T]hen they wonder why the girls don't respect them." Lillian's later letters show that she was equally critical of the matrons at Albion.[32] Other inmates demonstrated resistance by misbehaving on parole:

> —Julia was a great care throughout her parole . . . deceitful & deceptive. [No. 1581]

> —She was arrested while on parole and sentenced again to the W.H. of R. But we refused to take her again. [No. 1355]

> —Minnie gave entire satisfaction [while on domestic parole] for several months[,] saved her money[,] was quiet and unobtrusive. . . .
> The spirit of unrest [then] took possession of her and she absconded, and no trace of her has been found. [No. 89]

When No. 61 sold her discharge clothes, "bought a telescope," and ran away from the Wayfarers' Lodge in Buffalo, reformatory officials resignedly observed, "[A] perverse nature and bad blood [had] proved too strong for human endeavor."

On the other hand, Albion's records also provide evidence that numerous inmates were grateful for its help. Some, especially those who were very young, alone in the world, or in poor health, seem not to have found incarceration onerous. A few, for example, requested to stay for their full terms, without parole. Inmate No. 1257 resisted leaving Albion for an unpleasant home situation: her mother had been committed to an insane asylum, and there were small children whose care would fall on her. "When it came time for her to go . . . she cried and it was with difficulty that the Parole Officer persuaded her to go." Some parolees ran back to the institution from uncongenial domestic placements. One woman, after having been paroled twice, returned "and asked to be admitted. She was a wreck, physically and morally—her clothing torn and soiled, and evidently [she] had no place to go for the night nor money to pay her way." The reformatory gave her medical attention and sheltered her for another six months. After marrying, some former inmates brought their husbands to visit the reformatory and meet its superintendent. A woman who had escaped later wrote from a distant state to announce that she was happily married; her resentment at being confined, in other words, was not incompatible with a desire to demonstrate that she could achieve the institution's ideals.[33] Many women wrote back after release. "My dear Mrs. Boyed," began a letter received by superintendent Boyd in 1907,

> have [you] entirely forgotten Nellie that one time lived in your pleasant Home for Homeless Girls.
>
> I have been thinking for some time that I would write to you. . . . Of course you have heard from Mrs. Green that I am married and have a good Husband. . . . Are any of the Ladies [officers] with you now that were in the years of 1894 or 95 . . . how I would like to see them as well as your self. . . . I have a very pleasant home and appreciate it I think as I ought to. Yours in haste and with love,
>
> Nellie (I am Ever) L _____[34]

Albion succeeded in persuading inmates like Nellie to identify with its standards for correct female behavior. These were, essentially, middle-class standards. While many members of the working class may also have endorsed them, women sentenced to Albion had not—deviations from these values had led to their incarceration. In reforming (and in wanting to demonstrate reformation), successful cases had by definition come to identify with middle-class concepts of female propriety. Class identification was very much in flux at the turn of the century. As Charles Rosenberg has explained,

> [S]tatus definitions in 19th century America were . . . particularly labile. . . . A good many Americans must, it follows, have been all

the more anxious in their internalization of those aspects of life-style which seemed to embody and assure class status. And contemporaries clearly regarded overt sexuality, especially in women, as part of a life-style demeaning to middle-class status.[35]

When women who had been apprehended for sexual misconduct and other signs of independence from middle-class "status definitions" became chaste or sober or (like Nellie) "appreciative" of husband and home, the middle-class won an ideological victory. Its values had been affirmed; its symbols of status had been accorded validity by women of the working-class.

The reformatory probably influenced the values not only of those sentenced to it but also of women in the broader community. Albion's records show that some inmates knew each other before commitment and continued to associate after release. But to be a prisoner was unusual; since acquaintanceship networks existed among inmates, these networks must have been even more extensive between inmates and women never incarcerated. Through such connections, Albion would have come to play a role in the consciousness of working-class women in its area. Women who never set foot inside it would have been aware, through word of mouth, that there existed a state institution prepared to punish them for deviations from middle-class definitions of womanliness.

Informal as well as formal police actions reinforced the social values endorsed by Albion, reminding women in the community of the institution's potential for punishment. This kind of informal social control is almost invisible today since it was seldom noted in official records. Yet glimpses of it can be caught from time to time in reformatory documents. One hint appears in the registry record of inmate No. 2441, a woman confined for vagrancy. She had had no previous arrests, according to the registry, but had been "taken to the Police Station twice and talked to for being out late, attending dances." Whereas this particular woman was evidently not influenced by police efforts to get her to behave properly (she did, after all, end up at the reformatory), others so treated may have been. Of No. 1775, paroled in 1919, we are told,

> Edna was very erratic and unreliable during her parole. She was reported [to the reformatory] by the Binghamton police as being on the streets at a late hour very frequently with different men. Chief Cronin was asked several times [by reformatory officials] to arrest her and instructed his men to that effect.

Other police chiefs probably also ordered their men to keep women like Edna in line. Thus, through informal procedures as well as formal arrests, the police helped uphold the reformatory's values; they, too, gave women incentives to submit and behave.

THE DEFINITION OF GENDER

Most other women's reformatories also aimed at rescue and reform and used techniques of social control similar to those of Albion. From Maine to North Carolina, New York to Nebraska, reformatories for women removed errant women from the streets, trained them in domestic skills, and returned them to the home. Through parole supervision they also encouraged inmates on conditional release to maintain "self-control" at work and in sexual relationships; and if located in states with facilities for the feeble-minded, they also used transfers to such institutions as an auxiliary disciplinary measure. All prisons of the reformatory type seem to have exercised tight control over mail, visitors, and disposition of children. Like Albion, most other reformatories were multifunctional institutions that served as hospitals, refuges, schools, vocational training and placement agencies, and counseling centers—as well as prisons. Officials at many were rewarded by former inmates who returned, after discharge, to give thanks and demonstrate that they had indeed reformed.[36]

The prisoners of these institutions were burdened by multiple disadvantages. They and their families fell near the bottom of the class hierarchy. In addition to being poor, the prisoners suffered the disability of being women in a society that barred women from many occupations, paid them less than male workers, and imposed male authority everywhere. Race was yet another factor relegating black or Indian women to the base of the social structure, while nativist prejudices pushed the foreign-born toward the margins of society. Most reformatory prisoners were young, a further drawback in terms of status. Those who were single—and they were probably in the majority at other reformatories as well as at Albion—were at another disadvantage in a society that placed a premium on marriage for women.

The prisoners were, then, located at the bottom of many power dimensions in their society, those defined by social class, sex, age, marital status, and (for some) race or ethnicity. But they did not stay put in these lowly positions. They had no authority, yet as the many cases of incorrigible daughters, wandering wives, and unreliable servants in reformatory reports indicate, they balked at obedience. Lacking autonomy, they nonetheless acted independently. Bereft of status, many refused to behave as inferiors. Their very handicaps, in fact, created a situation of some fluidity. As women who had to work, they had achieved a degree (albeit minimal) of economic self-sufficiency. Denied the luxury of being kept, they were to some extent freed from cultural imagery that associated "good" women with fragility and submissiveness. Youth in combination with physical maturity and lack of marital attachment probably encouraged them to seek sexual pleasure outside marriage. Thus their characteristics and situations promoted disengagement from their era's standards for propriety.

Among the factors that fostered establishment of women's reformatories, two were of special importance: changes in gender roles in nineteenth- and early twentieth-century America and the simultaneous widening of divisions between social classes. During the nineteenth century, as production came to be located outside the family, women were increasingly isolated within the home. Their labor was devalued and a premium came to be placed on feminine characteristics such as domesticity, demureness, purity, and piety. But the ideal of true womanhood was more easily approximated by women of the middle than of the working class. The former were likely to have servants and other aids to gentility, and if they became restless they could take up causes like temperance and prison reform. Intensification of gender roles had different implications for working-class women, however. For them, true womanhood was more difficult to achieve and less rewarding. As the nineteenth century flowed into the twentieth, some middle-class women (including those who founded and ran reformatories) participated in the gradual break from traditional roles. But for them, activity in the world was more likely to be compatible with respectability; charitable work, for instance, had long been a hallmark of the lady, and social feminism posed no real threat to male authority. But activities available to working-class women in search of self-fulfillment meshed less well with traditional notions of rectitude. Indeed, some of them, such as drinks in saloons, late night cigarettes with sailors, and casual affairs, became grounds for imprisonment.

Persuaded of innate temperamental differences between the sexes, the reformers naturally set about establishing separate prisons for women run by women; and believing that woman's mission included rescue of the unfortunate, they naturally focused on fallen women—not serious felons or confirmed prostitutes but wayward "girls" who might be saved. Those among them active in social purity campaigns argued against the double standard of sexual morality for men and women. Yet all the reformers worked to found or operate prisons that in fact institutionalized the double standard. Their understanding of "woman's nature" led logically to advocacy of special help for the frailer sex.

This understanding was embodied in laws establishing reformatories that could incarcerate women for minor offenses, mainly "moral" in nature. In many cases, apparently, the understanding came to be internalized by inmates. This internalization provides an instance of the ability of law to perform hegemonic functions—to reproduce the ideological and political conditions of social hierarchy. As Diane Polan has explained, "In respect to patriarchy, a set of ideas . . . operate[s] hegemonically to the extent it succeeds in convincing women that their inferior political, economic, and social status is a result of a *natural* division of the world into separate spheres and *natural* differences between male and female personalities . . . rather than the result of exploitation and domination." From this perspective, inmates' acceptance of reformatory values can be seen as a phase in the process that another writer describes as "the *embourgeoisement* of the working class," its absorbtion of middle-class attitudes toward status, security, property, the family—and gender roles.[37]

Two groups of women—the working-class offenders and the middle-class reformers—met, so to speak, at the gate of the women's reformatory. The struggle between them was economically functional to the reformers: it helped maintain a pool of cheap domestic labor for women like themselves and, by keeping working women in the surplus labor force, it undergirded the economic system to which reformers owed their privileged positions. But a purely economic explanation does not adequately account for the dedication with which the reformers went about their tasks of rescue and reform. The struggle also involved the definition of gender. The reformers had already absorbed the social controls they sought to instill. These reformers hoped to recast offenders in their own image, to have them embrace the values (though not assume the social station) of the lady. And through reformatories like Albion, some working-class women were taught to accept a new concept of womanhood that restricted their sexual and vocational choices. They were, in fact, reformed.

CONCLUSION ||||||||||||||||||||||||||||

Women's Prisons, Past and Present: The Intractable Inequities

When in the 1840s Dorothea Dix surveyed prisons from Maine to Virginia, she counted a total of 167 female prisoners. Had she repeated her inspection in 1981, Dix would have found more than 14,000 women in state and federal prisons. But she also would have discovered that, in a number of significant respects, incarcerated women of the present resemble those of the past. Women continue to constitute only a fraction of the entire prisoner population. In nineteenth-century prisons and penitentiaries, they made up 10 percent or less (sometimes as little as 1 percent) of the total populations; today, they account for but 4 percent of all state and federal prisoners. Across time and in nearly all regions, black women were imprisoned in custodial institutions in proportions that far outstripped their representation in the general population; today, over 50 percent of incarcerated women are black. Like their predecessors, the majority of current female inmates entered prison in their twenties; they are less likely to be married than free women; and they worked for wages before imprisonment, mainly at service and other poorly paid jobs. The profile of incarcerated female felons, then, has remained quite stable over time.[1]

Several factors have helped foster these continuities in the characteristics of incarcerated women. First, female prisoner populations have been much smaller than male populations because crime rates for women are lower. In the United States, men have always held a near monopoly on criminal activity. Women more than men have been trained to be passive, self-effacing, and supportive of others. While today more women work for wages than in earlier periods, their lives still center on the home. They have fewer opportunities and less inclination to commit crimes. From time to time, judges have hesitated to send women (at least white women) to state penitentiaries, but chivalry alone cannot account for the enormous differences over time between male and female rates of incarceration. Women have committed, and continue to commit, many fewer crimes.

Second, there is clearly a strong association between rates of incarceration and a group's socio-economic disadvantages. Women sent to prison today, like those of the past, carry multiple burdens. Often they are black and poor. Many have young children whom they must support. Their race, class, and family responsibilities apparently encourage involvement in crime. Analysis of the characteristics of women held in late nineteenth- and early twentieth-century prisons indicates that they lacked the interpersonal ties that evidently restrained others from criminal activity. They tended to be mobile: many were immigrants, while others were black women migrating north. Many had no links to adult relatives or church friends who might have cushioned the hardships of their lives. Women incarcerated today have faced similar difficulties. Unlike most white, middle-class women, they have few resources to draw upon in hard times. If middle-class women become entangled in abusive relationships, they have more avenues of escape than do poor women, whose only recourse may be to strike back. If inclined to use drugs, middle-class women have access to physicians who prescribe legal substances. The fewer alternatives and social marginality of impoverished and minority women, then, partially account for their greater involvement in crime and, hence, their higher rates of incarceration. In addition, criminal justice officials seem to react more severely to such women. This study has found ample evidence of such bias. After the Civil War, southern judges sent black women to prison for minor thefts while finding alternative dispositions for all but the most serious white female offenders. The reformatory movement drew in large numbers of working-class women, even though their misbehaviors were trivial. And officials seem to have reacted less harshly (or less "protectively," as some would have put it) to married than to single women, who also tended to be black and poor.

SEX DISCRIMINATION IN WOMEN'S PRISONS: ITS NATURE AND ORIGINS

Problems specific to women in prison also have remained fairly constant from the establishment of the first penitentiaries into the present. Women continue to be slighted by a correctional bureaucracy that is overwhelmingly male and predominantly occupied by the larger male populations. When held in the same institution with men, women are still vulnerable to sexual exploitation by male staff. As in the past, female prisoners discover that medical services are geared toward men; they seldom have adequate access to physicians trained in obstetrics or gynecology. Women in prison today, like their nineteenth-century counterparts, have fewer programs than men. Because reformatories were deliberately built in rural areas, women often are more isolated than men from families, legal aid, and community resources. Unlike men sentenced to prison, women seldom have been able to rely on a spouse to care for their children; therefore they have suffered more anxiety about the welfare of their families. And incarcerated women continue to encounter gender stereotyping in programs and staff attitudes. Thus, across time, women in prison have shared the experience of partial justice—treatment inferior to that provided for males.[2]

It is true that incarcerated women were (and are) sometimes housed in less forbidding quarters and subjected to milder routines than men—the other sense of *partial justice*. At Auburn in the early nineteenth century, officials permitted women to talk while imposing on men the rule of constant silence. The environments of turn-of-the-century women's reformatories, with their cottages and rolling acres of unwalled farmland, were gentler than those of men's prisons. And today, women are less likely than men to be assigned to maximum security institutions.[3] But nearly every advantage enjoyed by female prisoners has had its dark side. Women could talk in some early nineteenth-century penitentiaries because they had no custodians whatsoever; unsupervised, they were also freer to attack one another. Within the bucolic settings of turn-of-the-century reformatories, women were confined for trifling offenses for which men were not sent to state prisons. Women today are less likely than men to experience maximum security confinement; but because most states operate only one prison for them, women have less access to institutions graded by security level, to specialized facilities such as those for mentally disturbed prisoners, and to placements near their families and friends. Less stringent treatment, then, presents its own set of disadvantages.

Gender and small numbers have been the sources of partial justice for incarcerated women since the early nineteenth century. Assumptions about women have led to inferior job assignments, lower wages, and the underfunding and understaffing of female departments. The small size of female state prisoner populations has also made women inmates marginal, encouraging officials to devote their attention and resources to the larger groups of males. Reformatory advocates initially overcame the problem of neglect. However, they delivered their specialized programs to only a narrow segment of female offenders. These programs, moreover, actually intensified gender stereotyping.

HISTORICAL DIFFERENCES WITHIN THE WOMEN'S PRISON SYSTEM

The recent growth of interest in the origins and development of prisons has generated a number of historiographical debates about the best way to analyze the evolution of such institutions. Currently the most hotly contested issue involves the amount of attention that should be paid to reform-ers' intentions, in comparison to the social control effects of their activities.[4] But of equal importance is another issue: how broadly can (or should) the findings of histories of specific prisons or prison systems be applied? Nearly every work in the field to date has focused on institutions for males. More-over, disproportional attention has been paid to the early penitentiaries of the Northeast. As a result, we have been presented with monolithic portraits of "the" prison system that fail to recognize variations by such factors as period, region, and inmates' sex, race, and age. Among women's prisons, the most marked variation was in type of institution. As noted in Part I, for a crucial period of about sixty years the women's prison system divided into two branches, one custodial and the other reformatory. Although the men's system also developed reformatories, they were far less differentiated from traditional prisons and had less impact on the development of the men's system as a whole.

There are several ways to analyze the branching of the women's prison system into two tracks. One is by race: as observed in Chapter 6, the division between custodial and reformatory institutions was to a considerable extent a split along racial lines. The misdemeanants who at first filled the refor-matories were mainly whites, women considered worthy of the expense and effort of rehabilitation. Most custodial units for women, on the other hand, held disproportionate numbers of blacks. This was not the case in the antebellum South, where slaves were usually punished on the plantation. But after the Civil War, southern states incarcerated large numbers of blacks and worked them even more ruthlessly than masters had previously worked slaves. In the South in particular, white women were screened out of prisons and jails. Racism was not the only factor affecting the disproportionately black composition of female custodial populations, for black women ap-parently committed felonies at higher rates. But in all regions of the country, judges seem to have been more reluctant to send white women to custodial institutions. And in these prisons, racism continued to determine treatment.

The division of the women's prison system into two tracks was also a regional one. Most northeastern and midwestern states founded refor-matories, but only three institutions of this type were established in the South, and of them, only one survived. In the West, California alone created a reformatory, and that institution, established near the movement's close, received felons from the start. Unlike California, many states that financed a women's reformatory also operated a custodial unit for female felons, but elsewhere, custodialism alone prevailed.

These regional differences reflected the greater receptivity of north-eastern and midwestern states to proto-Progressive and Progressive re-forms. For instance, states of these areas were most open to the late nineteenth-century prison reform movement. In them, social feminism gained a foothold, leading to the engagement of middle-class women in civic house-keeping activities such as temperance, child rescue and women's prison reform. Largely because of the efforts of these women, the social purity movement also prospered in the Northeast and Midwest, sowing concern about sexual morality in general, prostitution in particular. Social purity activities strengthened the women's reformatory movement, which seemed to offer a way to rescue fallen women and thus shore up family morality.

Northern states took the lead in these reform efforts partly because they were experiencing enormous turmoil through social class realignments. Industrialization, most rapid in the North, widened the distance between the middle and working classes. As the former expanded and acquired its base of wealth, its members sought ways to solidify and signify their class identity. Middle-class women needed servants not only to run their homes but also to symbolize their social station. The presence of servants, more-over, freed them for "progressive" reform activities which, as observed in Chapter 3, were often conservative in effect, extending new social controls over the poor. At the same time, working-class women were entering the labor force in ever growing numbers. Many came to prefer factory work to domestic service because it paid better and gave them more control over their lives. Many also began to develop new social interests, demonstrating an independence in courtship and amusements that defied Victorian recti-tude. These changing work and social preferences aroused anxiety among members of the middle class, some of whom helped establish reformatories to instill traditional concepts of domesticity and propriety.

Bifurcation of the women's prison system was also a matter of imagery: the two branches accreted around different archetypes of the female of-fender. These archetypes had their roots in early nineteenth-century dogma about gender, according to which women were the guardians of social morality, the conscience of civilization; through gentle suasion, women harnessed the brutish instincts of men. Women who departed from this scenario seemed to threaten the moral foundations of society. When such unnatural creatures committed crimes, they deserved to be treated like men. And if they were treated less well than male prisoners, that too was fitting, for such women had betrayed their own sex, the men whom they misled, and their community. That many incarcerated women were black reinforced such associations, for (another image that shaped the development of wom-en's prisons) women of color were regarded as more masculine. Thus the custodial branch of the women's prison system grew out of the archetype of the deceitful Dark Lady who, behind her apparent femininity, hid op-posite traits: self-centeredness, ability to scheme and use cunning, willing-ness to employ force, and voracious sexuality.

The reformatory movement required a different image of the female offender. To justify their work, reformers drew on popular imagery of the "true" woman and of women as inherently childlike to depict the female offender as a fragile, immature creature who had been victimized by poverty or bestial men. This Fair Lady had erred, but she was not beyond redemption. This archetype meshed well with petty offenders—ruined virgins, servants misused by masters, destitute inebriates, working girls who filched from employers. Thus, the reformers focused their attention not on felons but on misdemeanants, fallen women who might be saved—and on young white women, a group that seemed tractable and deserving. The type of offender with whom reformers proposed to work increased their credibility: skeptics who doubted that women were capable of handling "real" criminals were more willing to grant them permission to supervise misdemeanants. Then, too, reformers were no doubt more comfortable dealing with minor offenders instead of felons. Unlike the evil Dark Lady, misdemeanants could be viewed as bad children. They provided material for the motherly ministrations of reformers who sought to extend their domestic talents into the public sphere.[5]

Merger of the Two Systems

By the early 1930s, the women's reformatory movement had drawn to a close. In states where maintenance of gender roles had aroused deep concern, the movement had succeeded in establishing separate, feminized prisons for mildly deviant women. Prostitution—the phenomenon that had posed so great a challenge to middle-class notions of true womanhood—was no longer a source of national alarm. The social feminist movement that had supplied the leaders in women's prison reform had abated. And after the economic catastrophe of 1929, states that had been operating both a custodial unit and a reformatory for women decided they could no longer afford two institutions. Moreover, they needed the space that female felons had been occupying in or near their central prisons for expanding numbers of male prisoners. Some states (such as Ohio) had already combined their female custodial and reformatory populations. During the Depression, other states followed their example, transferring felons to reformatory grounds. In time, misdemeanants were forced out, leaving the reformatories to the populations of felons that inhabit them today.

As custodial and reformatory institutions for women merged about 1935, they combined their previously distinctive styles of differential treatment. To the merger custodialism brought its customary practice of neglecting female convicts. No longer were women in prison the object of intense rehabilitative efforts by women outside the walls; no longer did legislatures fund elaborate programs for female inmates. Women held in reformatories came to be disregarded, just as women in custodial institutions had always been, by a correctional system designed around the demands of the larger male population. Within prisons that had begun as reformatories, reformatory conventions also left a residue, a legacy of differential care based on gender. Women confined in these institutions continued to be treated as children; they were provided few opportunities for industrial training or for earning wages; their programs persisted in stressing personal grooming and domestic skills. As the two styles of treatment blended, they produced the type of care currently characteristic of women's prisons that originated as reformatories.

Over the last several decades, this type of care has also become characteristic of women's prisons that never passed through a reformatory stage. Traditionally, women in custodial prisons were treated similarly to men, if somewhat less well; but recently their care has come to resemble more closely that of women held in institutions that began as reformatories. This convergence appears in both architecture and program. When in the 1960s and 1970s states in the South and West established their first separate prison for women or built a second, some adopted a campus model, constructing unwalled institutions with low glass and concrete buildings.[6] These look less grim than the older, central prisons in which men continue to be confined. They may be nearly as tight in security, but because watchtowers and bars have been replaced with closed-circuit television and other technological surveillance mechanisms, these prisons physically look more like open reformatories than penitentiaries. In earlier periods, custodial institutions often required hard labor from women, assigning them to field work in the South, to prison factories elsewhere. But modern, campus-type custodial prisons provide few opportunities for work. In them, as in women's prisons that were once reformatories, "programs" often consist of little more than a classroom, an ironing board, and a hair dryer for the cosmetology course. The differences that used to distinguish custodial prisons from reformatories are disappearing, leaving us today with a relatively homogeneous women's prison system. Architecturally it looks more benign than the men's system; within the walls, it provides fewer and narrower programs.

PROSPECTS FOR THE FUTURE: THE COMING CRISIS

Today, the inequitable treatment experienced by female prisoners for nearly two centuries faces its first radical challenge. Within the past twenty years, incarcerated women have begun attacking disparities through the courts. Not only have they recognized that sex discrimination is grounds for legal battle; they have also identified, as matters for litigation, problems specific to female prisoners, most importantly the greater difficulties that childcare responsibilities place on them. Their new awareness and willingness to struggle has already thrown the correctional system into a severe dilemma, and there is every indication that in the years just ahead, women will press that system to the crisis point.

Successful challenges began in the mid-1960s, when women in prisons that had originated as reformatories publicly questioned the logic behind the longer sentences imposed on them than on men convicted of identical crimes. To encourage rehabilitation, those who founded reformatories had written into the establishing legislation provisions that made it possible to hold women on sentences with no minimums and uniform maximum terms. The reformatory movement itself was long dead by the 1960s, but in some states its sentencing structures had survived, continuing to regulate the terms of women. Thus while a man received a minimum and a maximum sentence determined (within statutory limits) by the judge, a woman convicted of the same offense received no minimum and a fixed maximum that could not be reduced through judicial discretion. "[E]ither on their faces or in practical application," writes Carolyn Temin in her analysis of reformatory laws, "they resulted in women getting longer sentences than men." In 1968, courts in Pennsylvania and Connecticut struck down differential sentencing laws, holding that these violated the equal protection clause of the fourteenth amendment by making women liable to terms longer than those of men convicted of the same crime.[7]

More recently, women have successfully challenged discriminatory treatment within the walls. Landmark decisions in this area, as summarized by a U.S. Comptroller General's report, include the following:

In *Glover* v. *Johnson* [478 F. Supp. 1075 (1979)] the court found that women inmates had fewer and inferior educational and vocational programs than did male inmates throughout the State [Michigan]. In addition, the court found women had been denied access to supplemental programs such as work pass incentive and good time. The court ruled that women prisoners have the right to a range and a quality of programing substantially equivalent to that offered men but based on the needs and interests of female inmates.

In *Barefield* v. *Leach,* No. 10282 (D. N.M. 1974), the court found the State [New Mexico] had failed to provide parity in vocational programing, assignment to wage paying work within the institution, and adequate facilities for vocational projects. The court ordered the State to achieve a reasonable parity.

In *Grosso* v. *Lally,* No. 4-74-447 (D. Md. 1977), the parties entered a consent decree in which the [Maryland] Division of Corrections agreed that programs, conditions, and opportunities for women would be "no less favorable, either quantitatively or qualitatively" than for men. Women were granted participation in community corrections and work release programs, equivalent eligibility requirements and wage rates, and vocational programs. The decree also allowed women's participation in educational and drug programs.[8]

These three decisions required states to raise women's treatment to the men's level. Varying that theme, a 1982 Kentucky decision declared that the state could not react more punitively to women than to men. In that case, a federal district court found the Kentucky state prison system guilty of sex discrimination because it subjected women, but not men, to a behavior modification program. This approach stripped incoming inmates of all privileges, which were then gradually reinstated as rewards for good behavior. (Such behavior modification systems can be found in other women's prisons and in institutions for children and the mentally retarded; officials continue to group women with incompetents and to assume that men have a greater need for autonomy.) The decision decreed that the Kentucky prison system must stop imposing more rules and greater deprivations on women than men. It further ordered that system to improve women's access to programs and legal aid.[9]

A final example indicates how such cases may link the issue of sex discrimination with the special problems of incarcerated mothers. This class action suit, filed in the Massachusetts Supreme Judicial Court in May 1983, claimed that the Department of Correction provided a greater variety of placements for men and that, as a result, women were denied access to their children. The case was brought by Maryann Chisholm, a widowed inmate who requested transfer from the women's prison at Framingham to a minimum security forestry camp near the home of her mother and five children. From this camp, she would have been eligible for furloughs and work-release, and thus able to spend more time with her family. Chisholm's request was denied because the statute creating forestry camps limited them to men. "The law states that any prisoner, except those at MCI-Framingham and prisoners convicted of first degree murder and child rapists can be transferred to the forestry camps," Chisholm's lawyer complained. "Women, like child rapists and murderers, are shunned. . . ." Chisholm's suit also claimed that female prisoners have less access than males to psychiatric care. A positive decision in this case (still pending at the time of this writing) would force Massachusetts to make major revisions in its prison system. Cases being filed at an accelerating rate by women across the country could have the same effect.[10]

Current litigation is thus pushing states to the decision point: will they allocate the funds necessary to counteract deeply ingrained patterns of sex discrimination? Despite favorable outcomes in some recent cases, it is by no means clear that states will conclude that women's interests outweigh their own. Instead of improving care of women, they may downgrade that of men—a route indicated as permissible by a California court in a 1979 prison sex discrimination case.[11] Administrative decisions in favor of lowgrade equality would impose particular difficulties on women, for outward evenhandedness enables prison systems to overlook women's special medical and childcare needs. Finally, even if states do attempt to upgrade treatment of women and deliver equitable (though not necessarily uniform) care, tight budgets may cripple their efforts.

Routes Toward More Equitable Treatment

Solutions do exist to these intertwined problems of gender devaluation and unequal numbers. One is to channel women out of prisons into community corrections—restitution programs, halfway houses, special treatment centers. As this study has shown, states have historically been all too quick to incarcerate women when less drastic solutions would have been less costly and more efficacious. Punishment of women has often been triggered by racial or moral fears rather than by seriousness of offense. Some women in prison are physically dangerous, but many are not. Arguably, even those serving time for homicide pose little threat to the community. Many killed a spouse or lover in the course of a quarrel, and some may have been acting in self-defense;[12] the likelihood of their killing someone else is negligible. These and other women, such as drug abusers, could be handled more constructively and less expensively in halfway houses or on probation; if left in the community, they could support themselves, care for their children, and receive better services. Greater emphasis on community corrections would reduce the number of women in prison, making more funds available for those left behind the walls.[13]

A second solution is for local, state, and federal prison systems to pool their resources for dealing with women. This would increase the number of institutions in which female prisoners of any one jurisdictional level might be confined, and thus more women could be placed near their families and support agencies. Cooperative measures would also enable women's institutions to specialize. When only one prison is available for a group, it must take security measures and provide staff for all programs. Increasing the number of institutions would relieve women's prisons of the impossible task of trying to meet many needs simultaneously, and it would supply female prisoners with a greater range of facilities.

A third response is co-corrections—the so-called "co-ed" prisons that, since 1971, have been established by the federal prison system and a number of states. In co-correctional institutions, male and female inmates live apart but share programs and space under one administration. The advantages of such an arrangement are numerous: activities and services previously available only to men become accessible to women as well; women's institutions no longer need to compete with men's for a share of limited budgets; institutional life becomes more like that of the outside world; and the threat of sex discrimination suits diminishes. According to its proponents, the co-correctional approach improves inmates' demeanor, leads to group counseling sessions that are more productive because they involve both sexes, and—through creating a more normal environment—eases the transition to freedom.[14]

Although co-corrections offers a cost-effective way to upgrade the quality of programs for incarcerated women, it is not a panacea for all the problems that have long beset this group. Most decisions to "go co-ed" have been made to solve bureaucratic needs (overcrowding at a men's institution and simultaneous underpopulation at a women's prison, for example) rather than out of concern to improve the lot of female prisoners. Decisions to maintain or terminate co-correctional programs are usually made by male administrators and tend to be dictated by concern for male prisoners, thus perpetuating the historical neglect of women's needs. Women may be used as tools for institutional control (for instance, co-corrections is viewed as a means for reducing the incidence of homosexual assault among male prisoners). Although women held today in mixed-sex institutions are better protected from sexual attacks than were women held in men's institutions in earlier times, the burden of prohibitions against sexual contact continues to fall on women. Moreover, co-correctional institutions provide more options for men than for women: men gain the option of mixed-sex facilities without losing that of prisons for their sex alone; but because female prisoners are much fewer in number, when a state "goes co-ed," women usually lose the possibility of being held at a prison for women only.[15]

These drawbacks do not mean that the idea of integrating resources for female and male prisoners should be abandoned; rather, they point to the need for refining the co-correctional concept. The most promising variant is the "coordinate" model recently adopted by Alaska. In the words of Esther Heffernan, who first proposed the coordinate system to that state, "the women's institution should be organizationally distinct, with classification levels, programs and policies . . . which reflect the differing functions of the women's institution. However, both the men['s] and women's units should be administratively coordinated, with the shared and common use of . . . food, educational, work, recreational, medical, and program area and services."[16] Alaska adopted the coordinate system because it had too few female prisoners to warrant "a full fledged co-correctional program."[17] The women's unit, built adjacent to an existing men's institution and named Meadow Creek, has its own library, classroom, and visiting and recreational areas. Though smaller than a full-scale prison, Meadow Creek thus has the potential for serving as a single-sex institution for women who elect against integration or become disciplinary problems when mixed with the men. According to a recent report, the inmates of the coordinated men's and women's units essentially share

one program, maximizing the cost effectiveness of that program and benefitting as individuals in the process. Men and women inmates are together in therapy and counseling groups, in religious activities, in academic classes and on some work assignments. They have two meals together each day. From two to three evenings per week they share the gymnasium as spectators or participants in volley ball and basketball.[18]

Key to the success of the Alaska experiment is the fact that each unit has its own superintendent (one male, one female). The dual superintendency is one of several precautions that have been taken to prevent the women's institution from becoming "a subservient dependency."[19]

All three of these proposals—more extensive use of community corrections; pooling of local, state, and federal resources; and coordinate institutions—offer at least a partial solution to the hitherto intractable problem of sex discrimination within the prison system. All three, however, are hampered by the same impediment: they are geared toward women. Both officials and the public balk at using community corrections more extensively for men, partly for the excellent reason that men are more violent; but it is doubtful that they would bother to develop community corrections for women only. Local, state, and federal officials probably will not make the effort necessary to merge their resources for female offenders. And the concept of coordinate prisons requires sharing power with women. There are few signs that the prison system or the public has enough commitment to equal rights to put these solutions into action. It is more likely that in the future, as in the past, incarcerated women will continue to be punished not only for their crimes but also for their minority statuses in a system planned for men.

APPENDIX A ||||||||||||||||||||||||||||||

Development of
The Women's Prison System,
1935–1980

It is far more difficult to obtain information on institutions established
during the third stage in the development of the women's prison system,
1935 to the present, than on those founded during the earlier stages. Many
nineteenth- and early twentieth-century prisons published bulky annual or
biennial reports full of details on inmates and management. Moreover, there
are a number of types of documents that can be used to supplement these
reports and check their accuracy. But since states began to centralize their
prison systems (a development that, generally speaking, began around 1900),
the quantity and quality of information on individual institutions has di-
minished. In addition, most states have stopped publishing full reports on
their prisons in legislative document series; instead, when departments of
correction issue annual reports, these tend to be mimeographed and difficult
to obtain. Relative to their predecessors, moreover, contemporary prisons
and correctional bureaucracies are reluctant to share information with out-
prison system in recent decades are created by the accelerating tendencies
to change the names and locations of women's prisons. Finally, in recent
years several state prisons for women, after having "gone co-ed" for a
period, have reverted to female-only status; it is difficult to classify such
institutions, for they are not really "new" prisons for women.

The following table presents a list of prisons for adult women established between 1935 and 1980. However, the table may be incomplete. No
outline of the recent development of the women's prison system can be
made with full confidence until researchers find ways to circumvent the

deficiencies in the currently available published data. In all probability, this picture will have to be built up piecemeal, by researchers in the individual states gaining the confidence of prison authorities and examining local records.

Prisons for Women Established 1935–1980, by Region

	ORIGINAL NAME	LOCATION	DATE ESTABLISHED	DATE OPENED
*Northeast**	—	—	—	—
Midwest				
Mo.	State Penitentiary for Women	Jefferson City	1955	[1955]
Mich.	Huron Valley Women's Facility	Ypsilanti	[1972]	1977
South				
Ky.	Women's Prison	Peewee Valley	[1938?], 1964	1938
Md.	Women's Prison	Jessup	1941	1940
W. Va.	State Prison for Women	Pence Springs	1947	1948
Ark.	State Reformatory for Women (moved in 1975 to Pine Bluff)	Cummins Farm	1951	1951
Fla.	(Orig. name not determined; later Florida Correctional Institution)	Lowell	[1956?]	1956
La.	Women's Prison	St. Gabriel	[1961?], 1970	1961
S.C.	Harbison Correctional Institution for Women (moved in 1975 to Columbia)	Irmo	[1964]	1964
Tenn.	Prison for Women	Nashville	1965	1965
Ga.	Rehabilitation Center for Women (moved in 1976 to Hardwick)	Milledgeville	[1968]	[1968]
Okla.	Women's Unit	McAlester	[1971]	[1971]
Okla.	Mabel Bassett Correctional Center	Oklahoma City	[1973]	1973
Tex.	Mountain View	Gatesville	[1975]	1975
Ky.	Daniel Boone Career Development Center	Burlington	[unkn.]	1976
Fla.	Broward Correctional Institution	Ft. Lauderdale	[1977?]	1977?

Prisons for Women Established 1935–1980, by Region (continued)

	ORIGINAL NAME	LOCATION	DATE ES-TABLISHED	DATE OPENED
West				
Nev.	(Orig. name not deter-mined; later Women's Correctional Center)	Carson City	[1961]	1964
Ore.	Women's Correctional Center	Salem	[1962], 1971	1965
Colo.	Women's Correctional Institution	Canon City	1967, 1975	1968
Wash.	Correctional Institu-tion for Women	Gig Harbor	1967	1971?
Wyo.	Women's Center	Evanston	[unkn.]	1977
N.M.	Radium Springs Center for Women	Radium Springs	[unkn.]	1978
Ariz.	Center for Women	Phoenix	[1979]	1980

*In 1968, Rhode Island transferred its adult female prisoners to the institution at Framingham, Mass.; in 1972, (according to the *Providence Journal*) or 1978 (according to the American Correctional Association's *Directory 1980*) it brought them back, creating a women's subdivision of the correctional center at Cranston by renovating part of the former Training School for Girls.

Sources: The table was compiled from a search for enabling legislation in the laws of the continental United States; internal documents of and correspondence with departments of corrections; the 1980 edition of the American Correctional Association's *Directory of Juvenile and Adult Correctional Departments, Institutions, Agencies and Paroling Authorities;* and other publications such as articles in the *Quarterly Journal of Corrections* and Glick and Neto's *National Study of Women's Correctional Programs (1977).*

Note: Sometimes the sources conflict with one another; question marks are used to indicate instances in which it proved impossible to confirm a date. Dates of establishment are bracketed in those cases in which the prison was established administratively rather than through legislative action. Dates of opening are bracketed in instances in which women were in fact held at that location before the institution opened as a women's prison. Co-correctional institutions, halfway houses, and pre-release centers are excluded from the table.

APPENDIX B ||||||||||||||||||||||||||||||

States in the Regional Divisions

For the investigation of regional differences in the development of women's prisons, regions were defined as follows:

Northeast

Connecticut
Maine
Massachusetts
New Hampshire
New Jersey
New York
Pennsylvania
Rhode Island
Vermont

South

Alabama
Arkansas
Delaware
Florida
Georgia
Kentucky
Louisiana

Maryland
Mississippi
North Carolina
Oklahoma
South Carolina
Tennessee
Texas
Virginia
West Virginia

Midwest

Illinois
Indiana
Iowa
Kansas
Michigan
Minnesota
Missouri
Nebraska

North Dakota
Ohio
South Dakota
Wisconsin

West

Arizona
California
Colorado
Idaho
Montana
Nevada
New Mexico
Oregon
Utah
Washington
Wyoming

Note: The study excluded Alaska and Hawaii.

APPENDIX C |||||||||||||||||||||||||||||

Offense Categories—Definitions

VIOLENT CRIMES
Accessory to murder, arson, assault, attempted murder, manslaughter, murder, and robbery. *Violent Crimes, Other* (Tables 5.2 and 5.3) include poisoning (Tenn. Pen.); attempted kidnaping, attempted suicide, kidnaping, maiming, poisoning, possession of firearms after a felony conviction, and rape, second degree (Auburn); accessory to rape of a minor, carrying concealed weapon, poisoning, stoning train, and throwing stones at a steam vessel (Ohio Pen.); attempted suicide and rape, second degree (Albion); carrying concealed weapon, kidnaping, maiming, rape and incest (one case), and stabbing (Ohio Ref. for Women).

PROPERTY CRIMES
Burglary, concealing/receiving stolen property, forgery/counterfeiting/passing bad checks, grand larceny, larceny, and petit larceny. *Property Crimes, Other* (Tables 5.2 and 5.3) include felonious breach of trust, horse theft, obtaining money under false pretenses, and stealing corn (Tenn. Pen.); blackmail and extortion (Auburn); blackmail, buying stolen property, embezzlement, extortion, horse stealing, obtaining goods through false pretenses, and pocket picking (Ohio Pen.); thieving and defrauding (Albion); auto theft, blackmail, embezzlement, extortion, obtaining goods/money un-

der false pretenses, pocket picking, and thieving (Ohio Ref. for Women).

PUBLIC ORDER CRIMES

Aiding and abetting carnal knowledge of a minor, aiding and abetting violation of age of consent law, attempted abduction, attempt to entice for immoral purposes, bigamy, crime against nature, incest, loitering, mayhem, miscegenation, and narcotics law violation (Tenn. Pen.); bigamy, compulsory prostitution, narcotics law violation, sodomy, unlawful marriage, and vagrancy (Auburn); abortion, aiding and abetting carnal knowledge of a minor, attempted abortion, bigamy, enticing minor into house of ill fame, incest, inducing illicit intercourse, malicious mischief, nonsupport of children, and obscenity (Ohio Pen.).

For the reformatories, public order crimes were classified by categories as follows: *Alcohol-related offenses* include drunk and disorderly, habitual drunkenness, and intoxication (Albion); intoxication, possessing liquor, and violation of liquor law (Ohio. Ref. for Women). *Childcare-related offenses* include abandonment, abduction, child neglect, corrupting/endangering morals of a child, and enticing minor into house of ill fame (Albion); abandonment, contributing to delinquency, neglecting one's child, and nonsupport (Ohio Ref. for Women). *Disorderly conduct* includes disorderly person, disturbing the peace, malicious mischief, public nuisance, and vagrancy as well as disorderly conduct charges (Albion); disorderly person, loitering, malicious mischief, and vagrancy as well as disorderly conduct charges (Ohio Ref. for Women). *Drug-related offenses* include "drugs" and sale of hypodermic needle (Albion); "drugs" and violation of narcotics law (Ohio Ref. for Women). *Marriage-related offenses* include adultery and bigamy (both institutions). *Sex-related offenses* include exposure of person, frequenting disorderly house, immorality, keeping house of ill-repute, prostitution, and waywardness (Albion); fornication, immorality, inducing illicit intercourse, keeping disorderly house, pandering, prostitution, and unlawful transportation of a female (Ohio Ref. for Women). *Status-type offenses* include delinquency, keeping bad company, truancy, under immoral influence, ungovernable child, and without guardianship (Albion); delinquency (Ohio Ref. for Women). *Public Order Crimes, Other* (Table 5.3) include concealing birth of a child, saloon visiting, and unlawful entry (clearly distinguished from burglary) (Albion); abortion, suffering gaming, and using obscene language (Ohio Ref. for Women).

OTHER OFFENSES Aiding escape, attempt to commit a felony, attempted perjury, false pretenses, felony, perjury, transporting (Tenn. Pen.); aiding escape, bribery, criminal anarchy, false pretenses, and perjury (Auburn); aiding escape, impersonation, perjury, and transporting (Ohio Pen.); aiding escape, escape, libel, perjury, violations of various city ordinances, violation of probation, and violation of special sections of New York State Penal Law (Albion); aiding escape, contempt of court, false pretenses, habitual offender, harboring a felon, and issuing a false statement (Ohio Ref. for Women).

APPENDIX D ||||||||||||||||||||||||||||||

Data Collection From Registries of Prisoners: Materials and Sampling Procedures

To supplement information on prisoners in official reports, data were collected directly from the prisoner registries of five institutions:

(1) Tennessee State Penitentiary, Nashville
(2) New York State Prison for Women at Auburn
(3) New York Western House of Refuge at Albion
(4) Ohio Penitentiary, Columbus
(5) Ohio Reformatory for Women, Marysville.

Several considerations dictated selection of these institutions. First, geographical diversity seemed desirable; thus one state was chosen from the South, one from the Northeast, and one from the Midwest. (The study originally was to use data collected by other researchers from California prisoner registries, but these materials were not computerized in time for inclusion.) Second, the plan called for comparison of the demographic, offense, and sentence characteristics of women held in custodial institutions and reformatories within the same state; both Ohio (which held female state prisoners at its penitentiary *until* opening of its reformatory) and New York (which *simultaneously* held women at the Auburn prison and Albion reformatory) provided this opportunity. (Tennessee, like most southern states, did not establish a women's reformatory.) Third, communication with archivists indicated that the prisoner registries for the five institutions in

199

these three states were not only available but also in relatively good condition. (Unfortunately, examination of the records of the Ohio Reformatory for Women revealed that these documents were less rich in detail than those of the other institutions.)

Data collection procedures, including sampling methods, were influenced by a number of factors: the format of the materials (for example, whether female prisoners were listed together in ledgers or rather, as at the penitentiaries of Ohio and Tennessee, included in predominantly male listings, making it necessary to search for female names and other identifiers); the extent of the materials (the more female cases, the greater the need to use skip-intervals); and limitations on the coders' time. About fifteen days were allotted for data collection from the registries of each institution. The first two days were spent assessing the materials and coding some cases. Estimates were then made of the total number of female cases available and the amount of time it would take to locate and code a single case. Division of the first figure by the second gave an idea of how many cases could be covered in the remaining time. At that point, a decision was made whether to sample and how many cases to skip when sampling.

In some instances, constraints posed by materials, time, and research questions made it necessary to skip years as well as cases. Data were collected on female prisoners incarcerated for periods five years before and after the opening of new units or institutions for women, for the original plan (which proved partially infeasible) was to determine if the opening of a new unit or institution affected characteristics such as offense type and time served. (This original plan also explains the use of periods of unequal duration in tables and commentaries giving breakdowns by period of commitment.) It also seemed advisable to cover roughly the same periods for all prisons. Such considerations governed determination of years skipped when it was impossible to collect data on the entire sequence of female cases. Data collection stopped with cases received in 1934, a point about which two of the institutions closed and one that appeared to be a major dividing point in the development of the women's prison system. In the instance of the Ohio Reformatory for Women, however, an enthusiastic assistant continued coding cases received into 1943. Figure 1 illustrates the periods covered and sampling procedures.

> Age at reception
> Date of birth
> Race
> Place of birth
> Parents' place of birth
> Prior occupation
> Religion

Marital status
Conviction offense(s)
Sentence
Type of sentence (simple, concurrent, or consecutive; extra punishment
    such as fine)
Date received
Date sentenced
Prior record
Date released
Method of release (death, escape, pardon, parole, etc.)
Crime partners

A few federal prisoners were held at several of the prisons. They were excluded from the samples, since the study was concerned with state prisoners only.

In what follows, the data sources and sampling procedures are identified for each of the five institutions.

TENNESSEE STATE PENITENTIARY

The primary source used for the study of female prisoners in Tennessee was the Tennessee State Archives' series of prisoner registries. These consist of volumes labeled K through T, plus a number of subsidiary volumes. Volumes U and following are held by the Department of Correction; use was made of volume U in addition to those in the archives.

The registries present a nearly unbroken series of consecutive admissions to the penitentiary, both female and male. There is some overlap among the earlier volumes, and the advent of a new clerk was sometimes accompanied by a new and idiosyncratic method of case enumeration. However, there was no change in the basic format, volume U recording data on the same variables, and in the same order, as did volume K. Thus the records are uniform as well as nearly complete.

Data were collected on a total of 965 cases, using every case received during the following periods:

1831 through 1874 (first female not committed until 1840)
1879 through 1905
1912 through 1922
1929 through 1934.

That is, for Tennessee, years were skipped, but no cases were skipped within the sampling periods.

The Tennessee State Archives hold a rich variety of other materials that supplement the prisoner registries. Particularly tantalizing were State Supreme Court case records that reveal the particulars of offenses listed merely as "larceny," "murder," and so on in the registries; some of these were used for Chapter 5.

NEW YORK STATE PRISON FOR WOMEN AT AUBURN

The New York State Archives include in their holdings a number of volumes relating to the State Prison for Women operated at Auburn between 1893 and 1933. Of these, the most useful were the following:

☐ Register of Convicts Received between May 1893 and March 1918

☐ Register of Convicts Received between August 1928 and June 1933

☐ Register of Convicts Discharged between June 1893 and December 1919

☐ Bertillon Register on inmates admitted from July 1909 until the prison's closing in 1933

☐ Commutation Ledger covering October 1920 to April 1930.

These volumes were used, sometimes simultaneously, to piece together records of prisoners included in the sample.

Information was collected on a total of 669 cases. Every case received from May to December 1893 was covered; these first cases included women convicted earlier but held in county penitentiaries until the opening of the State Prison for Women made possible their transfer to a state institution. Because they apparently do not appear in any other state data source, it seemed advisable to collect as much information as possible on these convicts. Beginning with January 1, 1894, the sample included every other admission (odd numbers). In all, the following periods were covered:

1893 through 1903
1912 through 1922
1926 through 1933.

Special samples were taken from the Bertillon register for specifics on some property and all homicide cases.

NEW YORK WESTERN HOUSE OF REFUGE AT ALBION

The New York State Archives hold seven volumes of prisoner registries of the Albion reformatory, covering the period from January 1894 (when the first inmate was received) through June of 1931 (when the institution ceased to function as a reformatory). These records are complete, highly detailed, and in excellent condition.

Data were collected on a total of 1,583 cases, using every other case (odd numbers) received. Owing to student assistance with coding, in the case of Albion it was possible to cover every year.

In addition to the prisoner registries, the archives hold an evidently complete set of case files on Albion's inmates—167 cubic feet of them, each in a folder tied with a bright pink ribbon. These case files, which include letters from and to inmates (the prison's administration exercised tight control over correspondence), photographs, test scores, and other documents, provide an extremely rich source of information on reformatory inmates and their reactions to institutional efforts to rehabilitate them. Although it was not possible to examine these case files systematically, when time allowed reference was made to some of unusual interest.

OHIO PENITENTIARY

The Ohio State Archives hold an excellent series of registries on prisoners (male and female) admitted to the Ohio penitentiary. There are twenty-one volumes in this series, covering admissions from 1834 through March 1900. Each volume is indexed, but it proved easier to identify female cases by looking for the "W" with which they were tagged in the registries themselves. In addition to this series, the archives hold a volume, clearly a copy of an earlier and now-lost registry, which records details on prisoners received from 1815 to 1834; this was used along with the series of registries. Registries for cases received after May 1900 (volumes 22 onward) are held by the Ohio penitentiary: these were used to pick up where the archives' series leaves off.

Information was collected on a total of 609 cases, using every female case admitted from 1888 through 1916 (after which women were no longer received at the penitentiary unless slated for execution) except for cases admitted from May 1910 through December 1911. This interval was skipped owing to unexpected lack of time; the original calculation of the probable number of females committed to the Ohio penitentiary proved to be an underestimation.

OHIO REFORMATORY FOR WOMEN AT MARYSVILLE

The Ohio State Archives also hold a two-volume set of registries for prisoners admitted to the reformatory at Marysville. The first prisoner committed directly to the reformatory was received on September 1, 1916. However, the reformatory also received, at first, transfers from the Ohio penitentiary (women committed as early as 1913), and data on these women are recorded in the first volume of the Marysville registries. The first registry covers cases committed originally to the penitentiary or directly to the reformatory between May 1913 and December 1926; volume 2 covers cases committed between January 1927 and April 1943. These records, though useful, are not nearly as detailed and complete as those of New York's reformatory at Albion. Moreover, they are often confusing about sentence length and time served.

Information was collected on a total of 780 cases, using every fifth case committed (either originally to the penitentiary or directly to the reformatory) in the following years:

1913 through 1921
1926 through 1943 (March).

Notes

Abbreviations used in the Notes:
AR—annual report
BR—biennial report
In both cases, the date following the abbreviation is that of the last year spanned by the report. When such reports form a regular part of a series of legislative or organizational documents, no fuller citation is given.

NOTES TO PREFACE

1. James A. Inciardi, Alan A. Block, and Lyle A. Hallowell, *Historical Approaches to Crime: Research Strategies and Issues* (Beverly Hills: Sage, 1977), p. 9.

2. See, for example, Ralph R. Arditi, Fredrick Goldberg, Jr., M. Martha Hartle, John H. Peters, and William R. Phelps, "The Sexual Segregation of American Prisons," *Yale Law Journal* 82 (1973): 1229–73; U.S. Comptroller General, *Women in Prison: Inequitable Treatment Requires Action* (Washington, D.C.: Government Printing Office, 1980).

3. Estelle B. Freedman, *Their Sisters' Keepers: Women's Prison Reform in America, 1830–1930* (Ann Arbor: University of Michigan Press, 1981); Eugenia C. Lekker-kerker, *Reformatories for Women in the United States* (Batavia, Holland: Bij J. B. Wolters' Uitgevers-Maatschappij, 1931); Steven L. Schlossman, *Love and the American Delinquent: The Theory and Practice of "Progressive" Juvenile Justice, 1825–1920* (Chicago: University of Chicago Press, 1977); Barbara Brenzel, "Lancaster Industrial School for Girls: A Social Portrait of a Nineteenth-Century Reform School for Girls," *Feminist Studies* 3 (1/2) (Fall 1975): 40–53, and "Domestication as Reform: A Study of the Socialization of Wayward Girls, 1856–1905," *Harvard*

Educational Review 50 (2) (May 1980): 196–213; Mark Thomas Connelly, *The Response to Prostitution in the Progressive Era* (Chapel Hill: University of North Carolina Press, 1980); Ruth Rosen, *The Lost Sisterhood: Prostitution in America, 1900–1918* (Baltimore: Johns Hopkins University Press, 1982).

4. Christopher R. Adamson, "Punishment after Slavery: Southern State Penal Systems, 1865–1890," *Social Problems* 30 (5) (June 1983): 555–69; John A. Conley, "Economics and the Social Reality of Prisons," *Journal of Criminal Justice* 10 (1) (1982): 25–35; Michael Stephen Hindus, *Prison and Plantation: Crime, Justice, and Authority in Massachusetts and South Carolina, 1767–1878* (Chapel Hill: University of North Carolina Press, 1980); Patricia O'Brien, *The Promise of Punishment: Prisons in Nineteenth-Century France* (Princeton: Princeton University Press, 1982).

NOTES TO INTRODUCTION

1. See, for example, Norman Johnston, *The Human Cage: A Brief History of Prison Architecture* (New York: Walker and Co., 1973); Blake McKelvey, *American Prisons: A Study in American Social History prior to 1915* (orig. 1936; repr. Montclair, N.J.: Patterson Smith, 1972); and David J. Rothman, *The Discovery of the Asylum: Social Order and Disorder in the New Republic* (Boston: Little, Brown and Co., 1971).

2. On the difference between the types of offenses for which men and women were sent to reformatories, see Lekkerkerker, *Reformatories for Women*, pp. 9–10, and Nicole Hahn Rafter, "Chastizing the Unchaste: Social Control Functions of a Women's Reformatory, 1894–1931," in Stanley Cohen and Andrew Scull, eds., *Social Control and the State: Historical and Comparative Essays* (Oxford: Martin Robertson, 1983), note 6 and accompanying text. As later chapters explain, some reformatories for women held felons from the start, but in the early years, most received mainly misdemeanants and lesser offenders.

3. For example, military training and vigorous "physical culture" constituted important aspects of the program at New York's men's reformatory at Elmira; see Zebulon Reed Brockway, *Fifty Years of Prison Service: An Autobiography* (orig. 1912; repr. Montclair, N.J.: Patterson Smith, 1969).

4. Indiana, Massachusetts, and New York opened women's reformatories before 1900; the last established two nineteenth-century institutions of this type, one at Hudson and the other at Albion. In addition, New York founded a third women's reformatory at Bedford in 1892, but this institution did not receive prisoners until 1901. For a list of reformatories opened between 1900 and 1935, see Table 3.1.

5. This change occurred slowly. Well after 1935, women continued to be sent to state prisons for less serious offenses than men. In some states, they were liable to longer terms until quite recently; see Carolyn Engel Temin, "Discriminatory Sentencing of Women Offenders: The Argument for ERA in a Nutshell," in Susan K. Datesman and Frank R. Scarpitti, eds., *Women, Crime, and Justice* (New York: Oxford University Press, 1980): 255–76.

6. Maryann Bird, "The Women in Prison: No Escape From Stereotyping," *New York Times*, June 23, 1979, p. 14; U.S. Comptroller General, *Women in Prison*, cover page. For other analyses of the special problems of women's prisons, see Ralph R. Arditi et al., "The Sexual Segregation of American Prisons"; U.S. General Accounting Office, *Female Offenders: Who Are They and What Are the*

Problems Confronting Them? (Washington, D.C.: General Accounting Office, 1979); and Ruth M. Glick and Virginia V. Neto, *National Study of Women's Correctional Programs* (Washington, D.C.: National Institute of Law Enforcement and Criminal Justice, LEAA, U.S. Department of Justice, June 1977).

7. U.S. Comptroller General, *Women in Prison*, p. ii.

8. Glick and Neto, *National Study of Women's Correctional Programs*, p. xxiv; U.S. General Accounting Office; *Female Offenders*, p. 68; U.S. Comptroller General, *Women in Prison*, p. i ("many officials").

NOTES TO CHAPTER 1

1. Rothman, *Discovery of the Asylum*, p. 105. On the debate about the origins of the penitentiary, see Michael Ignatieff, "State, Civil Society, and Total Institutions: A Critique of Recent Social Histories of Punishment," in Michael Tonry and Norval Morris, eds., *Crime and Justice: An Annual Review of Research*, vol. 3 (Chicago: University of Chicago Press, 1981), pp. 153–92.

2. For exceptions to the rule of disregard of women within penitentiaries, see W. David Lewis, *From Newgate to Dannemora: The Rise of the Penitentiary in New York, 1796–1848* (Ithaca: Cornell University Press, 1965); and McKelvey, *American Prisons*.

3. New York, Auburn State Prison, *AR 1832:* 17 (emphasis in original).

4. New York, Inspectors of State Prisons, *An Account of the State Prison or Penitentiary House, in the City of New-York* (New York: Isaac Colling and Son, 1801), p. 18 (both quotations).

5. For the complaints, see New York Committee on State Prisons, *Report of the Committee on State Prisons, relative to a prison for female convicts* (New York Sen. Doc. No. 68, 1835), p. 1 (no classification, "constant . . . intercourse"); New York, Mount Pleasant State Prison, *AR 1835:* 5 (food), *AR 1836:* 5 (need for a matron); New York Committee on State Prisons, *Report of the Committee on State Prisons* (New York Sen. Doc. No. 32, 1833), p. 3 (cholera and ensuing events). New York, Mount Pleasant State Prison, *AR 1836:* 5, notes the desire of New York City officials to rid themselves of the women at Bellevue.

6. Harriet Martineau, *Retrospect of Western Travel*, vol. 1 (London: Saunders and Otley, 1838), pp. 124–25.

7. On the unfortunate pregnancy of Rachel Welch, see Lewis, *From Newgate to Dannemora*, pp. 94–95.

8. On the two Ohio state prisons that preceded its penitentiary, see Clara Belle Hicks, "The History of Penal Institutions in Ohio to 1850," *Ohio State Archeological and Historical Society Publications* 33 (1924): 359–426; Jacob H. Studer, *Columbus, Ohio: Its History, Resources, and Progress* (Columbus: n.p., 1873); and George H. Twiss, ed., "Journal of Cyrus P. Bradley," *Ohio Archeological and Historical Publications* 15 (1906): 240–42.

According to Orlando F. Lewis, *The Development of American Prisons and Prison Customs, 1776–1845* (orig. 1922; repr. Montclair, N.J.: Patterson Smith, 1967), p. 262, Ohio's prison of 1818 included five underground, unheated cells, and it was here that the women were kept. No other historian of the building refers to women in the underground cells, however, and according to William Crawford's plan of the institution (*Report on the Penitentiaries of the United States,* [orig. 1835; repr. Montclair, N.J.: Patterson Smith, 1969], Plan 18), its women resided in a small building inside the yard.

9. Ohio Penitentiary, *AR 1850:* 133.

10. Gerrish Barrett as quoted by Lewis, *Development of American Prisons and Prison Customs,* p. 263; D. L. Dix, *Remarks on Prisons and Prison Discipline in the United States,* 2d ed. (orig. 1845; repr. Montclair, N.J.: Patterson Smith, 1967), p. 48; Sarah Maria Victor, *The Life Story of Sarah M. Victor for Sixty Years. Convicted of Murdering Her Brother, Sentenced to be Hung, Had Sentence Commuted, Passed Nineteen Years in Prison, Yet is Innocent* (Cleveland: Williams Publishing Co., 1887), p. 317.

11. Dan J. Morgan, *Historical Lights and Shadows of the Ohio State Penitentiary and Horrors of the Death Trap* (Columbus: Champlin Printing Company, 1895), p. 91; Victor, *The Life Story,* pp. 298, 326, 327; Ohio Penitentiary, *AR 1880:* 91. The humming-bird is described in Victor, *The Life Story,* pp. 324–35.

12. Tennessee State Penitentiary, *BR 1859:* 232. On the Tennessee penitentiary in the early and mid-nineteenth century, see Jesse Crawford Crowe, "The Origin and Development of Tennessee's Prison Problem, 1831–1871," *Tennessee Historical Quarterly* 15 (2) (June 1956): 111–35; and E. Bruce Thompson, "Reforms in the Penal System of Tennessee, 1820–1850," *Tennessee Historical Quarterly* 1 (4) (December 1942): 291–308.

13. Tennessee State Archives, *Convict Record Book 1831–1874,* Record Group 25, Ser. 12, v. 86; Messages of Governor James K. Polk, Tennessee General Assembly, *House Journal,* 24th Assembly, 1st sess., 1841–1842: 23, as quoted in Crowe, "Origin and Development of Tennessee's Prison Problem," p. 117.

14. For a hint of forced prostitution at the Tennessee penitentiary late in the century, see Tennessee, *Acts and Resolutions 1897,* Ch. 125, sec. 28, making it a misdemeanor for any prison officer "to hire or let any female convict to any person on the outside as cook, washerwoman, or for any other purpose."

15. Montana and Utah. Utah opened two work-release facilities for women in the late 1970s but apparently continued to send women to the state prison until near the end of their terms. See American Correctional Association, *Directory 1980* (College Park, Md.: American Correctional Association, 1980), pp. 139, 233. Cf. Joan Potter, "In Prison, Women are Different," *Corrections Magazine* (December 1978): 15 ("Montana's 12 women are divided between a separate Life Skills Center in Billings and a coed facility in Missoula").

16. Francis Lieber, "Translator's Preface" to Gustave de Beaumont and Alexis de Tocqueville, *On the Penitentiary System in the United States and Its Application in France* (orig. 1833; repr. Carbondale: Southern Illinois University Press, 1964), p. 8.

17. Crawford, *Report on the Penitentiaries,* Appendix; Dix, *Remarks on Prisons,* pp. 107–8.

18. Beaumont and Tocqueville, *On the Penitentiary System in the United States,* p. 72.

19. Lieber, "Translator's Preface," p. 8.

20. Ibid., p. 12.

21. Crawford, *Report on the Penitentiaries,* pp. 26–27.

22. New York, Mount Pleasant State Prison, *AR 1841:* 28 (emphasis as in original). For reviews of the literature on current patterns of female crime, current explanations of female crime patterns, and the evidence for and against judicial chivalry, see Nicolette Parisi, "Exploring Female Crime Patterns: Problems and Prospects" and "Are Females Treated Differently? A Review of the Theories and Evidence on Sentencing and Parole Decisions," both in Nicole Hahn Rafter and Elizabeth A. Stanko, eds., *Judge, Lawyer, Victim, Thief: Women, Gender Roles, and Criminal Justice* (Boston: Northeastern University Press, 1982).

23. W. A. Coffey, *Inside Out, or an Interior View of the New-York State Prison* (New York, 1823), p. 61, as quoted in Lewis, *From Newgate to Dannemora,* p. 38; E. C. Wines and Theodore W. Dwight, *Report on the Prisons and Reformatories of the United States and Canada* (Albany: van Benthuysen & Sons, 1867), p. 71.

24. Dix, *Remarks on Prisons,* p. 108; Crawford, *Report on the Penitentiaries,* Appendix, p. 68.

25. Lieber, "Translator's Preface," pp. 9–11; Mary Carpenter, *Our Convicts,* vol. 1 (orig. 1864; repr. Montclair, N.J.: Patterson Smith, 1969), p. 207; Caesar Lombroso and William Ferrero, *The Female Offender* (first English ed. 1895; repr. New York: D. Appleton & Company, 1915). On the troublesome women in Ohio, see note 10 and accompanying text. On the archetype of the Dark Lady and its influence, see Paula Blanchard, *Margaret Fuller: From Transcendentalism to Revolution* (New York: Delacorte Press, 1978), pp. 193–94; and Rafter and Stanko, *Judge, Lawyer, Victim, Thief,* pp. 2–7 and chapter 11. Lewis's "The Ordeal of the Unredeemables" (*From Newgate to Dannemora,* chapter 7) also deals with nineteenth-century conceptions of female criminals and their effects upon prison treatment.

26. Lieber, "Translator's Preface," p. 13.

27. Wines and Dwight, *Report on the Prisons,* pp. 123–24.

28. On Mary Weed, see Negley K. Teeters, *The Cradle of the Penitentiary: The Walnut Street Jail at Philadelphia, 1773–1835* (Philadelphia: Pennsylvania Prison Society, 1955), pp. 47, 61.

29. Dix, *Remarks on Prisons,* p. 107.

30. Ibid., pp. 62–63. For background on the Association of Women Friends, see Teeters, *Cradle of the Penitentiary,* p. 107.

31. See Elizabeth Fry, *Memoir of the Life of Elizabeth Fry with Extracts from her Journal and Letters,* two volumes edited by two of her daughters (Philadelphia: J. W. Moore, 1847); and, for a discussion of the Female Department of the Prison Association of New York, see Freedman, *Their Sisters' Keepers,* pp. 28–35.

32. New York, *Laws of 1835,* Ch. 104.

33. New York, *Laws of 1841,* Ch. 200, sec. 3.

34. Wines and Dwight, *Report on the Prisons,* p. 107.

35. Lewis, *From Newgate to Dannemora,* p. 177.

36. Georgiana Bruce Kirby, *Years of Experience: An Autobiographical Narrative* (orig. 1887; repr. New York: AMS Press, 1971), pp. 190–91.

37. New York, Mount Pleasant State Prison, *AR of the Inspectors 1846* (New York Sen. Doc. No. 16, 1846): Appendix D, p. 94 (first quotation); Kirby, *Years of Experience,* pp. 193, 199, 218.

38. New York, Mount Pleasant State Prison, *AR of the Inspectors 1846:* Appendix D, p. 88 (Farnham's retort).

39. Tennessee, *Acts of the General Assembly 1843–44,* Resolution No. 16; New Jersey, *Report of the Commissioners to Examine the Various Systems of Prison Discipline and Propose an Improved Plan* (Trenton: The True American Office, 1869), p. 5; Prison Association of New York, *AR 1846:* 48.

40. Dix, *Remarks on Prisons,* pp. 13–14 (includes the Edmonds report; emphasis as in original).

41. Despite its mild name, the shower bath was one of the prison's cruelest punishments. The prisoner was bombarded by a powerful stream of water until close to drowning.

42. New York, Mount Pleasant State Prison, *Report of the Inspectors of the Mount Pleasant State Prison in answer to a resolution of the Assembly* (New York Ass. Doc. No. 139, 1846): Appendix C, pp. 113–14.

43. Clifford M. Young, *Women's Prisons Past and Present and Other New York State Prison History* (Elmira Reformatory: The Summary Press, 1932), p. 13 (ruling of 1865); New York, *Laws of 1877,* Ch. 172, secs. 1 and 2.

NOTES TO CHAPTER 2

1. See, for example, Joseph F. Scott, "American Reformatories for Male Adults," chapter 5 in Charles Richmond Henderson, ed., *Penal and Reformatory Institutions* (New York: Charities Publication Committee, 1910); and Brockway, *Fifty Years,* part II.

2. Barbara Welter, "The Cult of True Womanhood: 1820–1860," *American Quarterly* 18 (Summer 1966), pp. 151–74, defines true womenhood in terms of "four cardinal virtues—piety, purity, submissiveness and domesticity" (p. 152). Although Welter's analysis stops at 1860, the cult lasted through the turn of the century; see chapter 7.

3. Previously women were incarcerated in a building on the grounds of the state prison at Jackson, where some continued to be held until 1873.

4. Wines and Dwight, *Report on the Prisons and Reformatories,* p. 341.

5. Brockway, *Fifty Years,* pp. 106–7. Permission was "readily obtained" because, by using profits from the House of Correction, Brockway was able to construct and operate the shelter without extra cost to the city.

6. On the three years law, see Brockway, *Fifty Years,* chapter 8, and Detroit House of Correction, *AR 1869:* 11.

7. Detroit House of Correction, *AR 1869:* 46 (groups held by the shelter).

8. Ibid., *AR 1868:* 7.

9. Ibid., p. 44.

10. Ibid., p. 7.

11. McKelvey, *American Prisons,* p. 66.

12. Brockway, *Fifty Years,* pp. 108–9.

13. New York, Western House of Refuge for Women, Inmate Admission Ledgers (New York State Archives, Series 520B), Inmate No. 107; see chapter 7, text accompanying note 25, for a fuller quotation from this registry entry.

14. Emma A. Hall as quoted in Brockway, *Fifty Years*, p. 410.

15. Brockway, *Fifty Years*, pp. 110–11. Although the House of Shelter closed in 1874, women continued to be held at the Detroit House of Correction until 1977.

16. The proceedings of this historic meeting, together with a list of its delegates, the principles they endorsed, and a description of the so-called Irish system of penal discipline, were published as E. C. Wines, ed., *Transactions of the National Congress on Penitentiary and Reformatory Discipline* (Albany: Weed, Parsons and Company, 1871). This was the first convention of the body known today as the American Correctional Association; the ACA reprinted the volume in 1970 (N.p: n.p.).

17. Wines, *Transactions*, pp. 543, 547.

18. Ibid., p. 542 ("will of the convict"). Brockway's address to the convention, the most influential paper delivered during the meetings, was titled "The Ideal of the True Prison System for a State."

19. Indiana State Prison South, *AR 1869:* 7, *AR 1873:* 11; Sara F. Keely, "The Organization and Discipline of the Indiana Women's Prison," National Prison Association, *Proceedings 1898:* 276; Lekkerkerker, *Reformatories for Women*, pp. 98–99 (intermixture of the delinquent girls); *Indiana House Journal*, April 14, 1869 (Indianapolis: Alexander H. Conner, 1869), p. 55 ("very grave charges").

20. Rhoda M. Coffin, "Women's Prisons," National Prison Association, *Proceedings 1885:* 189.

21. Ibid., pp. 188–89 (capitalization as in original); undated note of ca. February 1908 by Charles F. Coffin (Lilly Library Archives, Earlham College).

22. Indiana Reformatory Institution for Women and Girls (hereafter IRIWG), *AR 1871:* 6; Lekkerkerker, *Reformatories for Women*, p. 99 (quotations). The girls were removed in 1907.

23. Indiana General Assembly, *Laws of 1869*, Ch. 32, sec. 7.

24. IRIWG, *AR 1877:* 5.

25. Lewis Jordan in IRIWG, *AR 1876:* 51–54; IRIWG, *AR 1877:* 5. Also see Mary Coffin Johnson, ed., *Rhoda M. Coffin: Her Reminiscences, Addresses, Papers and Ancestry* (New York: The Grafton Press, 1910), pp. 157–59.

26. Coffin, "Women's Prisons," p. 190; IRIWG, *AR 1873:* 15; Keely, "Organization and Discipline," p. 276. These accounts suggest that the reports of brutal sexual victimization that originally inspired establishment of the women's prison may have been somewhat exaggerated. But on the other hand, conditions may have improved at Jeffersonville in the years between the scandals of the 1860s and the opening of the reformatory in 1873.

27. Isabel C. Barrows, "The Reformatory Treatment of Women in the United States," in Henderson, *Penal and Reformatory Institutions*, pp. 153, 152; Keely, "Organization and Discipline," p. 278 ("not a weapon").

28. IRIWG, *AR 1874:* 16 ("it is best"), *AR 1875:* 27 ("to occupy the position"), *AR 1873:* 27 ("womanly examples").

29. Sarah E. Dexter, *Recollections of Hannah B. Chickering* (Cambridge, Mass.: Riverside Press, 1881), p. 317.

30. New York State Board of Charities, *AR 1897:* 61.

31. New York, Western House of Refuge for Women, *AR 1894:* 7.

32. See, for example, Barrows, "The Reformatory Treatment of Women," pp. 160, 165.

33. According to Lekkerkerker, *Reformatories for Women,* p. 96, the territory of the Massachusetts reformatory was supplemented by "the large farm of some hundreds of acres which was bought, put in order, and worked under her [Ellen C. Johnson, an early superintendent] private means."

34. See Introduction, note 2. When males were committed to adult reformatories for sex- or family-related crimes, their offenses were bigamy, transporting of a female for immoral purposes, nonsupport, and the like—not the "fornication or insubordination" types of offenses for which many women were sent to reformatories. According to the records of the Ohio reformatory for men at Mansfield (held by the Ohio State Archives, Columbus), some early twentieth century prisoners had been convicted of the status offense of "juvenile delinquency." These, however, were cases of males under eighteen years of age who had in fact committed felonies (breaking and entering, carrying a concealed weapon, pocketbook snatching, and so on), not misdemeanors or lesser offenses.

35. The laws that originally governed commitment to the reformatory (*General Laws and Resolves 1874,* Ch. 385, sec. 21 and Ch. 165, sec. 28) specified that rogues and vagabonds, idle and dissolute persons, stubborn children, run-aways, common drunkards, common nightwalkers, pilferers, and lewd, wanton, and lascivious persons might be sent to the reformatory. That repeaters could be excluded from the institution was specified by *General Laws and Resolves 1878,* Ch. 270, sec. 2. According to Freedman's sample of records of women sentenced to the Massachusetts reformatory between 1877 and 1912, 84 percent had been convicted of public order or chastity offenses (*Their Sisters' Keepers,* p. 81).

36. New York, *Laws of 1881,* Ch. 187 (Hudson), *Laws of 1890,* Ch. 238 (Albion), *Laws of 1892,* Ch. 637 (Bedford).

37. Barrows, "The Reformatory Treatment of Women," p. 147.

38. Massachusetts, *General Laws and Resolves 1874,* Ch. 385, sec. 21 and Ch. 165, sec. 28. On the switch to a one-year minimum, see Massachusetts Reformatory Prison for Women, *AR 1879:* 15, *AR 1880:* 11, and Massachusetts, *Prison Laws, and Resolves: A Manual for the Use of Prison Officials of Massachusetts* (Boston: Rand, Avery, & Co., 1880), Ch. 114, sec. 1.

39. Massachusetts, *Prison Laws and Resolves 1880,* Ch. 221, sec. 2, and Ch. 247, sec. 1; Massachusetts Board of Commissioners of Prisons, *AR 1878:* 60.

40. New York, *Laws of 1890,* Ch. 238, sec. 8, *Laws of 1896,* Article IX, sec. 146; New York, House of Refuge at Hudson, *AR 1888:* 5–6, *AR 1889:* 10; New York, *Laws of 1899,* Ch. 632, sec. 1.

41. New York, Western House of Refuge for Women, *AR 1895:* 17.

42. New York, House of Refuge at Hudson, *AR 1897:* 10.

43. New York, Western House of Refuge for Women, *AR 1898:* 17 (Boyd's view); New York State Board of Charities, *AR 1889:* 127–28, *AR 1895:* xxiv, 54, 56.

44. Brockway, *Fifty Years,* p. 355; Michel Foucault, *Discipline and Punish: The Birth of the Prison,* trans. Alan Sheridan (New York: Pantheon, 1977), p. 293.

45. Dedham Temporary Asylum for Discharged Female Prisoners, *AR 1864:* 6, as quoted in Mary J. Bularzik, "The Dedham Temporary Asylum for Discharged Female Prisoners 1864–1909," *Historical Journal of Massachusetts* 12(1) (January 1984), p. 28. The Board of Commissioners for Prisons presented arguments for

the women's prison in their annual reports; sometimes they invoked the example of the House of Shelter, which some of them had studied in Detroit.

46. The support of Sanborn, Wines, and (especially) Brockway is described in Isabel C. Barrows, "The Massachusetts Reformatory Prison for Women," in Samuel J. Barrows, ed., *The Reformatory System in the United States* (Washington, D.C.: Government Printing Office, 1900): 105–6 On the league that organized the petition campaign, see Massachusetts Board of Commissioners of Prisons, *AR 1876:* 61.

47. David M. Schneider and Albert Deutsch, *The History of Public Welfare in New York State, 1867–1940* (Chicago: University of Chicago Press, 1941), p. 103.

48. New Jersey, *Report of the Commissioners to Examine . . . Prison Discipline,* New Jersey State Prison, *AR 1890:* 19, 32, 62, *AR 1895:* 12.

49. Helen Worthington Rogers, "A History of the Movement to Establish a State Reformatory for Women in Connecticut," *Journal of Criminal Law, Criminology & Police Science* 19 (4) (February 1929), pp. 520–23; Rhode Island Advisory Board of Visitors to Institutions Where Women are Imprisoned, *AR 1905:* 9–13.

50. Rhode Island Advisory Board of Visitors to Institutions Where Women are Imprisoned, *AR 1905:* 18 (quoting Sarah E. Doyle), 12.

51. Josephine Shaw Lowell, "One Means of Preventing Pauperism," in National Conference of Charities and Correction, *Proceedings 1879:* 189. This entire article gives a good example of Lowell's thinking on the matter of institutions for women. Also see New York State Board of Charities, *AR 1886:* 171, and Nicolas F. Hahn [Nicole Hahn Rafter], "Too Dumb to Know Better: Cacogenic Family Studies and the Criminology of Women," *Criminology* 18 (1) (May 1980): 3–25. For the eugenic reasoning and activities of the SCAA, see New York State Charities Aid Association, *AR 1879:* 5, 59. Effects of the eugenics movement on women's reformatories are discussed in chapter 3.

52. On women's reform in general in this period, see Jill Conway, "Women Reformers and American Culture, 1870–1930," in Jean E. Friedman and William G. Shade, eds., *Our American Sisters: Women in American Life and Thought,* 2d ed. (Boston: Allyn & Bacon, 1976), pp. 301–12. On the distinction between radical and social feminism, see Lois W. Banner, *Women in Modern America: A Brief History* (New York: Harcourt Brace Jovanovich, 1974), chapter 3. On the "disestablishment" from the home of northeastern, middle-class women in particular, see Ann Douglas, *The Feminization of American Culture* (New York: Avon Books, 1977), pp. 55–56. Freedman's *Their Sisters' Keepers* is the best source of information on those social feminists who engaged in prison reform. In chapter 2, Freedman analyzes the background of these women, identifying factors that encouraged them to undertake prison work: their sense of religious mission; their liberal, middle-class and upper middle-class origins; and their earlier work against slavery and in health services during the Civil War.

53. Conway, "Women Reformers," p. 309; Banner, *Women in Modern America,* pp. 111–12.

54. Freedman, *Their Sisters' Keepers,* p. 47.

55. David J. Pivar, *Purity Crusade: Sexual Morality and Social Control, 1868–1900* (Westport, Conn.: Greenwood Press, 1973), p. 7.

56. Women's Prison Association of New York, *AR 1893:* 6.

57. For a discussion of the philosophy underlying the system of institutions for juvenile delinquents, see Schlossman, *Love and the American Delinquent,* pp. 7–17,

and Alexander W. Pisciotta, "Saving the Children: The Promise and Practice of *Parens Patriae, 1838–98*," *Crime and Delinquency* 28 (2) (July 1982): 410–25.

58. Schlossman, *Love and the American Delinquent,* esp. chapter 3; Brenzel, "Domestication as Reform."

59. Schlossman uses the term "anti-institutional institutions" in *Love and the American Delinquent,* p. 38, crediting John Thomas, "Romantic Reform in America, 1815–1865," *American Quarterly* 17 (Winter 1965): 656–82 with original use of the term. According to Brenzel, "Domestication as Reform," p. 203, three-quarters of the girls in her sample of commitments to Lancaster during its first fifty years of operation "had been accused of committing crimes considered morally threatening to social stability," such as "stubborn, wayward, and potentially degenerate behavior; vagrancy, running away, and staying out late at night."

60. New York, House of Refuge at Hudson, *AR 1887:* 5; Bradwell v. Illinois, 83 U.S. (16 Wall.) 130, 141 (1872), as quoted and cited in Mary Eastwood, "Feminism and the Law," in Jo Freeman, ed., *Women: A Feminist Perspective,* 2d ed. (Palo Alto: Mayfield, 1979), p. 386.

61. Massachusetts Board of Commissioners of Prisons, *AR 1873:* 43.

62. Detroit House of Correction, *AR 1868:* 40.

63. Freedman, *Their Sisters' Keepers,* pp. 14–21, analyzes attitudes toward and treatment of "the fallen woman" in the pre-1870 period. While there is much that is useful and sensitive in this discussion, her blanket use of the term "fallen women" to refer to all females incarcerated in state prisons in this period *and* the next (up to 1900; see her chapter 2) is, I think, somewhat misleading. Most women held in state prisons in the early and mid-nineteenth century were convicted of crimes for which men, too, were imprisoned—larceny, burglary, murder, and the like, not morals offenses. With a few exceptions, these "real" criminals continued to be held in predominantly male prisons up to and beyond 1900. But most reformatories concentrated on a different class, misdemeanants and lesser offenders who had violated moral standards for women. I prefer to reserve the term "fallen women" to refer to those prostitutes and wayward women, so as to make it clear that the reformers were dealing with a population different from that traditionally sent to state prisons.

64. Freedman, *Their Sisters' Keepers,* p. 20.

65. Ibid., pp. 20–21 and chapter 2.

NOTES TO CHAPTER 3

1. New Jersey Women's Reformatory Commission, *Report of the New Jersey Women's Reformatory Commission* (Trenton: MacCrellish & Quigley, 1905), p. 8.

2. On prisons' assimilation of medical practices during the Progressive period, see David J. Rothman, *Conscience and Convenience: The Asylum and Its Alternatives in Progressive America* (Boston: Little, Brown and Co., 1980), and Nicolas Fischer Hahn [Nicole Hahn Rafter], "The Defective Delinquency Movement," Ph.D. diss. (Albany: State University of New York, 1978), esp. chapters 5 and 7.

3. See Mark H. Haller, *Eugenics: Hereditarian Attitudes in American Thought* (New Brunswick: Rutgers University Press, 1963); Hahn, "The Defective Delinquency Movement," Part II; Peter L. Tyor, " 'Denied the Power to Choose the Good': Sexuality and Mental Defect in American Medical Practice, 1850–1920,"

Journal of Social History 10 (4) (Summer 1977): 472–89; Hahn, "Too Dumb to Know Better."

4. Katherine van Wyck, "Reformatory for Women—Wisconsin's Outstanding Need," in Wisconsin Conference on Charities and Corrections, *Proceedings 1912:* 95–96. On the antiprostitution movement, see Connelly, *Response to Prostitution,* and Rosen, *The Lost Sisterhood.* Effects of the antiprostitution campaign on women's reformatories are discussed in more detail in chapter 7; the treatment of venereal disease is discussed later in this chapter.

5. See Richard Hofstadter, ed., *The Progressive Movement 1900–1915* (Englewood Cliffs, N. J.: Prentice-Hall, 1963), "Introduction"; Richard Hofstadter, *The Age of Reform* (New York: Vintage Books, 1955), esp. pp. 204–5; Robert H. Wiebe, *The Search for Order 1877–1920* (New York: Hill & Wang, 1967); Egal Feldman, "Prostitution, the Alien Woman and the Progressive Imagination, 1910–1915," *American Quarterly* 19 (Summer 1967): 192–206.

6. In addition to the seventeen instances in which the reformatory movement was successful in the twentieth century, there were three in which it failed to achieve its goal. In 1917 Michigan passed a law establishing a State Training School for female misdemeanants and felons. Construction was begun on a site near Okemos, but the legislature refused to complete the project when objections were raised to its proximity "to developing young minds" at the nearby Agricultural College. See C. Ray Freeman, "The Ruins at Okemos," *The State Journal,* September 19, 1965. In 1919 Washington created a Women's Industrial Home and Clinic, designed to hold felons, misdemeanants, and delinquents. This opened in 1920 only to close the next year when the governor vetoed its maintenance appropriation. Similarly, California established an Industrial Farm for Women at Sonoma in 1919. This opened in 1921 but received few commitments, and after a fire in 1923 destroyed the main building, the Farm was closed. Vermont's State Prison and House of Correction for women is not considered a reformatory in this work for reasons explained in note 23, below.

7. North Carolina State Board of Charities and Public Welfare, *BR 1922:* 80, 82; see also *BR 1924:* 71–72.

8. Ibid., *BR 1926:* 7.

9. Maine State Board of Charities and Corrections, *AR 1914:* 14–20.

10. Virginia, Board of Directors of the Penitentiary, *BR 1923:* 5.

11. Minnesota State Board of Control, *BR 1912:* 16.

12. A. R. Bowen, ed., *The Institution Quarterly* 9 (4) (December 31, 1918): 226 (Illinois); Virginia State Department of Public Welfare, *AR 1928:* 13, *AR 1927:* 11–12; David Y. Thomas, *Arkansas and Its People: A History, 1541–1930,* vol. 2 (New York: The American Historical Society, 1930), pp. 504–5; and Arkansas, *General Acts, 1919,* Act 494, sec. 9. The interplay between the reformatory and antiprostitution movements is presented in especially rich detail in Rogers, "History of the Movement," esp. pp. 531–33.

13. Rogers, "History of the Movement," p. 541 ("from their reluctance"), p. 524 ("promised land"). The work of Caroline Alexander (later Wittpenn) and of others involved in the New Jersey movement is described in detail in Mary Ann Stillman Quarles, "Organizational Analysis of the New Jersey Reformatory for Women in Relation to Stated Principles of Corrections, 1913–1963," (Ph.D. diss., Boston University, 1966), pp. 38–41; see also New Jersey Women's Reformatory Commission, *Report of the New Jersey Women's Reformatory Commission.*

14. Florence Monahan, *Women in Crime* (New York: Ives Washburn, 1941), p. 35.

15. Katherine Bement Davis, "A Reformatory for Women," in Ohio Board of State Charities, *Ohio Bulletin of Charities and Correction* 17 (2) (July 1911): 43–48; Thomas, *Arkansas and Its People,* p. 505; van Wyck, "Reformatory for Women—Wisconsin's Outstanding Need," p. 94; Quarles, "Organizational Analysis of the New Jersey Reformatory for Women," p. 39.

16. Rhode Island Advisory Board of Visitors to Institutions Where Women are Imprisoned, *AR 1905:* 44; Rogers, "History of the Movement."

17. On the struggle that accompanied the founding of California's reformatory, see Monahan, *Women in Crime,* pp. 179–81, and Lloyd L. Voight, *History of California Correctional Administration From 1930 to 1948* (San Francisco: n.p., 1949), p. 9.

18. Rothman, *Discovery of the Asylum,* pp. xvi–xvii; Rothman, *Conscience and Convenience.* In the latter work, Rothman concludes that "innovations that appeared to be substitutes for incarceration became supplements to incarceration" (p. 9), "add-ons to the system, not replacements" (p. 12); but his main point is that about 1900, institutionalization fell into disfavor as a means of coping with socially problematic groups.

19. Steven Schlossman and Stephanie Wallach, "The Crime of Precocious Sexuality: Female Juvenile Delinquency in the Progressive Era," *Harvard Educational Review* 48 (1) (February 1978), p. 70.

20. Schlossman and Wallach pinpoint nativist prejudices and the theories of adolescence associated with the work of G. Stanley Hall, as well as the social purity movement, as factors particularly important in both the expansion of the institutional system for girls and the more severe treatment of girls than boys. In the case of the system for adult women, nativism and the related social purity movement played key roles; so did the fact that by 1900, the reformatory plan had matured to the point that it was ripe for widespread application.

21. Schlossman and Wallach, "The Crime of Precocious Sexuality," p. 91.

22. Connelly, *The Response to Prostitution in the Progressive Era,* p. 18.

23. Vermont established a custodial institution for women, the State Prison and House of Correction at Rutland, in 1921. Although this institution had a number of reformatory features during the energetic superintendency of Lena Ross (1921–1936), and despite its close resemblance to the women's institution of Rhode Island, it is here classified as a custodial prison because its establishment came about not through the agency of a reformatory movement but as a bureaucratic solution to the need to improve conditions at the state prison at Windsor. Through 1979, at least, tiny New Hampshire never accumulated enough female prisoners to warrant establishment of a separate prison for women. The handling of female state prisoners by these two states is described in more detail in chapter 4.

24. As of 1979, North and South Dakota still had not established separate prisons for women. Instead they continued to hold female felons in their central state prisons. Lack of need explains this lack of interest in independent women's institutions: in 1978, the two states together had only twenty-two female felons (U.S. Comptroller General, *Women in Prison,* pp. 40–41). Missouri opened its first separate prison for females, the State Penitentiary for Women, in 1955, and

Michigan continued to hold women at the Detroit House of Correction until opening the Huron Valley Women's Facility in 1977.

25. See Paul W. Garrett and Austin H. MacCormick, eds., *Handbook of American Prisons and Reformatories, 1929* (New York: National Society of Penal Information, 1929), pp. 769–76.

26. After the reformatory movement had ended, two southern states established penal institutions called "reformatories," but in neither case was title a reliable guide to type. In 1940 Maryland opened its Women's Prison, later renamed the Maryland State Reformatory for Women. Women's organizations had helped create pressure for establishment of this institution, and it did utilize the cottage plan. However, it did not institute indeterminate sentencing until 1945; it received felons as well as misdemeanants; and in other ways, too, it was a reformatory more in name than in fact. The Arkansas "reformatory" for women established in 1951 at Cummins Farm was even more of a custodial operation, bearing no resemblance whatsoever to the original reformatory plan.

According to Jane Zimmerman, "The Penal Reform Movement in the South during the Progressive Era, 1890–1917," *Journal of Southern History* 17 (November 1951): 462–92, there was considerable agitation for prison improvement in this region, but it focused on abolition of the lease system and on separation of youths from adult prisoners rather than on improving conditions for women.

27. One set of emissaries of the National Society of Penal Information, Garrett and MacCormick, published a state-by-state report in 1929 in which they criticized the conditions under which women were held. In Virginia, they objected to the housing of women in a unit adjoining the men's penitentiary but even more to the practice of "using them in a section of the prison industries. It is accepted as a sound prison principle that women prisoners should be removed from the prison for men and cared for in some institution for women" (*Handbook of American Prisons and Reformatories, 1929*, p. 946). Virginia founded its women's reformatory the year following publication of this report.

28. Arkansas was the only state that did not cooperate with the research for this study. We knew that reports had been issued by the Arkansas reformatory, but state prison officials refused to send copies.

29. In 1935 and 1947, respectively.

30. The relation of the "servant problem" to the reformatory movement is discussed in chapter 7, and the employment history of Albion's inmates is discussed in more detail in chapter 5.

31. See Anne Firor Scott, "The 'New Woman' in the New South," in Friedman and Shade, *Our American Sisters:* pp. 252–61.

32. Ohio Governor, *Report of the Special Committee of the 77th General Assembly of Ohio Appointed to Investigate Penitentiary Buildings, Management and Convict Labor* (Columbus: Ohio State Archives, Ser. 1590, December 1908), p. 4.

33. The development of case work and of recreational programs that actively involved inmates in team sports, dramatic productions, and the like are two other important differences between twentieth-century reformatories and those of the nineteenth. They are covered thoroughly in Lekkerkerker, *Reformatories for Women.*

34. James R. McGovern, "The American Woman's Pre-World War I Freedom in Manners and Morals," in Friedman and Shade, *Our American Sisters,* p. 350.

35. New York State Reformatory for Women at Bedford (hereafter NYRWB), *AR 1903:* 34.

36. Katherine Bement Davis, "Outdoor Work for Women Prisoners," National Conference of Charities and Correction, *Proceedings 1909:* 289–94; Freedman, *Their Sisters' Keepers,* p. 110.

37. Rothman, *Conscience and Convenience,* pp. 60, 49–50.

38. Wisconsin Industrial Home for Women, *BR 1924:* 366 ("immoral actions"), 367, 370, *BR 1922:* 327–28, *BR 1926:* 469 (according to which women with venereal disease were tricked into consenting "to 'plead guilty' . . . upon representations of attorneys, social workers and others interested, that the condition is not serious and three or four weeks time will 'complete the cure' "); W. R. Ward, "The Social-service Work of the State Industrial Farm for Women," *Proceedings [of the] Kansas Conference of Social Work . . . 1922* (Topeka: B. P. Walker, 1923), pp. 46–47 ("cleaning up"); Lekkerkerker, *Reformatories for Women,* p. 119 (segregation of Kansas "internes"); Kansas Industrial Farm for Women, *BR 1920:* 6 (strict sanitary measures necessary because 95 percent of the women have venereal diseases); Monahan, *Women in Crime,* p. 39 (outhouse guards).

39. Kansas Industrial Farm for Women, *BR 1926:* 21.

40. Garrett and MacCormick, *Handbook of American Prisons and Reformatories, 1929,* p. 575. I am grateful to Dr. Ronald Gold of the Toronto Hospital for Sick Children for his help in understanding the treatment of venereal disease in the early twentieth century. According to Dr. Gold, severe side effects of mercury treatments for syphilis "were so common that most patients did not complete the course of treatment. The same applies to salvarsan. Combined treatment with salvarsan (arsphenamine) and mercury was the standard regimen in the 1920s and the series of weekly injections for six weeks seems to have been a very popular method. However, because the side effects of mercury and of arsenic compounds were so severe, the U.S. Public Health Service began a study in the 1930s of not treating syphilis. . . . [D]octors had finally realized that mercury plus arsenic treatment may have killed as many patients as syphilis. The major fatal reaction was from the severe liver damage caused by salvarsan. . . .

"Mercury was usually given by intramuscular injection and was very painful. . . . The most common severe side effects of mercury treatment were kidney damage, stomatitis (inflammation and ulceration of the mouth), and severe skin rashes. . . . Arsphenamine . . . caused fatal adverse reactions more frequently." (Personal communication of January 27, 1980.)

41. See Alfred Binet and Theodore Simon, *The Development of Intelligence in Children* (orig. 1916; repr. New York: Arno Press, 1973), pp. 9–10, 316–28.

42. For good examples of the literature on mental defect in the teens, see Henry H. Goddard's *Feeble-mindedness: Its Causes and Consequences* (New York: Macmillan, 1914), and his *The Criminal Imbecile: An Analysis of Three Remarkable Murder Cases* (New York: Macmillan, 1915). On p. 9 of *Feeble-mindedness,* Goddard produced a table summarizing defective-delinquency studies to date. In nearly every group of tested inmates, over 50 percent proved "defective," up to 89 percent at an institution in Illinois. For an incisive critique of the intelligence-testers and defective-delinquency theory, see Edwin H. Sutherland, "Mental Deficiency and Crime" (1931) in Albert Cohen, Alfred Lindesmith, and Karl Schussler, eds., *The Sutherland Papers* (Bloomington: Indiana University Press, 1956); for a delightful discussion of the "Myth of the Menace of the Feebleminded," see Haller, *Eugenics,* chapter 7.

43. See note 12, above, and accompanying text (Bowen citation). An excellent discussion of the linkage between female sexuality and mental retardation appears in Tyor, " 'Denied the Power to Choose the Good.' " Schlossman and Wallach, "The Crime of Precocious Sexuality," pp. 79–80, discuss the different effects of the eugenics movement on boy and girl delinquents and conclude that it led to more frequent incarceration of the latter.

44. Pennsylvania State Industrial Home for Women, *Report of the Board of Trustees . . . For the Four Year Period Ending May 31st, 1928:* 11 ("work, classes, and recreation"). The reformatories that transferred "defective" inmates to institutions for the feebleminded included those of Massachusetts, New Jersey, New York, Pennsylvania (especially), and Wisconsin.

45. NYRWB, *AR 1904:* 28 ("women in the lowest grade"), *AR 1910:* 20–21, 62–65 (Rowland's study), 6, 18–19, 58 (disposition of the feebleminded).

46. Ibid., *AR 1911:* 11, and New York Foundation, *Forty Year Report 1909–1949* (New York: New York Foundation, n.d.), p. 62; Jean Weidensall, *The Mentality of the Criminal Woman* (Baltimore: Warwick & York, 1916), pp. 1–3, and NYRWB, *AR 1911:* 18 (purpose of Weidensall's work).

47. Katherine B. Davis, "Introduction" to Weidensall, *Mentality of the Criminal Woman,* p. xi. For another Davis account of these events, see Katherine B. Davis, "A Plan for the Conversion of the Laboratory of Social Hygiene at Bedford Hills into a State Clearing House for Women Convicted in the First, Second, Third and Ninth Judicial Districts," manuscript held by Rockefeller Archive Center, Bureau of Social Hygiene (hereafter RAC, BSH), Ser. 3, Bx. 25, f. 360, pp. 1–5.

48. Raymond B. Fosdick, *John D. Rockefeller, Jr., A Portrait* (New York: Harper & Brothers, 1956), p. 137.

49. John D. Rockefeller, Jr., "Introduction," in George J. Kneeland, *Commercialized Prostitution in New York City* (New York: The Century Co., 1913), pp. vii–viii.

50. Details on the bureau's income up to the year 1928 appear in Bureau of Social Hygiene, Inc., "Financial Report from April 1, 1911 to January 1, 1928," RAC, BSH, Ser. 2, Bx. 1, f. 69; the bureau is described as JDR, Jr.,'s, favorite philanthropy in Peter Collier and David Horowitz, *The Rockefellers: An American Dynasty* (New York: Holt, Rinehart & Winston, 1976), p. 107.

51. State of New York, Office of the Attorney General, "Reformatory for Women at Bedford. Power of Board of Managers" (Albany: n.d.; copy in RAC, BSH, Ser. 3, Bx. 25, f. 360), pp. 1–2.

52. Accounts of the laboratory's work appear in Mabel Ruth Fernald, Mary H. S. Hayes, and Almena Dawley, *A Study of Women Delinquents in New York State* (New York: The Century Co., 1920); Edith R. Spaulding, *An Experimental Study of Psychopathic Delinquent Women* (Bureau of Social Hygiene, 1923; repr. Montclair, N.J.: Patterson Smith, 1969); and Weidensall, *Mentality of the Criminal Woman.*

53. John D. Rockefeller, Jr., to John S. Kennedy, December 6, 1919, as quoted in John S. Kennedy, "Report to the Governor, relative to the Investigation and Inquiry into Allegations of Cruelty to Prisoners in the New York State Reformatory for Women, Bedford Hills," in New York State Commission of Prisons, *AR 1920* (hereafter cited as Kennedy, "Report"), p. 79; New York, *Laws of 1920,* Ch. 774, secs. 241–42; New York State Department of Correction, *Westfield State Farm, Bedford Hills, N.Y.: Its History, Purpose, Makeup and Program* (West

Coxsackie, N. Y.: New York State Vocational Institution, n.d. [1949?]), p. 9; and Lekkerkerker, *Reformatories for Women,* pp. 100 and 237 (discontent among defective delinquents); *New York Times,* February 15, 1923 (purchase of Rockefeller plant by state).

54. The term "psychopath," as Lekkerkerker points out *(Reformatories for Women,* p. 227), was "applied rather loosely" in women's prisons so as to include "all offenders who show more or less serious mental deviations or peculiarities which can neither be classed as frank psychoses leading to the legal qualification of insanity, nor as feeble-mindedness, and which may be the result of a great variety of causes. . . ." As this description suggests, "psychopathic" became a fashionable label for those who appeared abnormal but did not do poorly on mental tests or act totally mad. Lekkerkerker concludes by noting, "From the point of view of institutional management psychopaths are disciplinary problems." The reverse was also true: administrators tended to think that disciplinary problems must be psychopaths.

55. NYRWB, *AR 1915:* 29.

56. Spaulding, *An Experimental Study of Psychopathic Delinquent Women,* pp. 10 (note 1), 22, 133.

57. The report on the 1920 investigation of Bedford by the Commissioner of Prisons, for example, concluded with a whole-hearted endorsement of the medical model (Kennedy, "Report"), and the Prison Association of New York ended its report of 1919 with praise for Rockefeller and the clinics he had funded at Bedford and Sing Sing (*AR 1919:* 30).

58. Connecticut State Farm for Women, *BR 1924:* 8; Kansas Industrial Farm for Women, *BR 1920:* 6, Wisconsin State Board of Control, *BR 1936:* 515.

59. See Brenzel, "Domestication as Reform"; Freedman, *Their Sisters' Keepers;* Hahn, "The Defective Delinquency Movement," chapter 2; Pisciotta, "Saving the Children"; Rothman, *Discovery of the Asylum* and *Conscience and Convenience;* and Schlossman, *Love and the American Delinquent.*

60. First, misdemeanants and first-time felons could be sentenced to definite terms of not less than one year. Second, at the discretion of the courts, prisoners could be given indeterminate sentences, their minimum and maximum limits set by the law governing the specific offense in question. Third, misdemeanants and lesser offenders could also receive indeterminate sentences of up to five years. Fourth and fifth, the Industrial Home also received venereal disease cases, who were held till "cured," and pregnant women, who were committed for the term of their pregnancy. See Wisconsin, *Session Laws of 1913,* Ch. 723, sec. 4944–0 (first three types); Bernett O. Odegard and George M. Keith, *A History of the State Board of Control of Wisconsin and the State Institutions: 1849–1939* (Madison: State Board of Control, 1939); p. 228 (". . . the Board of Control has designated this home as one of the state institutions to which the judge of any court of record may commit any female person afflicted with a venereal disease and who has refused to take or continue treatments"); Wisconsin Industrial Home for Women, *BR 1926:* 477 (examples of cases sentenced for term of pregnancy or until cured of venereal disease).

61. This was less true in the South and in several midwestern states, where prisoners continued to engage in heavy farming.

62. Elizabeth Munger, third superintendent of the Connecticut reformatory, took over its direction in the late 1920s, stabilizing the administration after a number

of difficult years. According to Janet York (who began working at the State Farm in the 1940s and later became its superintendent), Munger had introduced an excellent system of classification which was still effective two decades later (personal interview, November 1980).

63. According to Eleanor Little of Guilford, Conn. (a close friend of Caughey's), Caughey's decision to resign was prompted partly by exhaustion, partly by tensions between her and trustee Mrs. Alexander. Anna M. Peterson, the first regular superintendent of the Connecticut reformatory, resigned after a protracted struggle with board member Helen W. Rogers who, like Mrs. Alexander in New Jersey, had been a leader in the movement to establish the reformatory. See the account of the trouble between Peterson and Rogers by Rogers' husband, A. K. Rogers, *An Episode in History of a Connecticut Institution* (New Haven: City Printing Co., 1923).

64. In fairness to these women, it should be added that the Ohio reformatory was a large and overcrowded institution. According to a report of 1929, "The reformatory, with 475 inmates, is the largest institution for women in the country. The population has long since grown beyond its intended limits" (Garrett and MacCormick, *Handbook of American Prisons and Reformatories, 1929*, p. 774).

65. Ibid., pp. 770, 775.

66. Lekkerkerker, *Reformatories for Women*, p. 280.

67. New York State Commission of Prisons, *AR 1920:* 32 ("charges of . . . wrong-doing"); New York State Joint Committee of the Legislature, *Report of Investigation concerning the Management, Conduct and Affairs of the Western House of Refuge for Women at Albion, N.Y.* (N.Y. Leg. Doc. No. 48, 1920); John S. Kennedy, "Report to the Governor Relative to the Investigation of the Management of the Western House of Refuge for Women at Albion," in New York State Commission of Prisons, *AR 1920:* 100–3. Daniels' temperament comes through vividly in her correspondence with inmates and their families. These letters remain in the case files held by the New York State Archives, Albany. For another example of Daniels' habitual tone, see New York, Western House of Refuge, *AR 1922:* 9–10.

68. On Helen Cobb's dismissal, see *New York Times,* March 19, 1920, p. 6 (Commissioner Kennedy recommends that superintendent be removed), and March 20, 1920, p. 12 (Cobb resigns). On changes in the board of managers, see NYRWB, *AR 1921:* 2–3.

69. For more on these letters, see chapter 7.

70. May Caughey as quoted in Quarles, "Organizational Analysis of the New Jersey Reformatory for Women," p. 57. Because little is known of Caughey (she is not included in Freedman's [*Their Sisters' Keepers*] profile of twentieth-century prison reformers, for example), it seems worthwhile to mention some of the biographical data given to me by Eleanor H. Little. May Caughey received a B.A. in history from the University of Michigan in 1906. She taught for two years (first in Mexico City, then in Wisconsin) before joining the staff of Sleighton Farm, a reform school for delinquent girls near Philadelphia, in 1908. Working under Superintendent Martha P. Falconer, Caughey was in charge of self-government and acted as a consultant on discipline for the cottage matrons until, in 1912, she became superintendent of the New Jersey Reformatory for Women. Worn out and at odds with board member Alexander, Caughey resigned in 1917.

Thereafter she studied at the New York School of Social Work and in 1923, while working for the Red Cross in New Haven, received her M.A. in Public Health from Yale (personal communication from Eleanor H. Little, October 12, 1982).

71. Several other reformatories also had systems of inmate self-government, especially those whose officers had been trained by Martha P. Falconer. Falconer had introduced self-government at the turn of the century at Pennsylvania's Sleighton Farm (formally, the House of Refuge). On self-government in women's reformatories, see Lekkerkerker, *Reformatories for Women*, pp. 437–51.

72. According to Mary Ann (Quarles) Hawkes (personal communication of October 15, 1982), Clinton was unusual in that its decline in the 1920s was reversed. This occurred when Edna Mahan took over in 1928. Imaginative and adventuresome, Mahan served as superintendent for the next forty years. See Quarles, "Organizational Analysis of the New Jersey Reformatory for Women."

73. NYRWB, *AR 1913:* 15. O. F. Lewis reported on Davis's solicitation of commitments before the American Academy of Political and Social Science in *The Survey* 24 (1910): 115.

74. New York State Board of Charities, "Report of the Special Committee appointed to investigate charges made against the New York State Reformatory for Women at Bedford Hills, N.Y.," in *AR 1915:* 853, 860, 869, 860–61 (civil commitments).

75. For information on the riots, see Philip Klein's report in Prison Association of New York, *AR 1916:* 308–18; Kennedy, "Report," pp. 67–99. The riots are also mentioned in several articles in the *New York Times*. See, in addition, New York State Governor, Message to the Legislature, March 18, 1920, in *New York State Assembly Journal 1920,* vol. 1, p. 908.

76. *New York Times,* November 18, 1919 (Carter's story); Kennedy, "Report," esp. p. 68; *New York Times,* July 25, 1920 (state police restore order).

77. The Bedford reformatory was by then renamed Westfield State Farm.

78. It should be noted that in recent years, some originally all-female institutions have received males too, thus becoming "co-ed" prisons. Moreover, today men are increasingly being appointed as superintendents of these prisons.

NOTES TO CHAPTER 4

1. It might be argued that the tendency of custodial units for women to detach themselves from the central prisons where they originated was an effect of the reformatory movement's stress on the need for separate treatment of women. However, this tendency was in fact a by-product of administrative considerations, not a result of a desire to reform.

2. In 1941 the New Hampshire legislature authorized the trustees of the state prison to contract with county institutions or prisons in other states to take custody of female prisoners. At first, the women were transferred to the Women's Reformatory (as the former State Prison and House of Correction for Women had been renamed) at Rutland, Vermont. More recently, they have been sent to Connecticut (see Joan Potter, "In Prison, Women Are Different," p. 15).

3. Garrett and MacCormick, *Handbook of American Prisons and Reformatories, 1929,* p. 586.

4. Missouri State Penitentiary, *BR 1882:* 244; U.S. Department of Commerce, Bureau of the Census, *Statistical Directory of State Institutions for the Defective, Dependent, and Delinquent Classes* (Washington, D.C.: Government Printing Office, 1919), pp. 222–25 (giving statistics for 1916); Missouri State Penitentiary, *BR 1900:* 6 ("female cell-building" a "disgrace"); Missouri Department of Penal Institutions, *BR 1928:* 14 (moved to "the administration building"). For first-hand accounts of prisoner life in the Missouri penitentiary, see Emma Goldman, *Living My Life,* vol. 2 (New York: Knopf, 1931), and Kate Richards O'Hare, *In Prison* (orig. 1923; repr. Seattle: University of Washington Press, 1976); both tell of prisoners who died as a result of the penitentiary's conditions.

5. Garrett and MacCormick, *Handbook of American Prisons and Reformatories, 1929,* pp. 534 ("still part of the prison for men"), 543 ("ball and chain"); U.S. Prison Industries Reorganization Administration, *The Prison Problem in Missouri* (Washington, D.C.: U.S. Government Printing Office, 1938), p. 113.

6. U.S. Department of Commerce, Bureau of the Census, *Statistical Directory of State Institutions,* pp. 234–37 (Oklahoma data), 206–9 (Idaho data).

7. Tennessee State Archives, Record Group 25, Ser. 4, v. 31, *Board of Inspectors of the Tennessee Penitentiary, 1877–1892:* 14 ("separate [sic] and apart"); Tennessee State Penitentiary, *BR 1882:* 9 (warden's complaints and recommendations).

8. Tennessee State Penitentiary, *BR 1884:* 15.

9. Ibid., *BR 1898:* 724 ("strong, solid fence" and "several inmates"); Tennessee, *Report of Joint Investigating Committee on Penal Institutions, December 1, 1906, to November 30, 1908, Inclusive* (in *Appendix to Senate and House Journals, 1909*), p. 18.

10. Tennessee State Penitentiary, *BR 1900:* 11.

11. Tennessee Department of Institutions and Public Welfare, Advisory Committee on Correctional Institutions for Adults, *Report on Correctional Institutions for Adults* (n.p.: n.d. [1938?]), pp. 62–63 (all quotations). Tennessee continued to hold women in this custodial adjunct to its main penitentiary until, in the mid-1960s, it established its first autonomous women's prison.

12. Goldman, *Living My Life;* O'Hare, *In Prison.*

13. A distinction is usually made between the practices of leasing convicts and of working them on state penal farms, not only because of obvious differences in the financial arrangements but also because, in the case of men, the type of work performed could be very different. In the case of women, however, farming was the main type of work whether the convicts were leased or forced to labor on state plantations; thus the two practices are grouped together here under the "farm camp" designation.

14. The slave tradition of dividing workers into "full-hands," "half-hands," and "dead-hands" and its perpetuation under the lease system are described in McKelvey, *American Prisons,* p. 186. McKelvey's entire chapter 8, "Southern Penal Developments: 1860–1900," provides an overview of the subject; see also Mark T. Carleton, *Politics and Punishment: The History of the Louisiana State Penal System* (Baton Rouge: Louisiana State University Press, 1971), and Zimmerman, "The Penal Reform Movement in the South."

15. Information on the incarceration of women in Texas before 1910 can be found in the biennial reports of the superintendent of Texas State Penitentiaries, and in Herman Lee Crow, " A Political History of the Texas Penal System, 1829–1951" (Austin: University of Texas, Ph.D. diss., 1964).

16. Superintendent of Texas State Penitentiaries, *BR 1900:* 13.

17. Ibid., *BR 1908:* 12, *BR 1910:* 21.

18. Officials of the Texas Prison System, *AR 1911:* 16, 54 (physician's report); Garrett and MacCormick, *Handbook of American Prisons and Reformatories, 1929,* pp. 914–15.

19. Louisiana State Penitentiary, *AR 1866:* 60, *BR 1907:* 61 (giving data for January 1, 1908).

20. For information on the history of women prisoners in Georgia, I used "History of the Georgia Female Offender," attributed to Linda Lyons of the Georgia Department of Offender Rehabilitation, and "Historical Development of Programs and Services," Section 2 of *The Female Offender in the 1980's: A Continuum of Services,* a typescript dated March 1980 and sent by Janet Valente, the Department's Director of Women's Services. Other sources include annual reports of the Georgia Prison Commission; Citizen's Fact Finding Movement of Georgia, *Georgia Penal System* (April 1938); Garrett and MacCormick, *Handbook of American Prisons and Reformatories, 1929;* and U.S. Prison Industries Reorganization Administration, *The Prison Labor Problem in Georgia* (Washington, D.C.: U.S. Government Printing Office, 1937).

21. Crow, "A Political History of the Texas Penal System, 1829–1951," p. 196.

22. Ibid., note 23.

23. See, for example, Crow, "A Political History of the Texas Penal System, 1829–1951"; Malcolm C. Moos, *State Penal Administration in Alabama* (University, Alabama: Bureau of Public Administration, University of Ala., 1942); and J. Thorsten Sellin, *Slavery and the Penal System* (New York: Elsevier, 1976), chapters 11 and 12.

24. Those independent custodial prisons for women that operated in reformatory states were New York's State Prison for Women at Auburn (opened 1893); the Illinois Women's Prison at Joliet (1919; the Illinois State Reformatory for Women at Dwight did not open till 1930, however); the North Carolina Women's Prison at Raleigh (1933); and New York's State Farm for Women at Valatie (1914). The two that operated as the sole women's prison in their state were the Vermont State Prison and House of Correction for Women (opened 1921) and Alabama's Wetumpka State Penitentiary (this became female-only in 1923; its inmates were moved in 1943 to the nearby, newly-constructed Julia Tutwiler Prison).

25. New York State Commission of Prisons, *AR 1896:* 42; New York Superintendent of State Prisons, *AR 1892:* 23. For a fuller history of the Auburn institution, see Nicole Hahn Rafter, "Hard Times: Custodial Prisons for Women and the Example of the New York State Prison for Women at Auburn, 1893–1933," chapter 11 in Rafter and Stanko, *Judge, Lawyer, Victim, Thief.*

26. Illinois Department of Public Welfare, *AR 1921:* 170. On the history of this institution, see Florence Nortridge Beatty, "The Women's Prison," *Welfare Magazine* 18 (July 1927): 921–26, and Illinois Department of Public Welfare, *AR 1929:* 249.

27. Malcolm C. Moos, *State Penal Administration in Alabama,* p. 29.

28. With the possible exception of that of North Carolina, on which I was unable to find information pertaining to administration.

29. New York, *Laws of 1893,* Ch. 306, sec. 11.

30. Ross may have taken some comfort from the fact that the Department of Public Welfare protested the degradation of her status; in 1933, the Department

observed that "all other states give the heads of their institutions the title of Superintendent. It [the change] places your Superintendent outside the circle, and bans her from professional clubs." (BR 1934: 72).

31. Women's Prison Association of New York (hereafter WPANY), AR 1902: 52, AR 1905: 37, 39.

32. WPANY, AR 1905: 39 (both quotations).

33. WPANY, AR 1906: 57–58.

34. New York State Conference of Charities and Correction, Proceedings 1914: 230; see also WPANY, AR 1907: 45.

35. WPANY, AR 1907: 46, AR 1908: 6.

36. New York, Laws of 1908, Ch. 467, sec. 2; WPANY, AR 1902: 52. See also WPANY, AR 1908: 5; New York State Conference of Charities and Correction, Proceedings 1910: 159, 189; and New York State Commission of Prisons, AR 1914: 126.

37. WPANY, AR 1916: 8.

38. New York, Laws of 1908, Ch. 467, sec. 5; New York Superintendent of State Prisons, AR 1915: 344 (Mealey's request).

39. New York, Laws of 1908, Ch. 467, sec. 8. Amendments of 1913 evidently made it possible to commit to Valatie some women with no prior convictions: these provided that females over sixteen convicted in the city of New York of public intoxication, disorderly conduct, vagrancy, or frequenting disorderly houses or houses of prostitution could also be sent to the State Farm (New York, Laws of 1913, Ch. 372, secs. 88 and 89). While these amendments did not specify that such commitments had to have prior records, neither did they specify that an exception was being made to the general commitment law governing Valatie.

40. New York State Commission of Prisons, AR 1918: 330, 332 (total number of commitments); New York Superintendent of State Prisons, AR 1915: 338–40, AR 1916: 344, AR 1917: 342–45.

41. New York State Commission of Prisons, AR 1918: 330, 332 (data on overcrowding); New York Superintendent of State Prisons, AR 1917: 22 (escapes).

42. WPANY, AR 1918: 37; New York State Commission of Prisons, AR 1916: 26.

43. New York State Commission of Prisons, AR 1920: 28; Young, Women's Prisons Past and Present, p. 36; WPANY, AR 1919: 23–37.

44. Frank Tannenbaum, Darker Phases of the South (orig. 1924; repr. New York: Negro Universities Press, 1969), pp. 104–5.

45. See McKelvey, American Prisons, pp. 190–91.

46. Nevada Department of Prisons, "Programming: Nevada Women's Correctional Center" (Carson City: Department of Prisons, November 1979): 1. I am grateful to Martha S. Conard, superintendent of the center, for sending a copy of this typescript document. The information on Molly Forsha comes from materials sent by Phillip Earl, curator of exhibits, Nevada Historical Society, to whom I am also indebted.

47. Austin H. MacCormick and Paul W. Garrett, eds., Handbook of American Prisons, 1926 (New York: G. P. Putnam's Sons, 1926), p. 99; Garrett and MacCormick, Handbook of American Prisons and Reformatories, 1929, pp. 131, 136–37.

48. MacCormick and Garrett, *Handbook of American Prisons, 1926,* p. 566; Austin H. MacCormick, ed., *Handbook of American Prisons and Reformatories: Vol. 2, Pacific Coast States, 1942* (New York: The Osborne Association, 1942), p. 415; see also pp. 424–25 in this volume.

49. O'Hare, *In Prison,* p. 62.

NOTES TO PART II: INTRODUCTION

1. My original plan called for use of the registries of New York's Reformatory for Women at Bedford, in part because Progressives considered it *the* model penal institution for women (see chapter 3), in part because it (unlike the Albion reformatory) is not covered in depth in the only other historical work that has looked closely at the demographic and offense characteristics of female state prisoners, Freedman's *Their Sisters' Keepers.* Most of Bedford's prisoner records, however, have been lost.

2. Freedman's *Their Sisters' Keepers* seems to be the only other work that uses data drawn directly from the registries of a women's prison. Freedman sampled from records of the Massachusetts reformatory, using cases received 1877–1912.

Another source of information on incarcerated women is the reports compiled annually or biennially by prisons for their state legislatures. But the use of these published reports presents a number of disadvantages. The reports used different data bases at different points in time, in some years reporting on the entire population in custody, for example, while in others giving data only on prisoners received during the preceding fiscal year. The kinds of data in the published reports, moreover, often varied from year to year and prison to prison. Institutions that held both men and women sometimes failed to report separately on female inmates, either including them in summary statistics or ignoring them entirely. Finally, internal inconsistencies in the data of published reports indicate considerable inaccuracy. Use of prisoner registries makes it possible to avoid these problems. The data presented here, however, are not without drawbacks of their own. Information was not available on each variable for every one of the total of 4,606 cases. Moreover, because the prisons opened and closed at varying points, and because time constraints necessitated the skipping of years in sampling from four of the five institutions, the periods covered are not identical. Yet these data drawn directly from the registries are more reliable than those in published reports.

NOTES TO CHAPTER 5

1. See, for example, Hindus, *Prison and Plantation,* chapter 3; for a review of the literature on southern subcultural violence, see Daniel Glaser, *Crime in Our Changing Society* (New York: Holt, Rinehart and Winston, 1978), pp. 218–22.

2. Tennessee State Archives, Sallie Griffin vs. State of Tennessee, August 31, 1916 (this and the other cases are cited as on the documents themselves). The relatively light sentence of ten to twenty years for premeditated and malicious murder does reflect the circumstances of the case.

3. Tennessee State Archives, Kate Nelson vs. State of Tennessee, Supreme Court, Knox County, 1928 (Knox County Criminal Case No. 10, Sept. Term, 1928).

4. Tennessee State Archives, Julia Booze vs. State of Tennessee, January 26, 1929; Stella Armstrong vs. The State, May 16, 1922 (Knox County Supreme Court).

5. Tennessee State Archives, Jennie Ransom vs. State of Tennessee, Jan. 4, 1886; Eva Mai Davis vs. State of Tennessee, Supreme Court at Nashville, Dec. Term, 1930.

6. Tennessee State Archives, Fanny Weaks vs. State of Tennessee, Supreme Court, Montgomery County, Feb. 23, 1895; see also Mattie Jamison et al. vs. The State, Tennessee Supreme Court, Feb. 14, 1905 (No. 26 Criminal Cause [sic], Davidson County) and Alice Simpson et al. vs. The State, Tennessee Supreme Court, Feb. 14, 1905 (No. 28 Davidson Criminal).

7. New York State Archives, Ser. 500 F–4, New York State Prison for Women at Auburn, *Bertillon Register*.

8. The percentage of victims in each category may in fact have been slightly higher than those given here because in 5 percent of the cases the Bertillon register gives no information on the sex or age of victims.

9. No information on means of killing is given in 17 percent of the cases. The percentages in the text are based on the total number of victims, not the number for whom means of death was known.

10. For a review of this literature, see Nicolette Parisi, "Exploring Female Crime Patterns: Problems and Prospects," chapter 5 in Rafter and Stanko, *Judge, Lawyer, Victim, Thief*.

11. The prisoner registries often provide indirect evidence of crime partners: when two women arrived at a prison on the same date, from the same jurisdiction, with identical offenses and sentences and similar demographic characteristics, it seemed safe to conclude that they had committed their crimes together. In these and other cases in which there was direct evidence of crime partnerships, note was made of the fact, together with indications of the number and sex of the partners. Through this method, which undoubtedly underestimates the number of partnerships, I found that 4, 7, and 11 percent of the samples from Auburn, the Ohio penitentiary, and the Tennessee penitentiary, respectively, had acted in concert with another woman. Nearly all had committed some form of property offense.

12. Marvin E. Wolfgang, *Patterns of Criminal Homicide* (New York: John Wiley, 1958); William Wilbanks, "Murdered Women and Women Who Murder: A Critique of the Literature," chapter 7 in Rafter and Stanko, *Judge, Lawyer, Victim, Thief*.

13. Unfortunately, no supplemental source was located in Ohio that would have revealed details on violent crimes committed by women held at the Ohio penitentiary.

14. Wolfgang, *Patterns of Criminal Homicide*, p. 85; Wilbanks, "Murdered Women and Women Who Murder," p. 170.

15. Similarly, Madeline Z. Doty, *Society's Misfits* (New York: The Century Co., 1916), reported that a woman held at Auburn in the early twentieth century for grand larceny had in fact picked a man's pocket of two dollars (pp. 69–70).

16. Also see Daniel A. Novak, *The Wheel of Servitude: Black Forced Labor after Slavery* (Lexington: University Press of Kentucky, 1978), chapter 1, and Carleton, *Politics and Punishment*.

17. According to the FBI's *Uniform Crime Reports* for 1981 (Washington, D.C.: U.S. Department of Justice, 1982), p. 178, larceny-theft was the main arrest category for women, constituting 21 percent of all female arrests in that year. On the continuing involvement of females in minor property crimes, see Darrell J. Steffensmeier, "Sex Differences in Patterns of Adult Crime, 1965–77: A Review and Assessment," *Social Forces* 58 (4) (June 1980): 1080–1108; Steffensmeier's focus is on trends, but his points about the nature of female crime nonetheless apply. He makes the point about women's exclusion from criminal subcultures on pp. 1101–2.

18. Hindus, *Prison and Plantation,* chapter 3.

19. The city ordinances for violation of which women ended up at Albion mainly prohibited prostitution. One section of the New York State Penal Law violated with some frequency by Albion inmates was sec. 43 of the Penal Law of 1915, a catchall clause prohibiting forbidden acts not specified elsewhere in the penal law.

20. See Introduction, note 2.

21. Connelly, *The Response to Prostitution,* p. 18, and Rosen, *The Lost Sisterhood,* pp. 42–43 (definition of "prostitution"). Rosen suggests on p. 3 that rates of prostitution had peaked by 1900.

22. The nature of this offense is obscure; perhaps it resembled child neglect. Ohio's concern with such matters is indicated by another offense that appears in the reformatory's registries: contributing toward dependency of a minor (!).

23. Ohio Reformatory for Women, *AR 1926:* 367.

24. The first woman at Auburn to receive an indeterminate sentence did so in 1901, according to New York Superintendent of State Prisons, *AR 1901:* 239; for details on the indeterminate sentencing law, see New York State Commission of Prisons, *AR 1902:* 82–83. According to Tennessee Board of Control, *BR 1918:* 43, that state's first parole and indeterminate sentencing law went into effect on February 21, 1913. The last case in the Ohio penitentiary sample to receive a fixed sentence was committed in July 1913; the first to receive an indeterminate sentence was received in October of the same year.

25. More specific, year-by-year data would enhance this analysis; nonetheless, that there was an overall downward trend seems clear.

26. Jim Crow legislation and other steps taken by southern whites to regain control over blacks after the Civil War intensified racial antagonisms; see Carleton, *Politics and Punishment,* p. 45, and Charles E. Silberman, *Criminal Violence, Criminal Justice* (New York: Vintage, 1980), pp. 176–77.

27. For the purposes of this study, *definite-type release* was defined to include cases marked as or released through "absolute discharge," "discharge," expiration of sentence without possibility of good-time credits, "final release," illegal commitment, pardon, payment of fine, release by order of attorney general or government agency, reversal of judgment, and special commutation by governor. *Indeterminate-type release* was defined to include "commutation," conditional pardon, discharge to care of relative, expiration of sentence with good-time credits, expiration of sentence with good-time credits possible but denied totally or in part, informal trial as domestic servant (preparole or, to use Ohio's terminology, "temporary parole"), parole, remission of fine followed by parole, reparole, and special commutation by governor followed by parole. *Other types of release* were defined to include court-order (including writ of habeas corpus), deportation, discharge because sick, expiration of sentence when source was unclear as

to whether good-time credits were awarded, held beyond expiration of sentence (apparently), release before evident legal date, release to begin a new sentence, release to federal authorities, and transfer to another penal or civil institution. Deaths were coded separately.

28. Ohio, *Legislative Acts 1925,* House Bill No. 236, secs. 2148–7 and 2148–12.

29. Victor, *The Life Story;* Goldman, *Living My Life.*

30. On the establishment of institutions for juvenile delinquents in Tennessee, see Randall G. Shelden, "Sex Discrimination in the Juvenile Justice System: Memphis, Tennessee, 1900–1917," chapter 4 in Marguerite Q. Warren, ed., *Comparing Female and Male Offenders* (Beverly Hills: Sage, 1981).

31. Glick and Neto, *National Study of Women's Correctional Programs,* p. xvii; see also Timothy J. Flanagan, David J. van Alstyne, and Michael R. Gottfredson, eds., *Sourcebook of Criminal Justice Statistics—1981* (Washington, D.C.: U.S. Government Printing Office, 1982), p. 480, showing that the majority of female prisoners in state and federal correctional institutions for adults on March 31, 1978 were between eighteen and thirty-four years old. Information on age at commitment is not strictly comparable to that on age of an entire population of prisoners; the two readings on age are, however, similar enough to permit the generalization.

32. For current statistics on the marital status of incarcerated women, see Glick and Neto, *National Study of Women's Correctional Programs,* pp. 112–15. For the historical study of five prisons, "single" was defined to include never married, separated, divorced, and widowed; "married" was defined to include married, common-law marriage, and cohabitation.

33. On some of the problems involved in defining women's social class, see chapter 7, note 3.

34. Glick and Neto, *National Study of Women's Correctional Programs,* pp. 134–39.

35. On control theory, see Travis Hirschi, *Causes of Delinquency* (Berkeley: University of California Press, 1969). Incarcerated women, of course, were not necessarily representative of all female offenders, and therefore criminological conclusions based on prisoner data, such as those suggested in the next paragraph, can only be tentative.

36. Lieber, "Translator's Introduction," p. 12. At the turn of the century, females constituted only 5.5 percent of the total prisoner population (U.S. Department of Commerce and Labor, Bureau of the Census, *Special Report. Prisoners and Juvenile Delinquents in Institutions 1904* [Washington, D.C.: Government Printing Office, 1907], p. 16). In 1980, females constituted 15.8 percent of all persons arrested, and in 1979, they constituted only 4 percent of all state prisoners (Timothy Flanagan and Maureen McLeod, eds., *Sourcebook of Criminal Justice Statistics—1982* [U.S. Department of Justice, Bureau of Justice Statistics, Washington, D.C.: U.S. Government Printing Office, 1983], pp. 399, 547).

37. For evidence on this point, see chapters 6 and 7.

38. For example, according to a report summarizing the conviction offenses of all prisoners received at New York's Newgate between 1797 and 1801, only 1.3 percent had been convicted of violent crimes, and all these were men convicted of arson (New York, Inspectors of State Prisons, *An Account of the State Prison,* p. 78). According to Vaux's data on Pennsylvania for the years 1817 through 1824 (information that covers both felons and misdemeanants), between 71 and 97 percent of female commitments were convicted of property crimes (Roberts

Vaux, *Notices of the Original, and Successive Efforts, To Improve the Discipline of the Prison at Philadelphia* . . . [Philadelphia: Kimber and Sharpless, 1826], pp. 70–75). And according to the Tennessee penitentiary's prisoner registries, of the eight women committed to that institution before 1850, only one had been convicted of a violent crime.

39. According to breakdowns of conviction offenses by period of commitment, in the period 1893–1903, of all women committed to the Tennessee penitentiary, Auburn, and the Ohio penitentiary, 36, 29, and 29 percent respectively had been convicted of violent crimes.

40. According to Flanagan et al., *Sourcebook of Criminal Justice Statistics—1981,* p. 484, 40 percent of all female state prisoners as of March 31, 1978, had been convicted of violent offenses.

41. According to Rita J. Simon, *The Contemporary Woman and Crime* (Rockville, Md.: National Institute of Mental Health, 1975), over recent decades, at least, the proportion of violent female offenders has remained low and stable.

42. Case No. 60.

NOTES TO CHAPTER 6

1. Kirby, *Years of Experience,* p. 200; Crawford, *Report on the Penitentiaries of the United States,* p. 26. Although Crawford did not explicitly say so, the context suggests that he had mainly northern prisons in mind.

2. Beaumont and Tocqueville, *On the Penitentiary System in the United States,* p. 196. On the public punishment of slaves, cf. Michael S. Hindus, "Black Justice Under White Law: Criminal Prosecutions of Blacks in Antebellum South Carolina," *Journal of American History* 63 (1977): 575–99.

3. On the mounting of racial tensions in the South at the turn of the century, see Carleton, *Politics and Punishment,* p. 45, and Silberman, *Criminal Violence, Criminal Justice,* pp. 176–77.

4. New York's State Prison for Women at Auburn did not open until 1893; the sample included some female state prisoners sentenced earlier and held in county penitentiaries until the women's prison opened. For information on sampling periods and methods used throughout this chapter, see Figure 1 and Appendix D.

5. Adamson, "Punishment after Slavery," p. 562. For other discussions of changes in the southern penal system after the Civil War, see Carleton, *Politics and Punishment;* Crowe, "The Origin and Development of Tennessee's Prison Problem"; Paul B. Foreman and Julien R. Tatum, "A Short History of Mississippi's Penal Systems," *Mississippi Law Journal* 10 (1938): 255–77; Frances Kellor, "The Criminal Negro. IV. Advantages and Abuses of Southern Penal Systems," *The Arena* (1901): 419–28; McKelvey, *American Prisons,* chapter 8; Novak, *The Wheel of Servitude,* chapter 1; Sellin, *Slavery and the Penal System,* chapter 11; A. Elizabeth Taylor, "The Origin and Development of the Convict Lease System in Georgia," *Georgia Historical Quarterly* 28 (March 1942): 113–28; and Zimmerman, "The Penal Reform Movement in the South." I draw on these sources throughout this chapter.

6. Louisiana, *Annual Report of the Board of Control of the Louisiana State Penitentiary: November 17, 1868,* p. 52, as quoted in Carleton, *Politics and Punishment,* p. 15; Kellor, "The Criminal Negro. IV. Advantages and Abuses of Southern Penal Systems," p. 420.

7. Kellor, "The Criminal Negro. IV. Advantages and Abuses of Southern Penal Systems," p. 421; North Carolina State Board of Charities and Public Welfare, *BR 1922:* 80; Lekkerkerker, *Reformatories for Women,* p. 199.

8. Hans von Hentig, "The Criminality of the Colored Woman," University of Colorado Studies, Series C 1 (3) (1942), pp. 255–59.

9. Carl E. Pope and R. L. McNeely, "Race, Crime, and Criminal Justice: An Overview," in R. L. McNeely and Carl E. Pope, eds., *Race, Crime and Criminal Justice* (Beverly Hills: Sage, 1981), p. 20. This essay presents an overview of evidence for and against current differential processing of blacks. Also see Haywood Burns, "Black People and the Tyranny of American Law," chapter 15 in Charles E. Reasons and Robert M. Rich, *The Sociology of Law: A Conflict Perspective* (Toronto: Butterworth, 1978); Ralph Frammolino and Susan Milstein, "Tilted Scales of Justice: Dallas Courts Levy Heavier Sentences When Victims are White," *Dallas Times Herald,* January 16, 1983; John R. Hepburn, "Race and the Decision to Arrest: An Analysis of Warrants Issued," *Journal of Research in Crime and Delinquency* 15 (1978): 54–73; National Minority Advisory Council on Criminal Justice, *The Inequality of Justice: A Report on Crime and the Administration of Justice in the Minority Community* (Washington, D.C., September 1980); Joan Petersilia, *Racial Discrimination in the Criminal Justice System* (Santa Monica, Calif.: Rand Corp., 1983); and Carl E. Pope, "Blacks and Juvenile Crime: A Review," in D. Georges-Abeyie, ed., *Blacks, Crime and Criminal Justice* (New York: Clark Boardman, forthcoming).

10. Michael J. Hindelang, "Race and Involvement in Common Law Personal Crimes," *American Sociological Review* 43 (February 1978): 93–109, and "Variations in Sex-Race-Age-Specific Incidence Rates of Offending," *American Sociological Review* 46 (August 1981): 461–74; Marvin E. Wolfgang, *Patterns in Criminal Homicide* (New York: John Wiley, 1958); cf. Roger McNeely and Carl Pope, "Race and Involvement in Common Law Personal Crimes: A Response to Hindelang," *The Review of Black Political Economy* 8 (4) (Summer 1980): 405–10. On differences between black and white female rates of offending, see also Diane K. Lewis, "Black Women Offenders and Criminal Justice: Some Theoretical Considerations," chapter 6 in Warren, *Comparing Female and Male Offenders,* and Vernetta D. Young, "Women, Race, and Crime," *Criminology* 18 (1) (May 1980): 26–34.

11. U.S. Department of Commerce and Labor, Bureau of the Census, *Prisoners and Juvenile Delinquents in Institutions 1904,* p. 24. On the relative impartiality of the criminal justice system's response to violent crimes, see Hindelang, "Race and Involvement in Common Law Personal Crimes," and Silberman, *Criminal Violence, Criminal Justice,* p. 161 and Appendix.

12. Silberman, *Criminal Violence, Criminal Justice,* p. 167.

13. Carleton, *Politics and Punishment,* pp. 44–45.

14. von Hentig, "The Criminality of the Colored Woman," pp. 254, 257–58.

15. Ibid., pp. 239–241, 255.

16. Richard J. Gelles, *The Violent Home* (Beverly Hills: Sage, 1974); Murray A. Straus, Richard J. Gelles, and Suzanne K. Steinmetz, *Behind Closed Doors: Violence in the American Family* (New York: Anchor Books, 1980).

17. Steffensmeier and Cobb have recently used urban migration to explain the 1934–1979 narrowing of the sex differential in arrests between black males and females, and they argue that young black women moving into urban areas "are

often more . . . marginally attached than the female citizenry as a whole." However, Steffensmeier and Cobb also believe that "the narrowing of the sex differential reflects changes in law enforcement practices and changes in statistical coverage as much or more than changes in actual behavior." See Darrell J. Steffensmeier and Michael J. Cobb, "Sex Differences in Urban Arrest Patterns, 1934–79," *Social Problems* 29 (1) (October 1981), pp. 45–47.

18. Lewis, "Black Women Offenders and Criminal Justice," p. 101; Donald Black, *The Behavior of Law* (New York: Academic Press, 1976), p. 53.

19. New York, Inspectors of State Prisons, *An Account of the State Prison or Penitentiary House*, p. 78; Ohio Penitentiary, *AR 1840:* 8; Tennessee State Penitentiary, *Report of . . . January, 1868:* 43. The pattern persists today; see Lewis, "Black Women Offenders and Criminal Justice."

   The 1870 census included prisoners but did not cross-tabulate by sex and race; hence Table 6.3 begins with 1880.

20. Here I am reasoning not only from the prisoner statistics but also from evidence that current offending rates are higher for black than white females; see the references cited in note 10, above.

21. See Michael J. Hindelang, *Criminal Victimization in Eight American Cities* (Cambridge, Mass.: Ballinger, 1976), especially pp. 197–99, for findings of victim surveys and a summary of findings of studies based on official (criminal justice agency) data.

22. See Black, *The Behavior of Law*, pp. 49–54; William J. Bowers, *Legal Homicide: Death as Punishment in America, 1864–1982* (Boston: Northeastern University Press, 1984), especially p. 126; William J. Bowers and Glenn L. Pierce, "Arbitrariness and Discrimination under Post-*Furman* Capital Statutes," *Crime and Delinquency* 26 (4) (October 1980): 563–635; Frammolino and Milstein, "Tilted Scales of Justice"; Michael L. Radelet, "Racial Characteristics and the Death Penalty," *American Sociological Review* 46 (6) (December 1981): 918–27; and Shelden, "Sex Discrimination in the Juvenile Justice System," p. 69. Gary Kleck reviews some of the evidence for devaluation of black victims and finds it unpersuasive in "Racial Discrimination in Criminal Sentencing," *American Sociological Review* 46 (6) (December 1981): 783–805.

   Frances Kellor made this point about victim valuation by quoting a southern official who "put into humorous English what is really, though often unconsciously, the practise. He said: 'If two white men quarrel and one *murders* the other, we imprison the culprit, and in due season pardon him; if a white man *kills* a negro, we let him off; if a negro murders a white man, we like as not lynch him; if a negro kills a negro we imprison him' " ("The Criminal Negro. IV. Advantages and Abuses of Southern Penal Systems," p. 420; emphasis in original).

23. U.S. Department of Commerce and Labor, Bureau of the Census, *Prisoners and Juvenile Delinquents in Institutions 1904*, p. 60. Thanks are due to Glenn L. Pierce of Northeastern University's Center for Applied Social Research for pointing out the possible connection between the greater proportion of black females (relative to black males) in prison populations and their greater access to white homes.

24. See, for example, Tennessee State Penitentiary, *BR 1882:* 18–72, *BR 1890:* 20–21, *BR 1898:* 915–17; the pre-Civil War data were derived from Tennes-

see State Archives, *Convict Record Book 1831–74*, Record Group 25, Ser. 12, vol. 86.

25. For a northern example, see Rafter, "Hard Times: Custodial Prisons for Women," pp. 243–46.

26. On the possible advantage of black women over black men in cases where execution was a possible outcome, see von Hentig, "The Criminality of the Colored Woman," p. 257.

27. Lewis, "Black Women Offenders and Criminal Justice," p. 102; Lombroso and Ferrero, *The Female Offender*, p. 153.

28. von Hentig, "The Criminality of the Colored Woman," p. 237, also found smaller differences between black and white women in property than in violent crime.

29. See, for example, Hindus, *Prison and Plantation*, pp. 63–67, attributing South Carolina's higher levels of violence to "southern violence and volatility" in general, "chivalric notions of honor" in particular. Hindus's discussion is especially useful in that it links the phenomenon that some criminologists call "subcultural violence" with the institution of slavery; "slavery itself," Hindus writes, "seemed to inspire a certain pugnacity" among whites (p. 66). Arguably, slavery also engendered pugnacity among blacks: it perpetrated daily outrages, deprived blacks of most means of retaliation other than violence, and encouraged short-term solutions (few others being available to slaves). Whatever the sources of the relatively high levels of violence among southern whites, slavery itself certainly may have encouraged blacks to adopt a cultural propensity toward violence that continues to manifest itself in high levels of black violent crime today.

30. Hindus, *Prison and Plantation*, pp. 48–84.

31. U.S. Department of Commerce and Labor, Bureau of the Census, *Prisoners and Juvenile Delinquents in Institutions 1904*, p. 23.

32. Shelden, "Sex Discrimination in the Juvenile Justice System," discerned a similar pattern. Focusing on dispositions by the Memphis juvenile court in the early twentieth century, Shelden found the court much more likely to commit white than black girls to child-saving institutions (which resembled Albion and other prisons for adult women that were oriented toward rehabilitation). "[T]he philosophy of the juvenile court that children and youth needed 'care and treatment' apparently did not apply to blacks" (p. 69).

33. These data cannot be used to reach firm conclusions about racial discrimination at sentencing because they do not include information on actual time served or prior record.

34. Kleck, "Racial Discrimination in Criminal Sentencing," pp. 798–99.

35. Ibid., p. 800. Shelden, "Sex Discrimination in the Juvenile Justice System," also found that blacks were treated more leniently than whites, a phenomenon that he attributes to devaluation of black victims and benign neglect of black public order offenders, among other factors; see especially pp. 68–69.

36. Sellin, *Slavery and the Penal System*, p. 162. On death rates, see Adamson, "Punishment after Slavery," p. 566; Carleton, *Politics and Punishment*, pp. 37, 46; Foreman and Tatum, "A Short History of Mississippi's State Penal Systems," pp. 262, 265–66; and Sellin, *Slavery and the Penal System*, pp. 150–51.

234

150

Notes to pages 150–154

37. U.S. Department of the Interior, Census Office (Frederick Howard Wines), *Report on the Defective, Dependent, and Delinquent Classes . . . as Returned at the Tenth Census (June 1, 1880)* (Washington D.C.: Government Printing Office, 1888), pp. 520–25. Novak, *The Wheel of Servitude*, p. 32, similarly notes that leasing affected black men more adversely than white men: in the South in the 1870s, "there was a general feeling that white men should not be included in chain gangs. . . . In general, the few whites who were actually sent to prison were charged with serious crimes, such as murder or arson, which often debarred them from work outside the prison. In states where such restrictions were not applied, it was almost impossible to get a jury to send a white man to be farmed out."

38. Tennessee State Archives, *Convict Record Book 1831–74*, Record Group 25, Series 12, vol. 86.

39. Georgia General Assembly, *Proceedings of the Committee Appointed to Investigate the Condition of the Georgia Penitentiary* (orig. 1870; repr. New York: Arno Press, 1974), pp. 122–23.

40. Kellor, "The Criminal Negro. IV. Advantages and Abuses of Southern Penal Systems," pp. 422–23.

41. The term "state slavery" is Carleton's (*Politics and Punishment*, p. 193).

42. Georgia Prison Commission, *AR 1899:* 14; William B. Cox, F. Lovell Bixby, and William T. Root, eds., *Handbook of American Prisons and Reformatories, Vol. I, 1933* (New York: The Osborne Association, 1933), p. 295 (conditions in Maryland).

43. North Carolina State Board of Charities and Public Welfare, *BR 1922:* 80–82 (to rescue white women); Thornton W. Mitchell of the North Carolina State Archives to Elena Natalizia, June 4, 1980 (information on history of North Carolina reformatory; letter in possession of Nicole H. Rafter). As noted in chapter 3 (note 28), I was denied access to the reports of the Arkansas State Farm for Women; however, according to the 1923 prisoner census, it received whites only.

44. New Jersey State Reformatory for Women, *AR 1913:* 8, 5, *AR 1915:* 12.

45. Ibid., *AR 1915:* 5, 12; Lekkerkerker, *Reformatories for Women*, p. 234.

46. New Jersey State Reformatory for Women, *AR 1915:* 12.

47. von Hentig, "The Criminality of the Colored Woman," p. 236, notes, "[T]he relatively high percentage of colored females sentenced for violation of the Narcotic Drug Act becomes explicable when we consider the close connection between prostitution [to which black women were driven by financial need] and drug consumption."

48. "Report Condemns Facilities at Women's Reformatory," *The Providence Journal*, December 24, 1928: 16 (both quotations).

49. New York State Board of Charities, "Report of the Special Committee appointed to investigate charges made against the New York State Reformatory for Women at Bedford Hills, N.Y.," in *AR 1915:* 853; Lekkerkerker, *Reformatories for Women*, p. 234. The literature on interracial homosexuality in female institutions is extensive; see, for example, Margaret Otis, "A Perversion not Commonly Noted," *Journal of Abnormal Psychology* 8 (1913): 112–14.

50. New Jersey State Reformatory for Women, *AR 1913:* 8; Lekkerkerker, *Reformatories for Women*, p. 522 (Pennsylvania music club); Dan J. Morgan, *Historical Lights and Shadows of the Ohio State Penitentiary*, p. 95.

NOTES TO CHAPTER 7

1. More precisely, criminologists such as Hirschi attempt to explain why law-abiders do *not* break the law; see Travis Hirschi, *Causes of Delinquency*, p. 10.

2. David J. Rothman, "Social Control: The Uses and Abuses of the Concept in the History of Incarceration," in Cohen and Scull, *Social Control and the State*, p. 113. For overviews of the history of the concept of social control in social science, see the "Introduction" to the Cohen and Scull volume, and Morris Janow-itz, "Sociological Theory and Social Control," *American Journal of Sociology* 81 (1) (1975): 82–108. Examples of the feminist perspective appear in Carol Smart and Barry Smart, eds., *Women, Sexuality, and Social Control* (London: Routledge & Kegan Paul, 1978).

3. The definition of *social class,* a thorny and unresolved issue in any case, be-comes even more difficult when one deals with women. There are various ways to define social class, but none adequately accounts for the peculiar position of women. As Erik Olin Wright and Luca Perrone have pointed out ("Marxist Class Categories and Income Inequality," *American Sociological Review* 42 [1] [February 1977]: 33), one traditional conceptualization of class is based on status hierarchies. Factors that confer status, however, are different for women and men (the former derive status from the latter, for instance). Class has also been identi-fied by "position within authority or power structures" (to continue with the Wright-Perrone classification). This approach slights women by ignoring their exclusion from structures of authority and power. To identify class in terms of "groups of people with common economic 'life chances,' " a third approach, overlooks differences between the economic "life chances" of women and men. A fourth, Marxian approach that defines class "primarily in terms of structural position within the social organization of production" disregards the importance of gender in the social division of labor. Some Marxist feminists have tried to overcome this problem by redefining production to include domestic labor.

However these conceptual problems are resolved, it is clear that large social class differences separated the prisoners of women's reformatories from those who attempted to retrain them. The prisoners were poor women: most came from families in which the father held a blue-collar job, and often their mothers worked as well, taking in laundry or going out to day labor. Moreover, most of the prisoners had worked for wages in low-level positions before incarceration. The women who established reformatories often had considerable personal wealth; those who served on reformatory boards of managers had the leisure to engage in this unpaid work and the connections required for a gubernatorial ap-pointment; and many of those who administered reformatories had graduated from elite colleges and universities.

4. Although Albion established the model, reformatories of the Progressive era looked for leadership to the women's prison at Bedford, N.Y., where superin-tendent Katherine B. Davis energetically publicized her institution's experiments.

5. The registries and case files are held by the New York State Archives in Al-bany; on sampling methods, see Appendix D. In the material that follows, cases are identified by the numbers used in the prisoner registries.

6. The phrase is taken from a registry entry for inmate No. 107; see note 25 below and accompanying text.

7. On true womanhood, see chapter 2, note 2. As the quotation that heads this section indicates (see note 6, above, and accompanying text), the idea of true

womanhood played an important role in the conceptualization of gender into the twentieth century.

8. On their parents' employment, see note 3, above; on their own job histories, see chapter 5.

9. New York, *Laws of 1890,* Ch. 238, sec. 8.

10. On the equation of even minor forms of "immorality" with prostitution, see Connelly, *The Response to Prostitution,* pp. 18 and 37. In chapter 2, Connelly links the hysteria over female immorality to the widening gap between ideal womanhood and the lifestyle of working-class women; see also Rosen, *The Lost Sisterhood,* especially p. 43. On the sexually rebellious "new" woman of the turn of the century, see Peter Gabriel Filene, *Him/Her/Self: Sex Roles in Modern America* (New York: New American Library, 1974), chapter 1. For letters by a woman who seems in many ways to have resembled the typical Albion inmate, see Ruth Rosen and Sue Davidson, eds., *The Mamie Papers* (Old Westbury, N.Y.: The Feminist Press, 1977).

11. Inmate No. 2253.

12. Inmate No. 2043.

13. Inmate No. 2183.

14. Inmate Nos. 1791 (in love with Mr. Ludwig) and 1829 (involved with the disreputable Washington).

15. On defective delinquency theory and intelligence testing within prisons, see chapter 3, notes 41–53 and accompanying text.

16. New York, Western House of Refuge (hereafter NYWHR), *AR 1894:* 10, 12 (managers' aims and views); New York State Commission of Prisons, *AR 1897:* 106, and NYWHR, *AR 1896:* 21 (abandonment of the washing machine).

17. NYWHR, *AR 1912:* 13, *AR 1917:* 18 (punctuation as in original).

18. Elliott Park Currie, "Managing the Minds of Men: The Reformatory Movement, 1865–1920" (University of California, Berkeley, Ph.D. diss., 1973), p. 202.

19. NYWHR, *AR 1917:* 14.

20. On the "servant problem," see David M. Katzman, *Seven Days a Week: Women and Domestic Service in Industrializing America* (New York: Oxford University Press, 1978), and Daniel J. Walkowitz, "Working-class Women in the Gilded Age: Factory, Community and Family Life among Cohoes, New York, Cotton Workers," *Journal of Social History* 5 (Summer 1972): 464–90.

21. New York State Commission of Correction, *AR 1927:* 87. The earning power of domestics relative to other female workers is a complex question, partly because domestics received room and board (see Katzman, *Seven Days a Week,* Appendix 3). However, notations in Albion's registries do indicate that domestics earned lower raw wages than the comparatively few prisoners paroled to factory positions. In the period 1915–1920, for instance, women on domestic parole were paid between three and five dollars a week, while those placed in factory jobs earned seven to fifteen dollars, and one woman hired by the General Electric radio shop in Schenectady received a weekly wage of twenty-five dollars. It would be interesting to know whether the reformatory's practice of paroling inmates to domestic positions depressed wages for other servants in the area.

22. NYWHR, *Information and Regulations* (Albion, N.Y.: n.d.; copy included in the case file of, e.g., inmate No. 1891).

23. Ibid.

24. Inmate No. 2051.

25. Inmate No. 107.

26. Inmate No. 2233. According to Mary, the child's father was a state trooper.

27. Mary W. Libby to Clement J. Wyle, October 24, 1941 (letter located by Linda Dwelley, Media Resources, Maine Criminal Justice Academy in Waterville, who planned to send the original to the state archives).

28. Inmate No. 1699.

29. Inmate No. 1701.

30. Mrs. J. A. H _____ to Mrs. Flora Daniels, February 28, 1924, in file of Virginia S., inmate No. 2157.

31. Similarly, institutions for juveniles served a variety of functions, providing academic and vocational training, health care, and other social services; see Schlossman, *Love and the American Delinquent,* pp. 22–25. Brenzel, "Lancaster Industrial School for Girls," points out that the girls' reform school provided services not otherwise available to the urban poor; thus, impoverished parents were willing to commit daughters to the institution. Parents who committed daughters to Albion may also have done so because the institution furnished social services to which they otherwise had no access.

32. Inmates Nos. 2253 and 2043.

33. Inmates Nos. 79 (the "wreck") and 1917 (escapee who wrote to report marriage).

34. Nellie L. to Mrs. M. K. Boyd, April 8, 1907, in case file of Inmate No. 18; punctuation as in original.

35. Charles E. Rosenberg, "Sexuality, Class and Role in 19th-Century America," *American Quarterly* 25 (1973), p. 143.

36. See, for example, Vermont Department of Public Welfare, *BR 1928:* 81, describing return visits to Vermont's reformatory-like prison for women, and Freedman, *Their Sisters' Keepers,* p. 104, illustrating the same phenomenon at the Massachusetts reformatory.

37. Diane Polan, "Toward a Theory of Law and Patriarchy," chapter 15 in David Kairys, ed., *The Politics of Law: A Progressive Critique* (New York: Pantheon, 1982), pp. 298–99; Walkowitz, "Working-class Women in the Gilded Age," p. 487.

NOTES TO CONCLUSION

1. Dix, *Remarks on Prisons and Prison Discipline,* pp. 107–8; U.S. Department of Justice, Bureau of Justice Statistics, *Prisoners 1925–1981,* Bulletin NCJ-85861 (Washington, D.C.: U.S. Department of Justice, December 1982), p. 2 (current number and proportion); Flanagan et al., *Sourcebook of Criminal Justice Statistics—1981,* p. 482; Glick and Neto, *National Study of Women's Correctional Programs,* pp. 113, 134–40.

2. For documentation of these problems, see the sources cited in the Introduction, note 6, and Judith Resnik and Nancy Shaw, "Prisoners of their Sex: Health Problems of Incarcerated Women," in Ira P. Robbins, ed., *Prisoners' Rights Source Book: Theory, Litigation, and Practice,* vol. 2 (New York: Clark Boardman, 1980).

3. Flanagan et al., *Sourcebook of Criminal Justice Statistics—1981*, p. 482.

4. See, for example, William A. Muraskin, "The Social-Control Theory in American History: A Critique," *Journal of Social History* 9 (June 1976): 559–69; Patricia O'Brien, "Crime and Punishment as Historical Problem," *Journal of Social History* 11 (June 1978): 508–20; and Rothman, "Social Control: The Uses and Abuses of the Concept."

5. Clarice Feinman is one of the few who have recognized the important role played by imagery in criminal justice. In *Women in the Criminal Justice System* (New York: Praeger, 1980), she centers her discussion around "the madonna/ whore duality," which she traces back to Greek mythology and Judeo-Christian theology. Feinman holds that the tendency to classify women into dichotomous groups, one good (fair, pure, and subservient), the other bad (dark, sexual, and independent) basically stems from male fear of female sexuality (pp. 1–2).

Perhaps naturally, prison histories that focus exclusively on men overlook the effects of sexual stereotyping on the design of institutions.

6. Most of the campus-style institutions have been built in the South and West because, until recently, many states in these regions had only makeshift quarters for women. A campus-type women's prison has also been constructed in Michigan, one of the few midwestern states that never built a reformatory; this is the Huron Valley Women's Facility, opened at Ypsilanti in 1977.

7. Temin, "Discriminatory Sentencing of Women Offenders," p. 258. Temin discusses the Pennsylvania, Connecticut, and related cases in detail.

8. U.S. Comptroller General, *Women in Prison*, pp. 8–9.

9. "Better Deal for Women in Prison," *New York Times*, August 1, 1982: E7.

10. "Inmate Mother to Sue Mass.," *Boston Globe*, May 23, 1983; "A Question of Female Inmates' Options," *Boston Globe*, June 10, 1983. On legal activism of incarcerated women, see Smith College School of Social Work, *Legal Issues of Female Inmates: A Report to the National Institute of Corrections* (Northampton, Mass.: Smith College School of Social Work, May 1982).

11. U.S. Comptroller General, *Women in Prison*, p. 9, citing Molar v. Gates, 159 Cal. Rptr. 239 (4th Dist. 1979).

12. Traditionally, courts have used the same standards for men and women in deciding whether a killing was justifiable because committed in self-defense. Yet there are signs that the law is evolving to take into account differences between the sexes—including differences in size and weight, perceptions of danger, and personal histories—in making such determinations; see Ann Jones, *Women Who Kill* (New York: Fawcett Columbine, 1980), chapter 6. If the law continues to evolve in this direction, some women who previously would have been found guilty and sentenced to prison will be found innocent.

13. This solution and the next two are discussed in more detail in U.S. Comptroller General, *Women in Prison*, pp. 27–33.

14. On co-corrections, see J. G. Ross, E. Heffernan, J. R. Sevick, and F. T. Johnson, *National Evaluation Program, Phase 1 Report: Assessment of Coeducational Corrections* (Washington, D.C.: National Institute of Law Enforcement and Criminal Justice, LEAA, U.S. Department of Justice, June 1978), and John Ortiz Smykla, ed., *Coed Prison* (New York: Human Sciences Press, 1980).

15. See Ross et al., *National Evaluation Program, Phase 1 Report*, and Esther Heffernan, "Female Corrections—History and Analysis," Opening Address:

Conference on the Confinement of Female Offenders, U.S. Bureau of Prisons, Lexington, Kentucky, March 28–30, 1978 (unpublished paper, p. 9).

16. Esther Heffernan, *Women Offenders in the Alaska Criminal Justice System,* unpublished report to Division of Corrections, State of Alaska, Department of Health and Social Services, July 15, 1979, p. 17. I am grateful to Dr. Heffernan for supplying me with copies of this report, the report cited in note 17, and some of her unpublished papers on female corrections.

17. Charles F. Campbell (then head of Alaska's Division of Adult Corrections), "Shared Resources: The Implementation of Co-Corrections at the Hiland Mountain and Meadow Creek Correctional Centers, Eagle River, Alaska," unpublished report dated July 1982, p. 1.

18. Ibid., p. 7.

19. Ibid., p. 16.

Selected Bibliography

ARCHIVAL MATERIAL

New York State Archives. New York State Prison for Women at Auburn.
Series 500F:
  Vol. 1. Register of Convicts Received, May 1983–March 1918.
  Vol. 2. Register of Convicts Received, August 1928–June 1933.
  Vol. 3. Register of Convicts Discharged, June 1893–December 1919.
  Vol. 4. Bertillon Register, July 1909–1933.
Series 500M:
  Commutation Ledger. Box 20, October 1920–April 1930.
  Definite Sentence Book. Box 20, December 1928–June 1932.
  Determinate Sentence Book. Box 20, vol. VII-C, June 1921–February 1929.
  Indefinite Sentence Books. Box 20, vol. VII-A, June 1897–November 1906;
    vol. VII-B, January 1915–July 1923; vol. VII-D, August 1923–December
    1928; vol. VII-E, December 1928–June 1932.

————. Western House of Refuge for Women. Inmate Case Files. Series 520A.

————. Western House of Refuge for Women. Inmate Admission Ledgers. Series
  520B, 1894–1931.

Ohio Penitentiary. Registers of Prisoners, 1900–16.

Ohio State Archives. Ohio Governor. Verbatim Report of the Proceedings . . .
  presented to the Joint Committee on Investigation of the Ohio Penitentiary,
  1908, and Report of the Special Committee of the 77th General Assembly
  of Ohio Appointed to Investigate Penitentiary Buildings, Management and
  Convict Labor. Series 1590, December 1908.

————. Ohio Penitentiary. Criminal Record. Series 1530, 1815–34.

————. Ohio Penitentiary. Registers of Prisoners. Series 1536, 1834–1900.

————. Ohio Reformatory for Women. Press Clippings. Series 1680.

————. Ohio Reformatory for Women. Registers of Prisoners. 2 volumes. Series 1677, 1916–43.

————. Ohio Reformatory for Women. Superintendent's Correspondence. Series 1676, 1925–51.

————. Ohio State Reformatory [for Men]. Admission Books. Series 1706, vols. 17–19, 1896–1926.

Rockefeller Archive Center, Pocantico Hills, North Tarrytown, N.Y. Bureau of Social Hygiene Collection. Series 3.

Tennessee State Archives. Board of Inspectors of the Tennessee Penitentiary. Minutes of Meetings. Record Group 25, Series 4, vol. 31, 1877–92.

————. Main Prison, Convict Record Books. Record Group 25, Series 7, vol. 47, 1873–98; Series 12, vol. 45, 1833–42; vol. 86, 1831–74; vol. 93, 1886–87; vol. 94, 1887–90; vol. 96, 1885–95; vol. 97, 1892–94; vol. 98, 1894–96.

————. Main Prison, Convict Record Books K-T. Vols. 92 (1897–1900), 95 (1887–1908 [sic]), 99 (1900–04), 100 (1904–12), 101 (1912–17), 102 (1917–22), 103 (1922–26), 104 (1926–29), 105 (1929–31), 106 (1931–33).

————. Maintenance of Convicts, Steward's Reports. Record Group 25, Series 3, vol. 28, 1896–97.

Tennessee State Department of Correction. Convict Record Book U, 1933–35.

FEDERAL, STATE, AND ASSOCIATION REPORTS

American Correctional Association. Directory 1980. College Park, Md.: American Correctional Association, 1980.

Colorado Department of Charities and Corrections. First Biennial Report, 1923–24.

Connecticut Board of Charities (Department of Public Welfare). Reports, 1905–28.

Connecticut Prison Association. Reports, 1912–18, 1934–35.

Connecticut State Farm for Women. Reports, 1917–30.

Detroit House of Correction. Reports, 1863, 1865–71, 1874–75.

Georgia General Assembly. Proceedings of the Committee Appointed to Investigate the Condition of the Georgia Penitentiary. 1870. Reprint. N.Y.: Arno Press, 1974.

Georgia Prison Commission. Reports, 1897–99, 1906–07, 1911–12, 1916–17, 1921, 1929–30.

Illinois Department of Public Welfare. Reports, 1920–40.

Illinois Prison Inquiry Commission. The Prison System in Illinois. N.p.: n.p., 1937.

Indiana Reformatory Institution for Women and Girls. Reports, 1871–77, 1879, 1883, 1888, 1902–03, 1907–08.

Indiana State Prison South. Reports, 1863–64, 1869–70, 1872–73.

Iowa Board of Control. Reports, 1908–28.

Kansas Industrial Farm for Women. Reports, 1916–26.

Kansas State Penitentiary. *Reports,* 1907–16.

Kentucky Board of Prison Commissioners. *Reports,* 1898–1917.

Kentucky State Board of Charities and Corrections. *Reports,* 1920–31.

Louisiana State Penitentiary. *Reports,* 1866–68, 1906–07, 1916–17.

Maine. Joint Special Committee on the Maine State Prison. *Report of the Joint Special Committee on Investigation of the Affairs of the Maine State Prison.* Augusta: Sprague, Owen & Nash, 1874.

Maine Reformatory for Women. *Reports,* 1917–26.

Maine State Board of Charities and Corrections. *Reports,* 1913–26.

Maine State Prison. *Reports,* 1901, 1905, 1911–16.

Maryland House of Correction. *Reports,* 1917–22.

Maryland Penitentiary. *Warden's Reports,* 1917–22.

Maryland State Board of Prison Control. *Reports,* 1917–22.

Massachusetts. *Rules and Regulations of the Reformatory Prison for Women.* Boston: Rand, Avery, & Company, 1879.

Massachusetts Board of Commissioners of Prisons. *Report in Relation to the Division of the Commonwealth into Prison Districts.* Senate Document no. 4. Boston: Albert J. Wright, 1877.

————. *Reports,* 1871–82, 1888.

Massachusetts Board of State Charities. *Reports,* 1868, 1872, 1874, 1876, 1879.

Massachusetts Reformatory Prison for Women. *First Annual Report.* Massachusetts Senate Document no. 51, 1879 (for other reports in this series, see the annual reports of the Massachusetts Board of Commissioners of Prisons).

Massachusetts Senate. *Report of the Committee on Prisons.* Massachusetts Senate Document no. 244, May 29, 1873.

Michigan Board of State Commissioners for the General Supervision of Charitable, Penal, Pauper, and Reformatory Institutions (State Board of Corrections and Charities). *Reports,* 1878, 1914.

Michigan State Prison. *Reports,* 1864, 1866, 1868, 1871–73.

Minnesota State Board of Control. *Reports,* 1908–28.

Minnesota State Board of Visitors for Public Institutions. *Reports,* 1908–12, 1916–18, 1924.

Minnesota State Prison (Stillwater). *Reports,* 1908–22.

Minnesota State Reformatory for Women (Shakopee). *Reports,* 1922–26, 1930.

Missouri Department of Penal Institutions (Penal Board). *Reports,* 1917–34, 1940, 1944.

Missouri State Board of Charities and Corrections. *Reports,* 1902–14, 1918, 1922–32.

Missouri State Penitentiary. *Reports,* 1866, 1882, 1900, 1904.

National Society of Penal Information. *Handbook of American Prisons.* G. P. Putnam's Sons, 1925.

Nebraska. Board of Control. *Reports*, 1921, 1925–27, 1931.

Nebraska Industrial Home. *Reports*, 1890–92, 1898, 1918.

Nebraska Reformatory for Women. *Biennial Report of the Superintendent of the State Reformatory for Women, York, Nebraska, For the Period Ending June 30, 1923* (other reports in this series appear in the biennial reports of the Board of Control of Nebraska).

Nebraska State Board of Charities and Correction. *Reports*, 1908, 1912, 1914–18.

New Hampshire State Board of Charities and Correction. *Reports*, 1901–12, 1922.

New Jersey. *Report of the Commissioners to Examine the Various Systems of Prison Discipline and Propose an Improved Plan.* Trenton: The True American Office, 1869.

————. *Report of the Joint Committee on Female Prison and Reformatory.* Trenton: MacCrellish & Quigley, State Printers, 1887.

————. *Report of the Prison Inquiry Commission.* Volume I. Trenton: 1918.

————. *Report of the Special Committee on Investigation of State Prisons to the Legislature, Session of 1890.* Trenton: MacCrellish & Quigley, State Printers, 1890.

————. State Charities Aid and Prison Reform Association. *Annual Report of the Board of Managers of the State Charities Aid and Prison Reform Association of New Jersey for the Year 1908.* Legislative Document no. 34, 1908.

————. State of New Jersey Department of Institutions and Agencies. *Handbook of State Institutions and Agencies.* Trenton: 1928.

New Jersey Department of Charities and Corrections. *Reports*, 1908–9, 1911–17.

New Jersey Prison Reform Association. *First Annual Report of the New Jersey Prison Reform Association.* Trenton: Phillips & Boswell, 1850.

New Jersey State Prison. *Reports*, 1890, 1895, 1900, 1905, 1908, 1910–11.

New Jersey State Reformatory for Women. *Reports*, 1913–15, 1917–20.

New Jersey Women's Reformatory Commission. *Report of the New Jersey Women's Reformatory Commission.* Trenton: MacCrellish & Quigley, State Printers, 1905.

New York. Auburn State Prison. *Reports*, 1832, 1835, 1839–40.

————. House of Refuge at Hudson. *Reports*, 1887–92, 1897.

————. Inspectors of State Prisons. *An Account of the State Prison or Penitentiary House, in the City of New-York.* New York: Isaac Colling and Son, 1801.

————. Mount Pleasant State Prison. *Report of the Inspectors of the Mount Pleasant State Prison in answer to a resolution of the Assembly.* New York Assembly Document no. 139, 1846.

————. Mount Pleasant State Prison. *Report of the Minority of the late Board of Inspectors of the Mount Pleasant State Prison.* New York Senate Document no. 17, 1848.

————. Mount Pleasant State Prison. *Reports*, 1830–31, 1835–41, 1843–47.

————. Prison Association of New York. *Reports*, 1846, 1876–94, 1896–97, 1899–1906, 1908, 1910, 1912–13, 1916, 1919, 1922–23, 1927–28, 1932–33.

————. Western House of Refuge for Women. *Information and Regulations.* Albion: n.d.

————. Western House of Refuge for Women (Albion State Training School). *Reports,* 1894–98, 1903, 1907, 1912, 1917–18, 1922, 1926, 1930–31.

————. Women's Prison Association of New York. *Reports,* 1890–93, 1895, 1897, 1899, 1901–2, 1904–14, 1916–20.

New York Committee on State Prisons. *Report of the Committee on State Prisons, on Petitions Praying for a Law Abolishing the Use of the Whip in Our Penitentiaries.* New York Senate Document no. 120, 1846.

————. *Report of the Committee on State Prisons, relative to a prison for female convicts.* New York Senate Document no. 68, 1835.

————. *Reports,* 1832–33.

New York Inspectors of State Prisons. *Reports,* 1848, 1851, 1876.

New York Senate Committee on State Prisons. *Report of the committee on State Prisons, on the resolution of the Senate relative to Mount Pleasant prison.* New York Senate Document no. 153, 1847.

New York State Board of Charities. *Reports,* 1878, 1881, 1883, 1885–87, 1889, 1892–93, 1895, 1897, 1900–9, 1914–15, 1917, 1919, 1924.

New York State Charities Aid Association. *Reports,* 1879, 1881–83, 1885, 1887, 1892.

New York State Commission on Prison Administration and Construction. *The Correctional Institutions for Women.* Albany: J. B. Lyon, 1932.

New York State Commission of Prisons. *Report of the Special Committee of the State Commission of Prisons Appointed to Investigate the Matter of Mental Disease and Delinquency.* Ossining: Sing Sing, 1918.

New York State Commission of Prisons (Commission of Correction). *Reports,* 1896–98, 1900, 1902, 1904–6, 1908, 1910, 1914–18, 1920, 1927–28, 1931, 1934.

New York State Conference of Charities and Corrections. *Proceedings,* 1900–03, 1905–6, 1908, 1910, 1914, 1916, 1918.

New York State Department of Correction. *Albion State Training School, Albion, N.Y.: Its History, Purpose, Makeup and Program.* West Coxsackie: New York State Vocational Institution, 1949.

————. "These Are Your N.Y. State Correctional Institutions. Auburn Prison." *Correction* 14 (6) (June 1949): 3–19.

————. *Westfield State Farm, Bedford Hills, N.Y.: Its History, Purpose, Makeup and Program.* West Coxsackie: New York State Vocational Institution, n.d. [1949?].

————. *Your New York State Department of Correction and its Institutions: Custody . . . Treatment . . . Training . . . Rehabilitation. . . .* N.p.: n.p., 1953.

New York State Governor (Roswell P. Flower). *Annual Message,* January 3, 1893.

New York State Joint Committee of the Legislature. *Report of Investigation concerning the Management, Conduct and Affairs of the Western House of Refuge for Women at Albion, N.Y.* New York Legislative Document no. 48, 1920.

New York (State) Prison Department. *Handbook of Information Regarding the Correctional Institutions of the State of New York.* Albany: J. B. Lyon, 1910.

New York State Prison Survey Committee. *Report.* Albany: J. B. Lyon, 1920.

New York State Reformatory for Women at Bedford. *Reports,* 1892–98, 1901–5, 1910–11, 1913, 1915, 1921.

New York Superintendent of State Prisons (Commissioner of Correction). *Reports,* 1892–97, 1899, 1901, 1903, 1911–17, 1923, 1927, 1932.

North Carolina State Board of Charities and Public Welfare, Division of Institutions and Corrections. *Reports,* 1932–40.

———. *Reports,* 1922–36.

Ohio. "Report of Special Legislative Committee on the Girls' Industrial Home." In Ohio Board of State Charities, *Ohio Bulletin of Charities and Correction* 17 (1) (February 2, 1911): 27–35.

Ohio Board of State Charities. *Thirty-Second Report for . . . 1901.* In Ohio Board of State Charities, *Ohio Bulletin of Charities and Correction* 16 (3a) (November 1910): n.p.

Ohio Penitentiary. *Reports,* 1820–21, 1832, 1840, 1850, 1860, 1870, 1880, 1890, 1900, 1909, 1912, 1915–18, 1921.

Ohio Reformatory for Women. *Reports,* 1917–21, 1926, 1930, 1936.

Oregon Commission to Investigate the State Penitentiary. *Report of the Commission To Investigate The Oregon State Penitentiary.* Portland: January 1917.

Pennsylvania Board of Public Charities. *A Paper on Prison Reform.* Harrisburg: B. F. Meyers, 1875.

Pennsylvania Board of Public Charities (Department of Public Welfare). *Reports,* 1889, 1893, 1908, 1910–14, 1922–24, 1928–30.

Pennsylvania Prison Society. *Journal of Prison Discipline and Philanthropy.* Issue Numbers 39, 40, 42, 47, 48, 50, 52, 53 (1900–14).

———. *The Prison Journal.* Vols. I (January 1921), IV (2) (April 1924), V (2) (April 1925), V (3) (July 1925).

Pennsylvania State Industrial Home for Women. *Reports,* 1924–30.

Pennsylvania State Penitentiary for the Eastern District. *Reports,* 1907, 1910–12, 1919–20.

Pennsylvania State Penitentiary for the Western District. *Reports,* 1910–14, 1920.

Rhode Island. *Governor's Message and Report of the Commission to Investigate the State Public Welfare Commission and all Departments Thereunder.* Providence: E. L. Freeman Company, 1929.

Rhode Island Board of State Charities and Corrections. *Reports,* 1905, 1910, 1915.

Rhode Island Penal and Charitable Commission. *Reports,* 1918–20.

Rhode Island Public Welfare Commission. *Reports,* 1924–30, 1933.

Rhode Island Advisory Board of Visitors to Institutions Where Women are Imprisoned (Women's Board of Visitors). *Reports,* 1885, 1905, 1907–8, 1912, 1915, 1917–20.

South Carolina State Board of Public Welfare. *Reports,* 1920–22, 1924–26.

Tennessee. *Report of Joint Investigating Committee on Penal Institutions, December 1, 1906, to November 30, 1908, Inclusive.* In *Appendix to the Senate and House Journals, 1909.*

———. *Report of the Joint Penitentiary Investigating Committee to the Fiftieth General Assembly, March 24, 1897.* In *Appendix to the House Journal 1897*: 871–934.

Tennessee Board of Control. *Report,* 1918.

Tennessee Board of Prison Commissioners. *Reports,* 1898–1912.

Tennessee Department of Institutions. *Reports,* 1924, 1928–30, 1934, 1943.

Tennessee State Penitentiary (Nashville). *Reports,* 1855–60, 1868, 1882, 1884, 1888–94 (series continues in reports of Joint Penitentiary Investigating Committee, Board of Prison Commissioners, Board of Control, and Department of Institutions).

Texas. Officials of the Texas Prison System. *Report,* 1911.

———. Superintendent of Texas State Penitentiaries. *Reports,* 1900–2, 1906–10.

U.S. Comptroller General. *Women in Prison: Inequitable Treatment Requires Action.* Washington, D.C.: Government Printing Office, 1980.

U.S. Department of Commerce, Bureau of the Census. *Prisoners 1923.* Washington, D.C.: Government Printing Office, 1926.

———. *Prisoners and Juvenile Delinquents in the United States 1910.* Washington, D.C.: Government Printing Office, 1918.

———. *Statistical Directory of State Institutions for the Defective, Dependent, and Delinquent Classes.* Washington, D.C.: Government Printing Office, 1919.

U.S. Department of Commerce and Labor, Bureau of the Census. *Special Report. Prisoners and Juvenile Delinquents in Institutions 1904.* Washington, D.C.: Government Printing Office, 1907.

U.S. Department of the Interior, Census Office. *Report on Crime, Pauperism, and Benevolence in the United States at the Eleventh Census: 1890. Part I. Analysis.* Frederick H. Wines, Special Agent. Washington, D.C.: Government Printing Office, 1896.

———. *Report on Crime, Pauperism, and Benevolence in the United States at the Eleventh Census: 1890. Part II. General Tables.* Frederick H. Wines, Special Agent. Washington, D.C.: Government Printing Office, 1895.

———. *Report on the Defective, Dependent, and Delinquent Classes of the Population of the United States, as Returned at the Tenth Census (June 1, 1880),* by Frederick Howard Wines. Washington, D.C.: Government Printing Office, 1888.

U.S. General Accounting Office. *Female Offenders: Who Are They and What Are the Problems Confronting Them?* Washington, D.C.: General Accounting Office, 1979.

U.S. Prison Industries Reorganization Administration. *The Prison Problem in Alabama, 1939; The Prison Labor Problem in Arkansas, 1936; The Prison Labor Problem in California, 1937; The Prison Problem in Colorado, 1940; The Prison Labor Problem in Delaware, 1936; The Prison Problem in Florida, 1939; The Prison Labor*

Problem in Georgia, 1937; The Prison Labor Problem in Kentucky: A Survey, 1936; The Prison Labor Problem in Maryland, 1936; The Prison Problem in Missouri, 1938; The Prison Labor Problem in Oregon, 1938; The Prison Labor Problem in Virginia, 1939; The Prison Labor Problem in West Virginia: A Survey: 1937. Washington, D.C.: Government Printing Office, 1936–1940.

Vermont. Officers of the Vermont State Prison. *Reports,* 1908–12, 1914–16.

Vermont Department of Public Welfare. *Reports,* 1922–28, 1930–36.

Vermont Director of State Institutions. *Reports,* 1914–22.

Virginia. Board of Directors of the Penitentiary. *Reports,* 1911–13, 1923–26, 1932–42.

———. State Board of (Department of) Public Welfare. *Reports,* 1925–31.

Wisconsin. *Rules and Orders for the Discipline and Government of the Wisconsin State Prison (Waupan).* March 1897.

Wisconsin Industrial Home for Women. *Reports,* 1922–26, 1932, 1936.

Wisconsin State Board of Control. *Reports,* 1900, 1910–36.

Wisconsin State Conference of Charities and Corrections. *Proceedings,* 1912, 1914.

Wisconsin State Prison. *Reports,* 1876, 1900, 1910–34.

Wisconsin State Prison Commisioners. *Report,* Wisconsin Legislative Document H, 1856.

BOOKS, ARTICLES, DISSERTATIONS, THESES

Abbott, Lyman. "The Care of Vicious Women." *The Outlook,* May 17, 1912: 101–02.

Abel, Theodora M. "Negro-White Interpersonal Relationships in a Limited Environment." *Transactions of the New York Academy of Sciences* 5 (1943): 97–105.

Adamson, Christopher R. "Punishment after Slavery: Southern State Penal Systems, 1865–1890." *Social Problems* 30 (5) (June 1983): 555–69.

Arditi, Ralph R., Frederick Goldberg, Jr., M. Martha Hartle, John H. Peters, and William R. Phelps. "The Sexual Segregation of American Prisons." *Yale Law Journal* 82 (1973): 1229–73.

Banner, Lois W. *Women in Modern America: A Brief History.* New York: Harcourt Brace Jovanovich, 1974.

Barnes, Harry Elmer. *A History of the Penal, Reformatory, and Correctional Institutions of the State of New Jersey.* Trenton: MacCrellish & Quigley, 1918.

———. *The Evolution of Penology in Pennsylvania.* Indianapolis: Bobbs-Merrill Co., 1927.

———. *The Story of Punishment: A Record of Man's Inhumanity to Man.* 1930. 2d ed. revised. Reprint. Montclair, N.J.: Patterson Smith, 1972.

Barrows, Isabel C. "The Massachusetts Reformatory Prison for Women." In *The Reformatory System in the United States,* edited by Samuel J. Barrows, pp. 101–28. Washington, D.C.: Government Printing Office, 1900.

———. "The Reformatory Treatment of Women in the United States." In *Penal and Reformatory Institutions,* edited by Charles Richmond Henderson, pp. 129–67. New York: Charities Publication Committee, 1910.

Beach, Lena A. "The Women's Reformatory." *Bulletin of Iowa Institutions* 25 (1923): 51–56.

———. "Treatment of Venereal Disease in a Reformatory for Women." American Prison Association, *Proceedings 1923:* 107–15.

Beatty, Florence Nortridge. "The Women's Prison." *Welfare Magazine* 18 (July 1927): 921–26.

Beaumont, Gustave de, and Alexis de Tocqueville. *On the Penitentiary System in the United States and its Application in France.* Translated by Francis Lieber. 1833. Reprint. Introduction by Thorsten Sellin. Carbondale: Southern Illinois University Press, 1964.

"Blair Dedicates New Women's Prison at Tipton." *St. Louis Post-Dispatch,* February 12, 1960.

Boom, Aaron M. "History of Nebraska Penal Institutions, 1854–1940." Master's thesis, University of Nebraska, 1951.

Booth, Maud Ballington. "Address." American Prison Association, *Proceedings 1915:* 241–45.

———. "Individualization in Prisons." American Prison Association, *Proceedings 1932:* 187–95.

———. "Women in Prison Reform." American Prison Association, *Proceedings 1913:* 271–79.

Bounds, V. L. *Changes Made in Prison Law and Administration in North Carolina 1953–1960.* Chapel Hill: University of North Carolina Press, 1960.

Brenzel, Barbara. "Domestication as Reform: A Study of the Socialization of Wayward Girls, 1856–1905." *Harvard Educational Review* 50 (2) (May 1980): 196–213.

———. "Lancaster Industrial School for Girls: A Social Portrait of a Nineteenth-Century Reform School for Girls." *Feminist Studies* 3 (1/2) (Fall 1975): 40–53.

Brockway, Zebulon Reed. *Fifty Years of Prison Service: An Autobiography.* 1912. Reprint. Montclair, N.J.: Patterson Smith, 1969.

Bularzik, Mary J. "The Dedham Temporary Asylum for Discharged Female Prisoners 1864–1909." *Historical Journal of Massachusetts* 12 (1) (January 1984): 28–35.

———. "Sex, Crime and Justice: Women in the Criminal Justice System of Massachusetts, 1900–1950." Ph.D. diss., Brandeis University, 1982.

Butler, Amos W. *A Century of Progress: A Study of the Development of Public Charities and Correction 1790–1915.* Indiana Reformatory Printing Trade School, 1915.

———. "Recent Developments in the Treatment of Criminals." In Ohio Board of State Charities, *Ohio Bulletin of Charities and Correction* 14 (2) (March 1908): 71–75.

Butler, Charlotte Sperry. "Women Delinquents: Their Custodial Care." *Welfare Magazine* 18 (April 1927): 438–40.

Butler, June Rainsford. "A Study of Some Reformatory Systems for Women Offenders in the United States, with Particular Reference to the Industrial Farm Colony at Kinston, North Carolina." Master's thesis, University of North Carolina, Chapel Hill, 1934.

Cady, J. A. "Industrial Reformatory for Women." *Proceedings of the Ninth Annual Session of the Kansas Conference of Charities and Correction, 1908:* 38–42.

Campbell, Charles F. "Shared Resources: The Implementation of Co-corrections at the Hiland Mountain and Meadow Creek Correctional Centers, Eagle River, Alaska." N.p.: Alaska Division of Adult Corrections, July 1982 (typescript).

"Care of Women Prisoners." *New York Times,* January 25, 1891, p. 3.

Carleton, Mark T. *Politics and Punishment: The History of the Louisiana State Penal System.* Baton Rouge: Louisiana State University Press, 1971.

Carpenter, J. Estlin. *The Life and Work of Mary Carpenter.* 2d ed. London: Macmillan and Co., 1881.

Carpenter, Mary. *Our Convicts.* 1864. Reprint. Montclair, N.J.: Patterson Smith, 1969.

Chernin, Milton. "A History of California State Administration in the Field of Penology." Master's thesis, University of California, 1930.

Codding, Mrs. J. K. "Recreation for Women Prisoners." American Prison Association, *Proceedings 1912:* 312–28.

Coffin, Mrs. C. F. [Rhoda M.]. "System of Discipline Suited to a Female Prison." National Prison Association, *Proceedings 1876:* 422–26.

———. "Women's Prisons." National Prison Association, *Proceedings 1885:* 186–96.

Comstock, Harriet J. "The Woman Offender in Illinois." *Welfare Magazine* 18 (March 1927): 311–13.

Conley, John A. "Economics and the Social Reality of Prisons." *Journal of Criminal Justice* 10 (1) (1982): 25–35.

Connelly, Mark Thomas. *The Response to Prostitution in the Progressive Era.* Chapel Hill: University of North Carolina Press, 1980.

Conway, Jill. "Women Reformers and American Culture, 1870–1930." In *Our American Sisters: Women in American Life and Thought.* 2d ed., edited by Jean E. Friedman and William G. Shade. Boston: Allyn & Bacon, 1976.

Cox, William B., F. Lovell Bixby, and William T. Root, eds. *Handbook of American Prisons and Reformatories, Volume I, 1933.* New York: The Osborne Association, 1933.

Cox, William B., and F. Lovell Bixby, eds. *Handbook of American Prisons and Reformatories: Volume 1, West North Central States, 1938.* New York: The Osborne Association, 1938.

Crawford, William. *Report on the Penitentiaries of the United States.* 1835. Reprint. Montclair, N.J.: Patterson Smith, 1969.

Croft, Elizabeth Benz. "New York State Prisons and Prison Riots from Auburn and Clinton: 1929 to Attica: 1971." Master's thesis, State University of New York at Albany, 1972.

Crofton, Sir Walter. "The Irish System of Prison Discipline." In *Transactions of the National Congress on Penitentiary and Reformatory Discipline,* edited by E. C. Wines, pp. 66–74. Albany: Weed, Parsons, and Company, 1871.

Crow, Herman Lee. "A Political History of the Texas Penal System, 1829–1951." Ph.D. diss., University of Texas, 1964.

Crowe, Jesse Crawford. "The Origin and Development of Tennessee's Prison Problem, 1831–1871." *Tennessee Historical Quarterly* 15 (2) (June 1956): 111–35.

Currie, Elliott Park. "Managing the Minds of Men: The Reformatory Movement, 1865–1920." Ph.D. diss., University of California, Berkeley, 1973.

Davis, Katherine Bement. *Factors in the Sex Life of Twenty-two Hundred Women.* New York: Harper & Brothers, 1929.

———. "Outdoor Work for Women Prisoners." National Conference of Charities and Correction, *Proceedings 1909:* 289–94.

———. "A Reformatory for Women." In Ohio Board of State Charities, *Ohio Bulletin of Charities and Correction* 17 (2) (July 1911): 43–48.

———. "Treatment of the Female Offender." In Seventh New York State Conference of Charities and Correction, *Proceedings 1906,* in New York State Board of Charities, *Annual Report 1906:* 785–90.

Dexter, Sarah E. *Recollections of Hannah B. Chickering.* Cambridge, Mass.: Riverside Press, 1881.

Dix, D[orothea] L[ynde]. *Remarks on Prisons and Prison Discipline in the United States.* 2d ed. 1845. Reprint. Montclair, N.J.: Patterson Smith, 1967.

———. *A Review of the Present Condition of the State Penitentiary of Kentucky, with Brief Notices and Remarks upon the Jails and Poor-Houses in Some of the Most Populous Counties.* Frankfort: A. G. Hodges, State Printer, 1846.

Doty, Madeline Z. *Society's Misfits.* New York: The Century Co., 1916.

Douglas, Ann. *The Feminization of American Culture.* New York: Avon Books, 1977.

Dugdale, Richard L. *"The Jukes." A Study in Crime, Pauperism, Disease and Heredity. Also Further Studies of Criminals.* New York: Putnam's, 1877.

Farnham, Eliza W. Notes and illustrations to M. B. Sampson. *Rational of Crime and its Appropriate Treatment. Being a Treatise on Criminal Jurisprudence Considered in Relation to Cerebral Organization.* From the 2d ed. New York: D. Appleton and Company, 1846.

Feldman, Egal. "Prostitution, the Alien Woman and the Progressive Imagination, 1910–1915." *American Quarterly* 19 (Summer 1967): 192–206.

Fernald, Mabel Ruth, Mary H. S. Hayes, and Almena Dawley. *A Study of Women Delinquents in New York State.* New York: The Century Co., 1920.

Ford, Charles A. "Homosexual Practices of Institutionalized Females." *Journal of Abnormal and Social Psychology* 23 (January–March 1929): 442–49.

Foreman, Paul B., and Julien R. Tatum. "A Short History of Mississippi's Penal Systems." *Mississippi Law Journal* 10 (1938): 255–77.

Fornshell, Marvin E. *The Historical and Illustrated Ohio Penitentiary.* N.p.: 1907–8.

Fosdick, Raymond B. *John D. Rockefeller, Jr., A Portrait.* New York: Harper & Brothers, 1956.

Foucault, Michel. *Discipline and Punish: The Birth of the Prison.* Translated by Alan Sheridan. New York: Pantheon, 1977.

Freedman, Estelle. "Their Sisters' Keepers: An Historical Perspective on Female Correctional Institutions in the United States: 1870–1900." *Feminist Studies* 2 (1) (1974): 77–95.

———. "Their Sisters' Keepers: The Origins of Female Corrections in America." Ph.D. diss., Columbia University, 1976.

———. *Their Sisters' Keepers: Women's Prison Reform in America, 1830–1930.* Ann Arbor: University of Michigan Press, 1981.

Freeman, C. Ray. "The Ruins at Okemos." *The State Journal,* September 19, 1965, Sec. E, p. 1.

Fry, Elizabeth. *Memoir of the Life of Elizabeth Fry with Extracts from her Journal and Letters,* edited by two of her daughters. 2 vols. Philadelphia: J. W. Moore, 1847.

Garrett, Paul W., and Austin H. MacCormick, eds. *Handbook of American Prisons and Reformatories, 1929.* New York: National Society of Penal Information, 1929.

Glick, Ruth M., and Virginia V. Neto. *National Study of Women's Correctional Programs.* Washington, D.C.: National Institute of Law Enforcement and Criminal Justice, Law Enforcement Assistance Administration, U.S. Department of Justice, June 1977.

Glueck, Sheldon, and Eleanor T. Glueck. *Five Hundred Delinquent Women.* New York: Alfred A. Knopf, 1934.

Goddard, Henry H. *The Criminal Imbecile: An Analysis of Three Remarkable Murder Cases.* New York: Macmillan Co., 1915.

———. *Feeble-Mindedness: Its Causes and Consequences.* New York: Macmillan Co., 1914.

———. *The Kallikak Family: A Study in the Heredity of Feeble-Mindedness.* New York: Macmillan Co., 1912.

Goddard, Henry H., and Helen F. Hill. "Delinquent Girls Tested by the Binet Scale." *Training School Bulletin* 7 (4) (June 1911): 50–56.

Goldman, Emma. *Living My Life.* Vol. 2. New York: Alfred A. Knopf, 1931.

Gould, Orin B. "Ohio Penitentiary, Columbus." In Ohio Board of State Charities, *Twenty-first Report,* 1907: 46–48.

Growdon, Clarence H. "The Mental Status of Reformatory Women." *Journal of Criminal Law, Criminology & Police Science* 22 (1931–32): 196–220.

Hahn, Nicolas Fischer [Nicole H. Rafter]. "The Defective Delinquency Movement." Ph.D. diss., State University of New York at Albany, 1978.

——. "Female State Prisoners in Tennessee: 1831–1979." *Tennessee Historical Quarterly* 39 (4) (Winter 1980): 485–97.

——. "Too Dumb to Know Better: Cacogenic Family Studies and the Criminology of Women." *Criminology* 18 (1) (May 1980): 3–25.

Haller, Mark H. *Eugenics: Hereditarian Attitudes in American Thought.* New Brunswick: Rutgers University Press, 1963.

Heale, M. J. "The Formative Years of the New York Prison Association, 1844–1862: A Case Study in Antebellum Reform." *The New York Historical Society Quarterly* 59 (October 1975): 320–47.

Heffernan, Esther. "Female Corrections—History and Analysis." Opening Address to Conference on the Confinement of Female Offenders, U.S. Bureau of Prisons: Lexington, Kentucky, March 28–30, 1978 (typescript).

——. *Women Offenders in the Alaska Criminal Justice System.* Report to the Division of Corrections, State of Alaska, Department of Health and Social Services, July 15, 1979 (typescript).

Henderson, Charles Richmond, ed. *Penal and Reformatory Institutions.* New York: Charities Publication Committee, 1910.

Herre, Ralph S. "The History of Auburn Prison from the Beginning to about 1867." Ph.D. diss., Pennsylvania State College, 1950.

Hicks, Clara Belle. "The History of Penal Institutions in Ohio to 1850." *Ohio State Archeological and Historical Society Publications* 33 (1924): 359–426.

Hindus, Michael S. "Black Justice Under White Law: Criminal Prosecutions of Blacks in Antebellum South Carolina." *Journal of American History* 63 (1977): 575–99.

——. "The Contours of Crime and Justice in Massachusetts and South Carolina, 1767–1878." *American Journal of Legal History* 21 (1977): 212–37.

——. *Prison and Plantation: Crime, Justice, and Authority in Massachusetts and South Carolina, 1767–1878.* Chapel Hill: University of North Carolina Press, 1980.

Howard, E. Lee. "The Delinquent Woman." In Ohio Board of State Charities, *Ohio Bulletin of Charities and Correction* 15 (1) (February 1909): 74–76.

Howington, Arthur F. " 'Not in the Condition of a Horse or an Ox': *Ford v. Ford,* the Law of Testamentary Manumission, and the Tennessee Courts' Recognition of Slave Humanity." *Tennessee Historical Quarterly* 34 (3) (Fall 1975): 249–63.

Hunter, Mrs. Mattie E. "Women's Organizations." National Prison Association, *Proceedings 1898:* 61–64.

Johnson, Mary Coffin, ed. *Rhoda M. Coffin: Her Reminiscences, Addresses, Papers and Ancestry.* New York: The Grafton Press, 1910.

Johnston, Norman. *The Human Cage: A Brief History of Prison Architecture.* New York: Walker and Co., 1973.

"Katherine B. Davis Heads Parole Commission." *The Survey* 35 (15) (January 8, 1916): 415–16.

Katzman, David M. *Seven Days a Week: Women and Domestic Service in Industrializing America*. New York: Oxford University Press, 1978.

Keely, Sara F. "The Organization and Discipline of the Indiana Women's Prison." National Prison Association, *Proceedings 1898*: 275–84.

Kellor, Frances. "The Criminal Negro. IV. Advantages and Abuses of Southern Penal Systems." *The Arena* (1901): 419–28.

Kelly, Howard A. *Medical Gynecology*. New York: D. Appleton and Co., 1909.

Kirby, Georgiana Bruce. *Years of Experience: An Autobiographical Narrative*. 1887. Reprint. New York: AMS Press, 1971.

Kneeland, George Jackson. *Commercialized Prostitution in New York City*. With a supplementary chapter by Katherine Bement Davis and Introduction by John D. Rockefeller, Jr. New York: The Century Co., 1913.

Lane, Winthrop D. "Prisons at the Breaking Point." *Survey* 62 (2) (September 1, 1929): 557–58, 584.

Lekkerkerker, Eugenia Cornelia. *Reformatories for Women in the United States*. Batavia, Holland: Bij J. B. Wolters' Uitgevers-Maatschappij, 1931.

Lewis, Orlando F. *The Development of American Prisons and Prison Customs, 1776–1845*. 1922. Reprint. Montclair, N.J.: Patterson Smith, 1967.

Lewis, W. David. *From Newgate to Dannemora: The Rise of the Penitentiary in New York, 1796–1848*. Ithaca: Cornell University Press, 1965.

———."Eliza Wood Burhans Farnham." In *Notable American Women 1607–1950*, Vol. 1, edited by Edward T. James, Janet Wilson James, and Paul S. Boyer, pp. 598–600. Cambridge, Mass.: Belknap Press of Harvard University Press, 1971.

Lieber, Francis. "Translator's Preface" to Gustave de Beaumont and Alexis de Tocqueville. *On the Penitentiary System in the United States and its Application in France*. 1833. Reprint. Carbondale: Southern Illinois University Press, 1964.

Lombroso, Caesar, and William Ferrero. *The Female Offender*. 1895. Reprint. New York: D. Appleton and Co., 1915.

Lowell, Josephine S. "One Means of Preventing Pauperism." National Conference of Charities and Correction, *Proceedings 1879*: 189–99.

Lubove, Roy. "The Progressives and the Prostitute." *Historian* 24 (1962): 308–30.

Lydston, G. Frank. *The Diseases of Society (The Vice and Crime Problem)*. Philadelphia: J. B. Lippincott Co., 1905.

MacCormick, Austin H., ed. *Handbook of American Prisons and Reformatories: Vol. 2, Pacific Coast States, 1942*. New York: The Osborne Association, 1942.

MacCormick, Austin H., and Paul W. Garrett, eds. *Handbook of American Prisons, 1926*. New York: G. P. Putnam's Sons, 1926.

Martineau, Harriet. *Retrospect of Western Travel*. Vol. 1. London: Saunders and Otley, 1838.

Mason, Gregory. "Commissioner Davis and her Critics." *The Outlook* (September 8, 1915): 76–79.

Maughs, Sidney. "A Concept of Psychopathy and Psychopathic Personality: Its Evolution and Historical Development." Part 2. *Journal of Clinical and Experimental Psychopathology and Quarterly Review of Psychiatry and Neurology* (2) (January 1941): 465–99.

McCord, Clinton P. "One Hundred Female Offenders: A Study of the Mentality of Prostitutes and 'Wayward' Girls." *Journal of Criminal Law, Criminology & Police Science* 6 (September 1915): 385–407.

McGovern, James R. "The American Woman's Pre-World War I Freedom in Manners and Morals." In *Our American Sisters: Women in American Life and Thought.* 2nd ed., edited by Jean E. Friedman and William G. Shade. Boston: Allyn & Bacon, 1976.

McKelvey, Blake. *American Prisons: A Study in American Social History prior to 1915.* 1936. Reprint. Montclair, N.J.: Patterson Smith, 1972.

McPartlin, Catherine. "The Need of a Women's Reformatory in Minnesota." *Proceedings of the Twentieth Minnesota State Conference of Charities and Correction* (1911): 53–57.

Meanes, Lenna L. "Problems in Connection with the Delinquent Woman." *Bulletin of Iowa Institutions, 1915* 17: 331–36.

Monahan, Florence. "Parole Preparation for Women Offenders." *Minnesota State Board of Control Quarterly* 24 (2) (November 1924): 33–41.

———. "Paths of the Handicapped." *Minnesota State Board of Control Quarterly* 29 (September 13, 1929): 27–28.

———. *Women in Crime.* New York: Ives Washburn, 1941.

Moos, Malcolm C. *State Penal Administration in Alabama.* University, Ala.: Bureau of Public Administration, University of Alabama, 1942.

Morgan, Dan J. *Historical Lights and Shadows of the Ohio State Penitentiary and Horrors of the Death Trap.* 1893. Reprint. Columbus: Champlin Printing Company, 1895.

Neff, Joseph S. *The Degenerate Children of Feeble-Minded Women.* Philadelphia: Department of Public Health and Charities, 1910.

"New York State's Prison Revolts." *Literary Digest* (August 10, 1929): 8–9.

Novak, Daniel A. *The Wheel of Servitude: Black Forced Labor after Slavery.* Lexington: University Press of Kentucky, 1978.

Odegard, Bernett O., and George M. Keith. *A History of the State Board of Control of Wisconsin and the State Institutions: 1849–1939.* Madison: State Board of Control, 1939.

O'Hare, Kate Richards. *In Prison.* 1923. Reprint. Seattle: University of Washington Press, 1976.

Otis, Margaret. "A Perversion not Commonly Noted." *Journal of Abnormal Psychology* 8 (1913): 112–14.

Park, Robert. *History of the Oklahoma State Penitentiary Located at McAlester, Oklahoma.* McAlester Printing and Binding Co., 1914.

Perry, Julia B. "Industrial Reformatory for Women." *Proceedings of the Ninth Annual Session of the Kansas Conference of Charities and Correction, 1908:* 42–47.

———. "Segregation and Care of the Delinquent Woman." *Proceedings of the Nineteenth Annual Session of the Kansas Conference of Social Work, 1918:* 8–13.

Pickworth, Felix H. "The Delinquent Woman." *Bulletin of Iowa Institutions, 1915* 17: 10–14.

Pisciotta, Alexander W. "Saving the Children: The Promise and Practice of *Parens Patriae,* 1838–98." *Crime and Delinquency* 28 (2) (July 1982): 410–25.

Pivar, David J. *Purity Crusade: Sexual Morality and Social Control, 1868–1900.* Westport, Conn.: Greenwood Press, 1973.

Platt, Anthony M. *The Child Savers: The Invention of Delinquency.* 2d ed. Chicago: University of Chicago Press, 1977.

Potter, Frank Hunter. "A Reformatory which Reforms." *The Outlook* (February 5, 1910): 303–7.

Quarles, Mary Ann Stillman. "Organizational Analysis of the New Jersey Reformatory for Women in Relation to Stated Principles of Corrections, 1913–1963." Ph.D. diss., Boston University, 1966.

Rafter, Nicole Hahn. "Chastizing the Unchaste: Social Control Functions of a Women's Reformatory, 1894–1931." In *Social Control and the State: Historical and Comparative Essays,* edited by Stanley Cohen and Andrew Scull. Oxford: Martin Robertson, 1983.

———. "Hard Times: Custodial Prisons for Women and the Example of the New York State Prison for Women at Auburn, 1893–1933." In *Judge, Lawyer, Victim, Thief: Women, Gender Roles, and Criminal Justice,* edited by Nicole Hahn Rafter and Elizabeth A. Stanko. Boston: Northeastern University Press, 1982.

Reeves, Margaret. *Training Schools for Delinquent Girls.* New York: Russell Sage Foundation, 1929.

"Reformatory for Women is Planned: House of Correction at Howard to be Remodelled Into Quarters for Female Charges." *The Providence Journal* (Rhode Island), December 30, 1923, p. 4.

"Report Condemns Facilities at Women's Reformatory: Deplores Unsanitary Conditions and Failure to Provide for Segregation." *The Providence Journal* (Rhode Island), December 24, 1928, pp. 13, 16.

Resch, John P. "Ohio Adult Penal System, 1850–1900: A Study in the Failure of Institutional Reform." *Ohio History* 81 (Autumn 1972): 236–62.

Resnick, Judith, and Nancy Shaw. "Prisoners of their Sex: Health Problems of Incarcerated Women." In *Prisoners' Rights Source Book: Theory, Litigation, and Practice.* Vol. 2, edited by Ira Boardman. New York: Clark Boardman, 1980.

"R.I. Reformatory Laws Criticised." *The Providence Journal* (Rhode Island), November 8, 1927, p. 27.

Riegel, Robert E. "Changing American Attitudes Toward Prostitution (1800–1920)." *Journal of the History of Ideas* 29 (July–September 1968): 437–52.

Robert, Jeanne. "The Care of Women in State Prisons." In *Prison Reform,* compiled by Corinne Bacon, pp. 91–102. New York: H. W. Wilson, 1917.

Rogers, A. K. *An Episode in History of a Connecticut Institution.* New Haven: City Printing Co., 1923.

Rogers, Helen Worthington. "A Digest of Laws Establishing Reformatories for Women." *Journal of Criminal Law, Criminology & Police Science* 13 (3) (November 1922): 382–437.

————. "A Digest of Laws Establishing Reformatories for Women in the United States." *Journal of Criminal Law, Criminology, & Police Science* 8 (24) (November 1917): 518–53.

————. "A History of the Movement to Establish a State Reformatory for Women in Connecticut." *Journal of Criminal Law, Criminology & Police Science* 19 (4) (February 1929): 518–41.

Rosen, Ruth. *The Lost Sisterhood: Prostitution in America, 1900–1918.* Baltimore: Johns Hopkins University Press, 1982.

Rosen, Ruth, and Sue Davidson, eds. *The Maimie Papers.* Old Westbury, N.Y.: The Feminist Press, 1977.

Rosenberg, Charles E. "Sexuality, Class and Role in 19th-Century America." *American Quarterly* 25 (1973): 131–53.

Rosenberg, Rosalind. "In Search of Woman's Nature, 1850–1920." *Feminist Studies* 3 (1/2) (Fall 1975): 141–54.

Rothman, David J. *Conscience and Convenience: The Asylum and Its Alternatives in Progressive America.* Boston: Little, Brown and Co., 1980.

————. *The Discovery of the Asylum: Social Order and Disorder in the New Republic.* Boston: Little, Brown and Co., 1971.

Sanborn, Franklin B. "How Far is the Irish System Applicable to American Prisons?" In *Transactions of the National Congress on Penitentiary and Reformatory Discipline,* edited by E. C. Wines, pp. 406–14. Albany: Weed, Parsons, and Company, 1871.

Schlossman, Steven L. *Love and the American Delinquent: The Theory and Practice of "Progresive" Juvenile Justice, 1825–1920.* Chicago: University of Chicago Press, 1977.

Schlossman, Steven, and Stephanie Wallach. "The Crime of Precocious Sexuality: Female Juvenile Delinquency in the Progressive Era." *Harvard Educational Review* 48 (1) (February 1978): 65–94.

Schneider, David M., and Albert Deutsch. *The History of Public Welfare in New York State, 1867–1940.* Chicago: University of Chicago Press, 1941.

Schupf, Harriet Warm. "Single Women and Social Reform in Mid-Nineteenth Century England: The Case of Mary Carpenter." *Victorian Studies* 17 (March 1974): 301–18.

Scott, Anne Firor. "The 'New Woman' in the New South." In *Our American Sisters: Women in American Life and Thought.* 2d ed., edited by Jean E. Friedman and William G. Shade. Boston: Allyn & Bacon, 1976.

Sellin, J. Thorsten. *Slavery and the Penal System*. New York: Elsevier, 1976.

Selling, Lowell S. "The Pseudo Family." *American Journal of Sociology* 37 (July–May 1931–32): 247–53.

Shelden, Randall G. "Sex Discrimination in the Juvenile Justice System: Memphis, Tennessee, 1900–1917." In *Comparing Female and Male Offenders*, edited by Marguerite Q. Warren. Beverly Hills: Sage, 1981.

Sickels, Lucy M. "The Need of a Reformatory or Refuge for Women." *Bulletin of Iowa Institutions, 1914* 16: 263–68.

Sletterdahl, Peter, ed. *Indiana's State Institutions*. Indianapolis: n.p., 1928.

Slocum, Helen. "The Causes of Prostitution." *The Woman's Journal* (January 18, 1879): 22.

Smith, Daniel Scott, and Michael S. Hindus. "Premarital Pregnancy in America 1640–1971: An Overview and Interpretation." *Journal of Interdisciplinary History* 4 (Spring 1975): 537–70.

Sneed, William C. *A Report on the History and Mode of Management of the Kentucky Penitentiary from its Origin, in 1798 to March 1, 1860*. Frankfort, Ky.: Jno. B. Major, State Printer, 1860.

Spaulding, Edith R. *An Experimental Study of Psychopathic Delinquent Women*. 1923. Reprint. Montclair, N.J.: Patterson Smith, 1969.

———. "The New Psychopathic Hospital." *The Delinquent* 6 (9) (September 1916): 5–7.

Stewart, William Rhinelander. *The Philanthropic Work of Josephine Shaw Lowell*. New York: Macmillan Company, 1911.

Stokes, John H. "The Treatment of Syphilis." In *Therapeusis of Internal Diseases*. Vol. 3, edited by George Blumer. New York: D. Appleton and Co., 1924.

Tannenbaum, Frank. *Darker Phases of the South*. 1924. Reprint. New York: Negro Universities Press, 1969.

Tarbell, Ida M. "Good Will to Women." *American Magazine* 75 (December 1912): 45–53.

Taylor, A. Elizabeth. "The Origin and Development of the Convict Lease System in Georgia." *Georgia Historical Quarterly* 28 (March 1942): 113–28.

Teeters, Negley K. *The Cradle of the Penitentiary: The Walnut Street Jail at Philadelphia, 1773–1835*. Philadelphia: Pennsylvania Prison Society, 1955.

Temin, Carolyn Engel. "Discriminatory Sentencing of Women Offenders: The Argument for ERA in a Nutshell." In *Women, Crime, and Justice*, edited by Susan K. Datesman and Frank R. Scarpitti, New York: Oxford University Press, 1980.

Terman, Lewis M. *The Measurement of Intelligence*. Boston: Houghton Mifflin Co., 1916.

Thomas, David Y. *Arkansas and Its People: A History, 1541–1930*. Vol. 2. New York: The American Historical Society, 1930.

Thompson, E. Bruce. "Reforms in the Penal System of Tennessee, 1820–1850." *Tennessee Historical Quarterly* 1 (4) (December 1942): 291–308.

"To Help Fallen Women." *New York Times,* January 2, 1892, p. 8.

Tyor, Peter L. " 'Denied the Power to Choose the Good': Sexuality and Mental Defect in American Medical Practice, 1850–1920." *Journal of Social History* 10 (4) (Summer 1977): 472–89.

van Courtland, Catherine E. "Report on the State Prison for Women." In Prison Association of New York, *Annual Report 1876:* 40–42.

van Wyck, Katherine. "Reformatory for Women—Wisconsin's Outstanding Need." Wisconsin Conference on Charities and Corrections, *Proceedings 1912:* 93–98.

"Vanity of Female Convicts." *New York Times,* September 9, 1894, p. 18.

Vaux, Roberts. *Notices of the Original, and Successive Efforts, To Improve the Discipline of the Prison at Philadelphia and To Reform the Criminal Code of Pennsylvania: With a Few Observations on the Penitentiary System.* Philadelphia: Kimber and Sharpless, 1826.

Victor, Sarah Maria. *The Life Story of Sarah M. Victor for Sixty Years. Convicted of Murdering Her Brother, Sentenced to be Hung, Had Sentence Commuted, Passed Nineteen Years in Prison, Yet is Innocent.* Cleveland: Williams Publishing Co., 1887.

Voigt, Lloyd L. *History of California Correctional Administration From 1930 to 1948.* San Francisco: n.p., 1949.

von Hentig, Hans. "The Criminality of the Colored Woman." University of Colorado Studies. Series C 1 (3) (1942): 231–60.

Walkowitz, Daniel J. "Working-class Women in the Gilded Age: Factory, Community and Family Life among Cohoes, New York, Cotton Workers." *Journal of Social History* 5 (Summer 1972): 464–90.

Ward, W. R. "The Social-service Work of the State Industrial Farm for Women." In *Proceedings [of the] Kansas Conference of Social Work, 1922:* 45–47. Topeka: B. P. Walker, 1923.

Waterman, Willoughby Cyrus. *Prostitution and its Repression in New York City, 1900–1931.* 1932. Reprint. New York: AMS Press, 1968.

Weidensall, Jean. *The Mentality of the Criminal Woman.* Baltimore: Warwick & York, 1916.

Welter, Barbara. "The Cult of True Womanhood: 1820–1860." *American Quarterly* 18 (Summer 1966): 151–74.

Williams, Katherine R. "Need for a Reformatory For Women in Wisconsin." *Wisconsin Conference on Charities and Corrections, 1912:* 99–102.

Wilson, Helen. *The Treatment of the Misdemeanant in Indiana, 1816–1936.* Chicago: University of Chicago Press, 1938.

Wines, E. C., and Theodore W. Dwight. *Report on the Prisons and Reformatories of the United States and Canada.* Albany: van Benthuysen & Sons, 1867.

Wines, E. C., ed. *Transactions of the National Congress on Penitentiary and Reformatory Discipline*. Albany: Weed, Parsons and Company, 1871.

Wisner, Elizabeth. *Public Welfare Administration in Louisiana*. Chicago: University of Chicago Press, 1931.

"Women's Prison Association—Two of the Plans It Advocated Put into Effect." *New York Times,* February 8, 1893, p. 10.

Young, Clifford M. *Women's Prisons Past and Present and Other New York State Prison History*. Elmira Reformatory: The Summary Press, 1932.

Zimmerman, Jane. "The Penal Reform Movement in the South during the Progressive Era, 1890–1917." *Journal of Southern History* 17 (November 1951): 462–92.

Index